FLAPPERS 2 RAPPERS
AMERICAN YOUTH SLANG

BY TOM DALZELL

Merriam-Webster, Incorporated
Springfield, Massachusetts

A GENUINE MERRIAM-WEBSTER

The name *Webster* alone is no guarantee of excellence. It is used by a number of publishers and may serve mainly to mislead an unwary buyer.

Merriam-Webster™ is the name you should look for when you consider the purchase of dictionaries or other fine reference books. It carries the reputation of a company that has been publishing since 1831 and is your assurance of quality and authority.

ISBN 0-87779-612-2

Printed and bound in the United States of America

123456QPH989796

For Dick,
who loved Mencken,
and for my mother.
For Jake
and for Julia,
for always.

ACKNOWLEDGMENTS

I am indebted to and gratefully acknowledge the contributions of the following:

Paul Dickson of Garrett Park and Madeline Kripke of New York, my slang mentors and good friends.

John Morse of Merriam-Webster, who understood this project from the start and who remembers Hy Lit.

Randy Roberts of the Western Manuscript Collection at the University of Missouri at Columbia, who has mastered the Peter Tamony Collection and who tirelessly worked with me.

Language writers Reinhold Aman, Robert Chapman, Trevor Cralle, Connie Eble, Gerard Cohen, Lewis Poteet, and Bruce Rodgers, all of whom were very generous with their encouragement and time.

Ward Gilman, Jennifer Goss, and Tom Pitoniak of the Merriam-Webster Editorial Department, who read the entire manuscript and offered many helpful suggestions; Bob Ciano and Jon Hensley of the Encyclopaedia Britannica Art Department, who acquired the art and created the design for the inside of this book; and Lynn Stowe Tomb of Merriam-Webster for her production assistance.

James Musser (Skyline Books), Jean Kapp Van Fleet (Bibliomania), and Sue Fox (Sacred and Profane Books), who found for me many of the books consulted.

Art and Helen Zoloth, scouts and clippers in a league of their own.

Simon Lake, Matt Levy, Noah Levy, the Liberatores (Tony, Lisa, and Anna), Molly "1900" Meadows, Paul Meadows, Frank "Queso Alto" Potestio, Mike Weinberg, and Emma Zoloth — book scouts, word scouts, and general purpose helpers.

Shawn Berlin, who cheered it on.

Mr. Baldwin, Mr. Muir, Mr. Lee, Dr. Regan, and Dr. Kelly, who brought mr to English and to popular culture.

CONTENTS

Introduction

▼

"Cool expressions change with each generation, dog, dig?"

—The spider to the dog (*Gordo,* by
Gustavo Arriola, Sunday, April 9, 1967)

In choosing to accept the mission of explor-
ing the slang of 20th century American
youth, I knew from the start of certain
obstacles that I would encounter.

For one, as the jive-talking spider with a goa-
tee and beret in *Gordo* recognized quite well,
slang changes quickly. While not all slang is
ephemeral, most is; likewise, youth itself is fleeting and transitory. Combine the passing nature of
youth and the passing nature of slang and the
result is a quickly passing youth slang. Connie
Eble, Professor of English at the University of
North Carolina and one of today's leading field
workers and analysts of college slang, finds that
most of the terms that she has gathered over the
last 23 years were collected only once; between
1972 and 1987, for example, she found a reten-
tion rate of less than 10%. Simply put, this
means that at any given moment, many slang
words in circulation will be quickly forgotten,
which in turn means that any collection of youth
slang is bound to include words which may not
seem authentic. So it is with this collection, as I
have taken a generally inclusive approach and
left the task of sifting and sorting to each reader.

Second, slang is primarily a spoken language,
not a written one, yet most of what endures is
written, not spoken. This makes a full and accurate analysis particularly difficult. Some of those
who have recorded the slang of the young in the
20th century certainly did a better job than others, but even the best work has its limits. To com-
pensate for this fact, I relied as much as possible
on the lyrics of songs, comic strips and comic
books, magazines, tapes of radio shows, and to a
lesser degree, the language used in television
shows and movies. Even so, I have never entertained the thought that a truly comprehensive
record of a century of youth slang is possible.

Third, I knew that there were certain difficul-
ties inherent in defining "youth." Within the
young population one finds substantial differences in language usage based on a number of
demographic factors. In general, though, I have
addressed the slang of middle-class American
youth, whatever their race or address or gender.
Slang acquisition seems to begin when children
approach adolescence. There are exceptions of
course, both on an individual basis (children
with older siblings are likely to acquire slang
earlier than those without older siblings) and on
a group basis (children in a subculture where
slang is more the norm than standard English
will acquire slang earlier than those who take
their slang cues from outside their own subculture).

Illustration by Victoria Roberts

Within the context of a broad definition of youth, I was ever aware of the pioneering role of younger youth in shaping slang. In the October 1964 issue of *American Speech*, Henry Kratz wrote in "What is College Slang?" as follows:

As a matter of fact, it is the members of the younger set, the group in junior and senior high school, who are probably most directly responsible for the spread of slang. They are much more susceptible to the world of television comedians and commercials, to comic strips and disc jockeys, and are much more receptive to the tasteless and synthetic ephemera which these media do so much to promote.

In a similar vein, in 1966 the *Toronto Star* rushed to the defense of teenyboppers, arguing that they were the true trend-setters because they were "The only people brave enough to try outrageous new fads" (*Toronto Star*, October 30, 1966). In the end, my definition of "youth" was somewhat amorphous, ranging from early adolescence to mid-20s.

A fourth question which I faced before beginning my work was what to do with the slang of college students. I quickly decided to exclude the purely collegiate slang—the technical vocabulary of academic life, the names students give their courses, the technical terms pertaining to the curriculum, the grading system, dormitory living, buildings, parts of the campus, fraternities and sororities, and college-specific social affairs. My two reasons for deciding to exclude this kind of slang were simple: a comprehensive examination of college slang is a project in and of itself, and too many of the slang words and expressions used on college campuses are more in the nature of a specialized vocabulary, admittedly highly informal, than true slang. The decade which posed the greatest problem in this regard was the 1930s; it is impossible to deny the collegiate nature of much of youth slang of the pre-Swing 1930s, yet I still chose to avoid the strictly college language.

Fifth, I knew coming into this project that etymology is a major obstacle in the study of slang, and I assumed that it would be an even greater obstacle with youth slang because of its intrinsically transient nature. Linguists speak of lexical polygenesis and multiple etymologies; one need

look no further than the discussion of "hip" and "hep" in Chapter Four to see the chaos that results from any serious attempt to pin down the etymology of slang. Not to put too fine a point on it, most slang words and expressions are simply etymological mysteries.

The last barrier that I anticipated was the organization of the material. I ultimately decided, with the exception of the rap idiom of the hip-hop culture, to proceed decade-by-decade, an artificial template if ever there was one. Language did not suddenly change between December 31, 1939, and January 1, 1940, and by approaching this subject by decades I do not suggest that it did. Cultural shifts, including slang, are measured more by generations than by years or decades, and generations are difficult, if not impossible, to measure. At times generational change can be seen in just a few years, while at other times it seems that a decade might pass without a generational shift. All in all, decades seemed like safe measuring posts for the century; fully cognizant of their shortcomings, I use them.

The Slang

Enough with the obstacles—what of the slang?

As I worked my way through the century, I came to several broad conclusions about youth slang from that of the Flapper to that of the Rapper. First, one cannot help but be struck by the powerful influence of African-American vernacular on the slang of all 20th-century American youth. Jazz musicians of the 1930s and rappers of the 1980s and 1990s defined the popular youth slang of the late 1930s, the 1940s, the counterculture 1950s, the 1960s, and the 1990s. There were other influences, to be sure, on the slang of America's young, but none as powerful as that of the streets of Harlem and Chicago.

As a second observation, it is my distinct belief that the young do not use slang to conceal the meaning of their speech from their parents and other authority figures. This theory has its advocates, most notably Robert Chapman, author of the *New Dictionary of American Slang*, whose standing in the world of slang is beyond question. Chapman believes that slang has "the function of defending the infant ego against constant assault and dismissal by the looming adults" and that it is constantly changed "in order to stay incomprehensible to The Other." Still, I believe otherwise. My sense is that most young people do not even use slang in front of adults. If slang is not used in front of adults, it cannot be said that it is used to cloak the meaning of what is said.

Instead, the primary purposes of youth slang, it seems to me, are threefold. First, slang serves to change the level of conversation towards the informal. Slang serves the important function of identifying other young people as members of a group; because you use certain words or expressions, I know that we are from the same tribe and that I can speak freely and informally with you. Second, slang establishes station. Aside from the high percentage of slang that is devoted to dividing the world into the accepted and the social outcast, slang also functions to imply the speaker's status. Slang for youth provides automatic linguistic responses to handle awkward social situations with peers. Beginning (hello) and ending (good-bye) conversations smoothly is a learned social skill, and the risk of embarrassing oneself and losing face is great. Youth slang confronts this problem by providing established, almost liturgical greetings and farewells. The third function of youth slang is to satisfy youth's drive for defying authority. Satiric, vulgar, witty, and skeptical, youth slang is often quite oppositional and marks a resistance to established authority.

My next observation on the slang of 20th-century American youth is that there is very little that is new. Certain words are cyclical; **groovy, mellow,** and **solid** all come to mind as examples of words that were popular with the youth of the 1940s, fell into disfavor in the 1950s, and then reemerged with a vengeance in the 1960s. Similarly, **fly** enjoyed some popularity in the 1940s but then went into hiding until it burst on the rap scene in the late 1980s. **Sweet** was widely used in the 1930s, lay low for several decades, and then became the single most frequently encountered word in Connie Eble's 23 years of slang-tracking at the University of North Carolina between 1972 and 1995. **Tasty** was a popular slang superlative of the 1920s, and it emerged again in the 1970s and 1980s.

How does this happen? How is it that **groovy** was so thoroughly forgotten as a big word of the 1940s and sounded so new when it leapt into the spotlight in 1965 or so?

Robert Chapman believes that there is no single cause for the reincarnation of slang "It's what the shrinks call 'overdetermined,' which is another way of saying we don't know."

Other words, such as **dope, drag, freak, rap,** or **trip** assumed different meanings in different decades, linguistic chameleons if you will. Of course, there is the incomparably adaptable *hip*, which has survived in one form or another (**hip, hep, hipster, hepster, hep-cat, hippy, hippie,** and **hip-hop**) for the entire century.

Many slang words used by youth today are just not as new as they seem. The following list of very modern-sounding words, given with their decade of origin, demonstrates just how old some of what we think new is: **anxious** (1940s), **brutal** (1940s), **cap** (1940s), **cherry** (1950s), **chill** (1960s), **clue** (1950s), **copacetic** (1920s), **dirt** (1930s), **drag** (1950s), **fade** (1930s), **flash** (1960s), **fly** (1940s), **frantic** (1940s), **frosted** (1950s), **hang** (1950s), **homey** (1940s), **hot** (late 19th century), **icy** (1940s), **jell** (1930s), **kill** (1950s), **killer** (late 19th century), **marble palace** (1930s), **nail** (late 19th century), **nerd** (1950s), **not!** (1930s), **no way** (1970s), **potent** (1940s), **rag** (late 19th century), **righteous** (1940s), **rink rat** (1940s), **scrub** (late 19th century), **slam** (late 19th century), **smooth** (1920s), **suck** (1930s), **sweet** (1930s), **tasty** (1920s), **turkey** (1940s), and **unreal** (1920s).

The same can be said about other decades. In the 1950s, for example, **nifty** and **swell** were seen as new adjectives of approval, yet they first became popular in the 1920s. Similarly, many words which we think of as quintessential creatures of the 1960s were coined much earlier—**far out** (1904), **groovy** (1940s), **head** for a drug user (1950s), **hung-up** as inhibited (1940s), **mellow** (1930s and 1940s), **nowhere** meaning out of touch with things (1950s), **out of sight** (late 19th century), **solid** (1940s), **trip** for a drug experience (1950s), **truckin'** (1940s), and **turn on** meaning to use drugs (1950s).

In the same vein, looking at the language of the teenage girl of the 1940s with her intensifying **too perfectly** or **too positively,** her melodramatic use of **drear, grim, loathsome,** and

stark, it is impossible not to hear the voice of the 1980s Valley Girl. **Definitely stark, actually! It's all too desperate!**

Lastly, even within a decade words can hold different meanings. If one takes the 1960s, there is a striking difference in meanings ascribed to different words by the mainstream youth culture on the one hand and the hippie counterculture on the other:

blow your mind
Mainstream: To love a record, thing, or person
Hippie: To be confronted with a strange mental experience

Bogart
Mainstream: To injure or hurt
Hippie: To hog a marijuana cigarette

digger
Mainstream: The leader
Hippie: A commune in San Francisco

happening
Mainstream: A good party
Hippie: An intentionally spontaneous gathering, usually involving drugs

strung out
Mainstream: Disturbed, worried
Hippie: Addicted to a drug

taste
Mainstream: A sample
Hippie: A sample of drugs being purchased

turn on
Mainstream: To arouse someone's interest in something
Hippie: To use drugs

uptight
Mainstream: Very good
Hippie: Inhibited

Most of what follows should be fairly self-explanatory; however, a few features of this book call for a little explanation. Words set in small capitals (SMALL CAPITALS) are cross-references and refer the reader to an entry in the main A-Z

sequence of entries within that chapter. All footnotes for a chapter appear at the end of that chapter. Also at the end of each chapter is a list of the principal references relied on in the writing of that chapter. Reference sources that are referred to and were relied on for chapters throughout the book are listed in the Bibliography that appears at the back of the book.

Enough ruminations from this middle-age white guy, though. Bring on the kids! Bring on the words! Are you ready for this yon teens—yon hipsters, yon flipsters, yon finger-popping daddies, all you uptown downtown all around town showcasing groovers? Pick up on this riff you sharp cats and kitties. Heed these syllables you ditty boppers. Drape yourself in shape 'cause here's a hot flash of ecstatic static, a king-size dose of spectacular vernacular and extraordinary vocabulary, some real gone jive guaranteed to sharpen your game! Let me lay this on you! Let these words wake you! I mean it and how—Boot it, shoot it, hang with this slang and reep these righteous words. Don't vegetate, percolate! Here it be!!!!! Let it roll, let it all roll!!!!

CHAPTER 1
Before The Flapper
▼

"23 Skidoo!"

To be sure, young people in the United States did not suddenly start using slang with the advent of the Jazz Age in about 1920. Slang has long been an integral component of American English, and the young have never distinguished themselves by confining their speech to standard English.

A viable slang idiom, though, is dependent upon a viable subculture, for the creation of slang is by its very nature a social and group process. Further, the transmission of slang among a group depends on either the mobility of the group (as is the case with the slang of workers or criminals) or the existence of means of mass communication, such as comic strips in newspapers, phonograph records, radio, movies, or television.

Before World War I, a viable youth subculture did not exist anywhere other than on the campuses of colleges and possibly within pockets of youthful vagrants, criminals, and workers. There was little mobility among the young (or in the nation for that matter), and the various forms of mass communication which would make the national spread of slang possible did not begin to emerge until the 1920s.

It is thus no surprise that before World War I the specialized study of the slang idiom of the young was limited to the study of the slang of college students. College slang was then (and to some degree is now) the product of institutional, not generational forces. Each college or university was a closed social system which developed its own traditions, customs, and language. While some words were nearly universal (such as **pony** for a literal translation of a work in a foreign language), many were institution-specific. Most of the vocabulary dealt with academic or institutional subjects such as campus landmarks, intra-college rivalries, academic subjects, and one's level of performance in studies. The big subjects treated by 20th-century youth slang (greetings and farewells, status, intoxication, and sex) were all but ignored by pre-1920 slang.

Illustrations by Victoria Roberts

College Slang in the 1850s

Probably the earliest treatment of the language used by young people in the United States was *A Collection of College Words and Customs* by John Bartlett (Cambridge: John Bartlett, 1851).[1] Bartlett addressed English and American institutions, and overall he paid as much attention to customs as to language. Much of the language that Bartlett recorded was jargon, while much of the actual slang dealt with college-specific subjects and situations. For example, there was a diverse slang idiom to describe a student's performance on recitations, ranging from the poor recitation (**barney, bull, lump, smash, ticker**) to the good (**rowl** or **shine**), showy (**squirt**), or perfect (**curl** or **sail**).

Some of the slang not pertaining specifically to college life as reported by Bartlett follows:

fish
To ingratiate oneself and curry favor through flattery

blood
Excellent

bos
Desserts

buck
Excellent

bull
To discuss at length

coax
To curry favor through flattery

collar
To appropriate

cork
An utter failure or stopper

Cuz John
A privy

dead
Unprepared, unable

decent
Tolerable

devil
To idle

dig
To study hard

diked out
Dressed up stylishly. *What a difference a century would make with this one!*

fag
To labor to the point of weariness. *And this one!*

fat
Containing money (said of a letter). *Heads up rappers, here comes a word!*

ferg
To regain one's poise

flummux
A failure

fork on
To appropriate to oneself

gas
To deceive or cheat

gonus
A dimwit

skunk
To fail to pay a debt

gorm
To eat voraciously

gum
A deception

 H

hard up
The object of a joke

hunch
A tip or implication

 L

lem
A privy

 M

minor
A privy

 N

number ten
A privy

long ear
A sober and religious
person

nuts
Despicable, foolish

 R

ragtail
An annoying person

ray
An insight or clue, as
in "He doesn't
have a ray."

 S

seed
A youth

seedy
Rowdy

short ear
A rowdy person

skin
To plagiarize

smouge
To procure without
permission

spoony
Silly, absurd, often
used to describe
someone who is
drunk

squirty
Gaudy

 T

temple
A privy

tight
Pleasantly intoxicated

tight fit
A good joke

 W

wire
A trick

College Slang Circa 1900

At the turn of the century, the American Dialect Society performed a comprehensive examination of the language used by college students throughout the United States. The two seminal articles were "College Words and Phrases" by Eugene H. Babbit, *Dialect Notes*, Volume II, Part 1 (1900) and "College Slang Words and Phrases," *Dialect Notes*, Volume IV, Part III (1915). From these two articles and several other sources, including Lyman Bagg's *Four Years at Yale* (New Haven, 1871), *Student Life at Harvard* (Boston, 1876), and "Student Slang" by Willard C. Gore in *Contributions to Rhetorical Theory*, edited by F. N. Scott (1895), one may cull a glimpse at the nonacademic and noninstitutional slang used by American college students at the turn of the century.

As would be the case in the 1930s, there were a startling number of words for toilet, including **bank, can, crystal, domus, Egypt, honey house, Jake** (a toilet for men), **Joe, marble palace, mine, old soldiers' home, Ruth** (a toilet for women), **shot tower, temple,** and **X**.

Precursors to *cool* as slang voicings of approval included **hot, peachy,** and **smooth;** with *hot* and *smooth* you have two major-league words of the century with essentially the meaning of "cool." A representative sampling of the slang from these several sources other than the academic- and institution-oriented follows:

A

aped
Drunk

B

babe
A pretty girl

baby
Anything nice

ball of fire
An energetic and brilliant person

ball up
To confuse or become confused

beef
To make an error

belly wash
Any soft drink

bird
A girl

bitch
The queen in a deck of cards

blob
A mistake

blub
To complain of

bone
A dollar

bones
Dice

break off
To disparage.

bug
A dimwit

bull
To make a mistake

bull-dog
The king in a deck of cards

bullet
The ace in a deck of cards

bum
1. A splurge
2. To beg

C

case
A dollar

chill, to have something down
To have complete mastery over something

chimney
Someone who smokes a lot

chump
A fool

cinch
Advantage

clinker
A biscuit

cold
Plain, certain

cooler
Sharp, witty. *Could this be the precursor of cool?*

crust
Aggressiveness

cush
Money

darb
Something that is very attractive

dead
1. Perfect
2. Very

devil
A good companion

dog
To dress with elaborate care

doggy
Dressy. *A big rap word in years to come.*

dough
Money

drag in
To arrive

drink
Any large body of water. *An interesting early example of a word that would later be borrowed from Harlem jive in the 1930s and then resurface in the language of the Beats in the late 1950s.*

drool
Nonsense

fairy
A pretty girl. *Within 30 years, the meaning would be transformed into a reference to an effeminate male.*

fertilizer
Nonsense

fiend
One who excels at anything

fish-scale
A nickel

flivver
A deception

fluke
An utter failure

foxy
Well-dressed

freak
Someone who is exceptionally proficient in a given area

frog
To cheat or deceive

fruity
Easy

fumigate
To smoke

horse
Corned beef

goo
Anything liquid or sticky

gravy
The best

hell-sticks
Matches

invisible blue
The police

CORNED BEEF

irrigate
To drink to excess

J

jitney
A nickel

josh
A joke

junk
A small celebration
with a spread of food

K

kill
To do very well

killer
One who does things
easily

L

lunch
Something that is
easy

N

nail
To master something
completely. *A term*

*with considerable
currency even in the
1990s.*

niggle
To hurry

O

oodles
A lot of

P

pape
A playing card

plunk
A dollar

prime
Complete and total

pumpkin
One's girlfriend

Q

quickstep
Diarrhea

R

rag
To tease or disparage.
*Again, a very modern
word even over the
decades.*

roachy
Of poor quality

roast
Severe criticism

root
A cigarette

rot
Money

S

scag
The butt of a
cigarette

scrub
A second-rate person

scruf
To disparage

shark
One who excels at
something

skate
To drink to the point
of intoxication

skin
To hurry

slam
Disparaging remarks

sore
Vexed

spon
Money

spread
A banquet

stew
Anything easy

porky
Very bad

stiff
Intoxicated

stove
A pipe for
smoking

suds
Money

swipe
To steal

T

tacky
Shoddy

ten-paper
Toilet paper

tin
Money

W

waddy
Unattractive and
unappealing

wop
A boor

Y

yap
The mouth

toy
A comical fellow

Word History: 23 Skidoo!

Although the phrase *23 Skidoo!* (sometimes spelled *23 Skiddoo!*) is now generally associated with the Roaring Twenties, it had in fact lost its popularity by the mid 1910s. During its heyday between 1900 and 1910, *23 Skidoo!* was an expression to behold. Wentworth and Flexner credit it as having been "perhaps the first truly national fad expression and one of the most popular fad expressions to appear in the United States."

As has been the case with any number of slang words and expressions that have followed, the great beauty of *23 Skidoo!* was its versatility. It could be and was used to mean almost anything, ranging from enthusiastic approval to dismissive rejection.

As also is the case with many slang words and expressions, there are competing etymological theories. In *A Dictionary of Catch Phrases* (New York: Stein and Day, 1977), slang lexicographer Eric Partridge advanced four different theories: (1) Frank Parker Stockbridge's theory that the expression was launched as a catch phrase line from *The Only Way,* a dramatization of Dickens's *Tale of Two Cities* in 1899, in which Sydney Carton's standing as the 23rd victim of the guillotine was announced by a character proclaiming "23," to which *skidoo* was added for effect in the retelling; (2) in the first few years of the century, memorabilia sold at vacation resorts and fairs were emblazoned with either *23* or *Skidoo,* and the two soon met; (3) Tom Lewis originated the fad word *23* in *Little Johnny Jones* in 1904, and *Skidoo* was tacked on later; and (4) *23* was possibly derived from a telegraphic shorthand code, not unlike trucker CB code, meaning "Away with you!"

A fifth theory is that the expression was coined by Thomas Aloysius Dorgan ("TAD"), a cartoonist and sportswriter who had an undeniably large role in the coining and spreading of slang. Although the expression was attributed to Dorgan (the simple *23* did appear in a comic published on February 16, 1902), it never appeared in his work.

* * *

[1]In "Words from the Diaries of North Carolina Students," *American Speech,* Vol. 26, No.3 (October 1951), M. B. Dickinson analyzes the slang used in student diaries between 1840 and 1863. Several words from his article are included in this word list of slang of the 1850s.

CHAPTER 2
The 1920s: The Flapper

▼

"Get Hot!"

A vivid image of the Flapper is firmly fixed in our collective cultural memory—the shocking and wild, bootleg-gin-drinking, cigarette-in-holder-smoking, necking and swearing, Charleston-dancing jazz baby; the short-haired or bobbed-hair young girl with a defiantly boyish figure, a fringed skirt, and stockings rolled and bunched below the knee as brazen witness to the fact that—gasp—she wore no corset. Her spunk, zest, and daringly outspoken free spirit reach out over the decades, leaving her raccoon-coated male counterpart in the shadows.

The Flapper was an equal and opposite reaction to the austerity and sacrifices forced upon America by World War I. The 1920s brought peace, economic prosperity, and a split-personality culture at odds with itself—at once Calvinist and hedonist, tradition-bound yet trend-crazy.

She first came into being as an Ivy League student type but was soon imitated by other students and then by young secretaries, office workers, and high school girls. This was, Stuart Berg Flexner wrote, "the first young generation to take itself seriously as a separate, distinct group— and the first to be analyzed, egged on, and

Illustrations by Victoria Roberts

exploited by the books, movies, newspapers, and magazines of its own day."

Girls throughout the country were drawn to the image of the Flapper. Rival organizations of Flappers—the National Flapper Flock and the Royal Order of the Flapper—sprang up, sponsoring fashion shows, picnics, and Flapper frolics.

By the early 1920s, the Flapper was drawing serious attention from the mainstream press. In an article headlined "Flapping Not Repented Of," the *New York Times* on July 16, 1922 reported that Flappers "came upon us and surrounded us all about." The *Times* described the Flapper as "shameless, selfish and honest," and as one who "takes a man's point of view as her mother never could." The Flapper's willingness to compete with men on their own terms was more than just a little shocking: "She'll don knickers and go skiing with you; or, if it happens to be Summer time, swimming; she'll dive as well as you, perhaps better...."

It should come as no surprise that she was not without her critics. H. L. Mencken, for one, dismissed the Flapper as "a young and somewhat foolish girl, full of wild surmises and inclined to revolt against the precepts and admonitions of her elders."

The Flapper's end came towards the end of the decade, despite the bold if reckless prophesy by *The Flapper* magazine in 1922 that "The Flapper Movement is not a craze, but something that will stay." On July 28, 1929, the *New York Times* recounted the end of the Jazz Age and pointed to current fashion trends in Paris as "the death sentence of the Flapper." Not without glee the *Times* writer heralded the coming of the Siren and passing of the Flapper: "Voices falter in their stridencies and reach for lower notes. Girls from the hinterlands clutch at brief skirts in a sudden agony of doubt as to the chic of bumpy knees...."

In 1922, the *New York Times* had guessed that the Flapper would be judged compassionately: "Watch her five years from now and then be thankful that she will be the mother of the next generation, with the hypocrisy, fluff and other

'hookum' worn entirely off." When it described the death sentence of the Flapper in 1929, the *Times* lauded with some apparent irony the accomplishments of the Flapper, who had "established the feminine right to equal representation in such hitherto masculine fields of endeavor as smoking and drinking, swearing, petting and disturbing the community peace."

Language of the Flapper

The 1920s was a decade that was extraordinarily prolific for the American language. New inventions and new ways of social behavior demanded new words. New words and expressions leapt into existence and were popularized in short order. *The Flapper* magazine predicted without hesitation that "many of the phrases now employed by members of this order [the Flapper movement] will eventually find a way into common usage and be accepted as good English just like many American slang words."

The Flapper movement was the first youth movement to generate its own slang dictionaries; as has been the case with many youth slang dictionaries since then, they were small, self-referencing efforts. One was published in *The Flapper* magazine with the explanation that "Stories in this magazine are made more clear to the uninitiated through means of a Flapper dictionary." The second was printed as a small booklet, with the sobriquet of "THE FLAPPER—When she speaks: know what she means." Arriving later on the scene was the *Philadelphia Evening Bulletin*, which on March 8, 1927, bellowed in a headline: "Flapper Filology—The New Language."

In 1934, Maurice Weseen in the *Dictionary of American Slang* recorded "flapperese" as meaning "the slangy language of modern youth." While one may suspect that the term "flapperese" enjoyed very little popular application, there is no doubt that the Flapper used a language of her own. Interestingly, little of the slang that she spoke is spoken today, either as slang or as standard colloquial English. *Copacetic* denoting excellence sur-

vives; *bozo* and *ducky* have not completely vanished; *mad money* is still fairly frequently used, and *unreal* is alive and well in essentially the same sense used by the Flapper. One surprise survivor is *lounge lizard*, which seems to show up in nearly every decade of the century but which clearly meant a ladies' man in the 1920s, as witnessed by its use by F. Scott Fitzgerald in *This Side of Paradise* (1920). If one accepts the narrating voice crafted by Anita Loos in *Gentlemen Prefer Blondes* as an accurate depiction of Flapper-inspired speech, the Flapper often began a sentence with "I mean," pausing to make her point; this has a very modern sound. Her distrust of anyone over 30, as evidenced by *Father Time* and *Rock of Ages* is more than vaguely evocative of the "Don't trust anyone over thirty" motto of the late 1960s.

Aside from these few expressions, her language seems to have faded with the years. In retrospect, it was not a particularly smart slang, and much has the sound of having been self-consciously modern, cunning, and forced. To call someone who never pays (coughs up) his share a *Smith Brother* (a cultural allusion to Smith Brothers cough drops) is cute, but perhaps too cute. The seemingly endless string of *cat's pajamas* and *bee's knees* is an example of the simple and artificial nature of much of the Flapper's slang, a criticism which applies with some regularity to the slang of the young.

The Flapper's slang was not without its bright moments, though. The use of *dincher* to mean a half-smoked cigarette has a certain cool ring to it even now and whatever the etymology of the word. To refer to a particularly tough or hard-boiled character as *eight minutes* or even *ten minutes* was undeniably witty. *High hatty* as meaning haughty is catchy, and the shout of *Get Hot!* to the Flapper tearing up the dance floor with the Charleston sounds as vibrant today as it did in 1923. As was the case with the slangy spelling of *phat* in the 1990s, the Flapper experimented with spelling at times: *Rhatz!* for "rats!" and *'stoo bad* for "that's too bad," a spirited expression in its own right.

A Flapper Word List

A

ab-so-lute-ly
Yes

absent treatment
Dancing with a timid
dance partner

air-tight
Very attractive
(see TIGHT)

airedale
An unattractive man

alarm clock
A chaperone

alibi
Flowers or a box of
candy

all wet
Wrong

And how!
I strongly agree with
you!

ankle
To walk

ankle excursion
A walk, especially a
walk home

apple sauce
Flattery. *One of the
many slang words
coined, or at least
with first recorded use,
by T.A. Dorgan (TAD)
in his comic strip.
This first appeared
in a TAD strip in
1919.*

armchair
A love nest

B

baby grand
Heavyweight

bally nipper
A tomboy

baloney
Nonsense

Banana oil!
I doubt that!

Bank's closed.
I will engage in no
kissing or petting.

barneymugging
Courtship or petting

bean picker
A person who patches
up problems (picks
up spilled beans)

bird
A man who is a high flyer

bell bottom
A sailor

bell polisher
A young man who
lingers in a dormitory
or apartment
vestibule late at
night

bent hairpin
Elderly maid

berries
1. Great
2. Money

big cheese
An important person

big timer
A charming and
romantic man

billboard
A flashy man or
woman

bimbo
A great person

blaah
No good

blooey
The condition when
one has gone to
pieces

blouse
To leave

blow
1. A wild party
2. To leave

blue serge
A sweetheart

blushing violet
A publicity hound

The Flapper
Intoxicated

Bar none, no adjective has commanded more slang synonyms over the ages than "intoxicated." Despite the 18th Amendment and its novel approach of augmenting the Constitution to limit, not protect, a right, the consumption of alcohol to the point of inebriation as a quest of the young was alive and well in the 1920s.

To the Flapper, alcohol was **giggle water** or **hooch,** a consciously slangy word (derived from the name of an Alaskan Indian tribe, the Hoochinoo, involved in the production and transportation of bootleg liquor) that was not confined in usage to the Flapper; to **lap** was to drink, most often at a **gin mill** (speakeasy). To be **half-cut** or **soaked with a bar rag** was to be pleasantly tipsy, while Flapper slang to describe the state of full-blown alcohol intoxication included **barreled, bolognied, canned, crocked, fried, jammed, jiggered, juiced, oiled, ossified, out like a light, pie-eyed, piffled, plastered, polluted, potted, shellacked, shot, splifficated, stewed to the hat,** and **tanked.** A Flapper who could hold her liquor was a **non-skid;** a **hip hound** was a serious drinker; a drunken GOOF was a **flask,** and an **apple alley** was a drunk sailor.

---

boob tickler
A girl who entertains her father's out-of-town customers

bookkeeping
The act of making a date

booklegger
A dealer in suppressed novels

brillo
Someone who lives fast and spends money freely

bunk
Nonsense

bust
A prize fighter

Butt me.
Please give me a cigarette.

button shining
Close dancing

cake basket
A limousine

canceled stamp
A shy girl at a dance or party

cash
A kiss

Cash or check?
Do I receive a kiss now or later?

cellar smeller
A young man with a knack for showing up where liquor is being served

charlie
A man with a mustache

cheaters
Eye glasses

Check.
Kiss me later.

Check your hat.
Call on me later.

cherry smashes
Feeble kisses

chin music
Gossip

ciggy
A cigarette

clothesline
Gossip

copacetic
Excellent

corn shredder
A man who is an awkward dancer

corridor vamp
Someone of either sex who ogles the opposite sex during school hours

cowpie
A car

cowpie warmup
A car ride

crape or **crape hanger** or **crepe** or **crepe hanger**
A zealous reformer

crasher
A person who attends a party without an invitation

cuddle cootie
A young man who takes a girl for a ride

cuddler
One who likes to pet

dapper
A Flapper's father

declaration of independence
Divorce

dewdropper
A young man who does not work and who sleeps all day

di mi
Goodness

dimbox
A taxi

dimbox jaunt
A taxi ride

dincher
A half-smoked cigarette

dipe ducat
A subway token

ditzek
Anything funny

dog jock
A man who walks his wife's dogs

dogs
Feet

dolled up
Dressed up

drag
Influence

drag a sock
To walk or dance

drop the pilot
To divorce

drugstore cowboy
A fashionably dressed idler who loiters in public places, trying

to pick up girls.
Another term coined by TAD.

ducky
Very good

dud
A studious boy or girl who does not socialize

dud up
To dress up

dumkuff
Nutty

E

earful
Enough, too much

Edisoned
Questioned

egg
A big timer

egg harbor
A free dance

embalmer
A bootlegger

eye opener
Marriage

F

face stretcher
An older unmarried woman trying to look young

eight minutes
A tough (hard-boiled) guy

false ribs
A corset

Father Time
Any man over 30

feathers
Light conversation

feet
A very clumsy dancer

fig-leaf
A one-piece bathing suit

fire alarm
A divorced woman

fire bell
A married woman

fire extinguisher
A chaperone

fish walk
A Flapper who walks with the rhythm of a sea animal

flat shoe
A fight between a Flapper and her GOOF

flat tire
A boring pest

floater
A person who makes trouble and then vanishes

floorflusher
An insatiable dancer

flop
A seat

flour lover
A girl who uses too much face powder

fluky
Odd

for a row of...
Some distance, as in "I was knocked for a row of carrots."

For crying out loud!
I can't believe that!

four flusher
One who fails to keep a promise or pay a debt

G

gams
Legs

gander
To dress up

garable
Plenty of talk

Get hot! Get hot!
Encouragement shouted to a Flapper giving her all to the Charleston

gimlet
A chronic bore

give the air
To break a date

give the knee
To dance cheek-to-cheek and toe-to-toe

glorious regalia
The flamboyant and chic clothes of a Flapper

glue
To take and keep

good mixer
A person who fits in well

goof
A boyfriend

goofy
In love, attracted to

grab a flop
To take a seat

greaseball
A foreign CAKE-EATER (See box on page 20.)

green apples
A homely woman

greenland
A park

ground-gripper
A sober-minded young person

grummy
Depressed

grungy
Envious

gussie
A shy person

H

handcuff
An engagement ring

hard-boiled
Tough (See EIGHT-MIN-UTES and the even tougher TEN-MINUTES.)

heebie-jeebies
Physical manifesta-tions of anxiety

heeler
An inferior dancer

hen coop
A beauty parlor

high hatty
Haughty, unapproachable

high cloud
A big shot, tough guy

highjohn
A boyfriend

hike
A walk

hikers
Knickerbockers

hokum
Nonsense

holaholy
A girl or boy who objects to necking

holy smokes
A probation officer

hoof
To walk

heeler
An inferior dancer

hoofer
A chorus girl

hope chest
A pack of cigarettes

hopper
A dancer

horn in
To get into a dance without an invitation

Hot dawg!
How great!

hot foot
A skilled dancer

Hot diggity dog!
How great!

hotsy-totsy
Pleasing

Houdini
To arrive on time for a date

grubber
One who borrows cigarettes

I

I should hope to kill you!
I emphatically agree with what you said!

icy mitt
Rejection

insured
Engaged

It's the bunk!
I doubt that!

J

Jane
A girl who meets her date on the stoop

lamp post
An ostentatious piece of jewelry

jay-bird
A man who takes risks

jumping tintypes
Moving pictures

K

keen
Attractive, appealing

killjoy
Anyone who is too solemn

kippy
Anything that's nice

kneeduster
A skirt

L

lalapazaza
A good sport

lallygagger *or* **lollygagger**
A young man who likes to pet

Lens Louise
A person who monopolizes conversations

lip stick
A cigarette

M

mad money
Carfare home to be used by a Flapper if she has a fight with her date

manacle
A wedding ring

mars
A theater star

meal ticket
A Flapper who invites a man to dinner when he calls

meringue
Personality

mooch
To leave

mop
A handkerchief

mug
A kiss

munitions
Face powder

mushroom
A parlor

mustard plaster
An unwelcome boy who loiters around

N

necker
A petter who puts her arms around a boy's neck

Nerts!
I am amazed!

nifty
Good

noodle juice
Tea

nosebaggery
A restaurant

Not so good!
I don't approve!

nut cracker
A nightstick

O

oatmeal mush
The shallow talk of a

Currency

The Flapper had a rich vocabulary when it came to talking about the coin of the realm. To her, a **boffo** or **brick** was a dollar, **prunes** were pennies, and **berries, chips, dough, green glorious, greens, jack, kale, mazuma, plunks, shekels,** or **sugar** meant money. An **anchor** was a large bankroll; a rich man was a **darb** (or **The Darbs**) or a **gold mine,** and so a **miner** or **gold-digger** was a woman who pursued men for their money, and a **forty-niner** was a man prospecting for a rich wife. **Hush money** was a young Flapper's allowance.

At the other end of the spectrum, a **hardware merchant** was a man who mixed keys with his change to give the impression of carrying a lot of coins, and a cheapskate was called a **false alarm,** a **gum-drop,** a **one-way kid,** a **pocket cleaner** or **pocket twister,** a **slimp,** a **slumper,** a **strangler,** a **twister** or a **wallet-clutcher.** If you had no money you were **soaped,** and probably a **grubber** (a person who borrowed cigarettes).

A **finagler** abruptly disappeared when the check arrived, while the **finale hopper** simply chose to arrive after things had been paid for; to **step off a wharf** was to order drinks without paying for them. Several words and expressions were used to describe someone who took his date to a free event and then walked her home to avoid the cost of carfare, including **flat-wheeler, heel and toe, Johnny Walker,** and **park bench duster.**

CAKE-EATER (See box on page 20.)

obituary notice
An eviction notice

Oh yeah!
I doubt that!

oilburner
A person who chews gum

oilcan
An imposter

old fops
People past middle age

Oliver Twist
A good dancer

once in a dirty while
From time to time

Ooo, you slaughter me!
That's funny!

orchid
Anything expensive

ostrich
A person who knows everything

out on parole
Divorced

overdose of shellac
Too much make-up

owl
A person who stays out late

peppy
Vigorous, energetic

petting pantry
A movie theater

pill
A teacher

pillow case
A young man who is full of FEATHERS

pine feather period
The period in a Flapper's life when she blossoms out

pipe down
To stop talking

playboy
A boyfriend, usually older

pos-a-lute-ly
Yes

pos-i-tive-ly
Yes

pricker
A gossip, slanderer

Priscilla
A girl who prefers to stay home

Produce the cash
Kiss me now

prune pit
Anything that is old-fashioned

punch rustler
One who spends most of the time at a party near the refreshment table

punch the bag
To talk without saying anything of consequence

put next to
To alert someone to something good

quilt
A drink that warms one up

R

razz
To make fun of

real McCoy
An authentic item

reel boy
A man who likes
movies

Rhatz!
How disappointing!

Ritz
Conceited

ritzy burg
Something that is not
classy

Rock of Ages
A woman over the
age of 30

rughopper
A young man who
never dates

rug shaking
Dancing the shimmy

show case
A rich man's wife
with jewels

S

seetie
Anything a Flapper
hates

sharpshooter
A young man who
spends a lot and
dances well

sip
A female dancer

slapper
A reformer, antagonist
of the Flapper

slat
A boyfriend

sloppy
A female dancer

slummer
A woman who revels
in studio parties

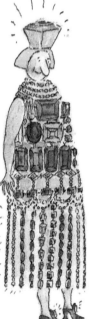

Smith Brother
A young man who
never pays (coughs
up)

smoke-eater
Someone who smokes
cigarettes

smooth
A young man who
does not keep his
word

smudger
A person who likes to
dance closely

snake charmer
A woman involved
in bootlegging

soft shoe
To follow behind
someone

spill
To talk

spill an earful
To talk too much

squirrel
To hide

stander
The victim of a
female grifter

static
Conversation that
means nothing

step off a wharf
To order drinks
without paying for
them

step out
To rise from girlhood
to Flapperdom

step on it
To make up
after a quarrel or
FLATSHOE

stilts
Legs

'stoo bad
An offer of sympathy
to a person enjoying
hard luck

storm and strife
The girlfriend of a
CAKE-EATER (See box
on page 20.)
*A rare example of
American use of
rhyming slang: "storm
and strife" rhymes
with "wife."*

streeted
Thrown out of a party

strike breaker
A young woman who
goes out with her
friend's boyfriend
while there is a lull in
their relationship

struggle
Modern dance

stuck on
In love

stutter bus
A truck

stutter tub
A motor boat

sugar daddy
Boyfriend, usually
older

swan
To glide gracefully

swanky
Good

swell
Good

Trotzky
An old woman with face hair. *Another example of intentional misspelling.*

T

take the air
To leave or be asked to leave

tasty
Good, appealing. *Definitely a modern-sounding word suggestive of the surfer culture, tasty is found in "Collegiate," a song written in 1925 by Moe Jaffe and Nat Bonx with the words "Hasty, hasty—we make life so tasty."*

ten cent box
A taxi cab

ten minutes
An exceptionally tough (hard-boiled) man

the nuts
Anything good

tight
Attractive

toddler
The faster sister of a FINALE HOPPER (See box on page 17.)

toss and hike
To reject one girl and pursue another

U

umbrella
A young man any girl can borrow for the evening

unreal
Special

upchuck
To vomit

upstage
Snobbish

urban set
A new gown

W

walk in
A young man who attends a party without an invitation

water-proof
A girl whose fine complexion requires no make-up

weasel
A young man who steals a girl from her boyfriend

wet blanket
Kill-joy

whangdoodle
Jazz

whiskbroom
A man with face hair

whoopee
Raucous, affable fun

windsucker
A braggart

wooden woman
A girl who will not go out

Woof! Woof!
An expression denoting ridicule

wrestle
A type of shimmy dance

wrinkle
A girl's mother

wurp
A killjoy

Z

Zowie!
An interjection after a sudden bump in the road

Word History: "Any Animal's Anything"

The expression **cat's pajamas** was one of the many Flapper slang expressions to combine an animal with a part of anatomy ("pajamas" being the nonanatomical exception to prove the rule) to convey outright perfection. The two feline metaphors **cat's meow** and *cat's pajamas*, both of which survive to some degree today, although with a quaint feel to them, were two of the most popular slang expressions of the 1920s and were the genesis of the long lineage of animal expressions that the Flapper favored, all meaning "something great."

As is the case with most slang words and expressions, a definitive etymology is impossible, and varying accounts of the expressions' origins exist.

In *The Random House Historical Dictionary of American Slang*, Jonathan Lighter traces *cat's meow* to 1921 and *cat's pajamas* to 1922. Conversely, Stuart Berg Flexner places *cat's pajamas* as the original phrase upon which all future variants were built, noting that when the phrase was coined in around 1920 "pajamas were still somewhat shockingly new."

Christine Ammer delves further back, writing in *It's Raining Cats and Dogs and Other Beastly Expressions* that the expression *cat's meow* "seems to have originated in American girls' schools during the late 19th century and become very popular during the roaring twenties, when

The Male Companion

When it came to describe the Flapper's male counterpart, no single term so well caught the public imagination nearly as well as "Flapper" did for the woman. Inasmuch as the 1920s youth scene was defined by the woman, it is hardly surprising that language followed reality. The dominant role played by the young woman of the 1920s is revealed by the definition-by-comparison of "flipperism" in *The Flapper's Dictionary* as "the revolt of the modern young man to keep up with the flapper." Good luck.

Social historians have seized upon **sheik** as the favored name of the young man in revolt in the 1920s, the young man who took his name and look from Rudolph Valentino's 1921 movie. While "sheik" was certainly used at the time, it was not the most common term employed. That honor would probably have gone either to **flipper** (apparently simply coined from **Flapper**) or **goof. Jazzbo, sharpshooter, slicker,** and **stroller** were all used to describe a regular fellow, while a **lounge lizard** was an especially attractive ladies' man.

The most lavish Flapper vocabulary was reserved, with some degree of disdain, for the **cake-eater,** a term whose first recorded use is attributed to Thomas Dorgan (TAD) in his comic strip of November 17, 1918, and described by *The Flapper's Dictionary* as

...any guy who is addicted to noodle juice parties, one who nibbles at cakes at such parties. One who wears his mop up his sleeve, opposite to a he-man. A sissy.

Other words used to describe the same less-than-he-man included **angel child, ballroom golfer, bun-duster, crumb-gobbler, crumb-snatcher, crumpet-muncher, Eskimo pie eater, grummy ostrich, parlor bolshevik, parlor hound, pastry snake, pastry vaulter, porcupine, puddle jumper, snake, sponge cake,** and **tea-crasher**. Even more contempt was reserved for a **wallie,** a cake-eater with veneered hair.

A **beasel hound, scandal walker,** or **subchaser** was a cake-eater who attempted to pick up a Flapper, while a **cuddle cootie** was a young man who took his Flapper for a ride in a bus or car. A **brooksy boy** was a classily, if sometimes over-dressed, young man.

Last and least, a **dud** was a flipper who did not live up to his name.

College Slang

The Flapper movement dominated the 1920s youth scene, but it was not the only show in town. College campuses generated their own slang, much of which was specific to a campus or the academic setting. Some of the college idiom, though, was general-purpose slang. It is not possible to say where Flapper slang stopped and college slang started, but the words that follow were found in college glossaries but not Flapper lists.

The young male student of the 1920s was very conscious of how he dressed, and he had a range of vernacular to describe it. If he was **smooth,** he was well dressed without qualification; the **doggy** student was well dressed, but in a self-conscious and conspicuous manner. A **Joe Brooks** was a perfect dresser; this expression and its cousin **Joe Zilsch** (John Doe student) evolved in the late 1920s and early 1930s into simply **Joe** (the average student). At the other end of things, if you were **wet** you were an odd dresser or you over-dressed, and most likely you were a braggart without any sense of humor, sophistication, or breeding.

When it came to matters of love and romance, one's **wife** was his steady girlfriend. If he wanted to go to a **drag** (a dance; **dragging** meant taking a girl to a dance) and had no date, not to worry—take a **blind date** (a social partner whom one has not met). Combine the two and you could **drag a blind**—take a blind date to a dance. **Necking** replaced "petting" to mean kissing, while a **party** referred either to a girl who necked or necking itself. Still in the sin department, alcohol was known as **mule**.

Female college students had their own extensive body of slang, which was characterized by elaborate, largely clipped references to professors, courses, and buildings. Of a more general nature was **baby** as an adjective, denoting that that which was being described was of an introductory or novice level. Something that was very good was **quite the berries,** while something that was quite amusing was a **hoot**. A lot of something was **oodles**. To **tub** was to take a bath.

Written sources on which this section was based include "The University Tongue" by Altha Leah Bass, *Harper's Monthly,* March 1922; "College Slang a Language All its Own" in *The Literary Digest,* March 14, 1925; "College Slang Words and Phrases From Bryn Mawr College" by Howard J. Savage in *Dialect Notes,* Volume V, pages 139-148; and "Collegians have Language All Their Own" in *Word Study,* December 1927.

Clara Bow, the fabled 'It girl,' was widely regarded as 'the cat's meow.'"

Whatever the origin, the animal metaphor proved to be fast-mutating. The same enthusiastic praise garnered by *cat's pajamas* was conjured by the combination of practically any animal and any part of its anatomy, real or imagined. Richmond P. Bond described the evolution of Flapper animal metaphors in *American Speech,* Vol. 2, No. 1 (October 1927):

"The cat's meow" is used to express approval of or satisfactory ability on the part of the thing or person referred to. Substitute for "meow" "whiskers," "eyebrow," "ankle," "tonsils," "adenoids" or "galoshes," "pajamas," "cufflinks," "roller skates," and the result is the same. The ant *and the gnat and the bee and the elephant are also called upon in such hours of need.*

While more examples could surely be found, the following list demonstrates the breadth and width of the Flapper's smart and slangy zoological metaphors—the **bee's ankles, bee's knees, bullfrog's beard, canary's tusks, cat's canary, cat's cuffs, cat's eye, cat's eyebrows, cat's kimono, cat's underwear, cat's whiskers** (the name of a song by Fred Tibbott and George Rex), **clam's garters, cuckoo's chin, dog's ankles, duck's quack, eel's hips, eel's ankle, elephant's adenoids, elephant's arches, elephant's instep, elephant's hips, elephant's wrist, frog's ankles, frog's eyebrows, gnat's elbow,**

Terms of Dis-Endearment

As Flappers shocked the nation, America was quietly transforming itself from a rural population to an urban one. The Flapper was ever-conscious of those with less sophistication in the ways of the world, and she had a diverse vocabulary to describe naive men from the country, or **the sticks**. The word **hick** had been around for centuries, but it gained tremendous ground in the 1920s. Other expressions and terms meaning the same included **apple knocker, apple shaker, brush ape, brush hound, bush hound, hay shaker, otig** or **dumbotig,** and **otis**.

A dense or dull boy or man could be called a **bozo** (quite modern even now), **gobby,** or **potato**. His female counterpart was known as a **bozark, dumbdora, meatball, mockadite,** or **tomato**. Words of disparagement free of any gender association included **kluck** (someone who was dumb but happy), **lob** (a dimwit), **low lid** (an unsophisticate), and a **slunge** (a person of the lowest kind), a word that has a definite ring of the 1970s Valley Girl to it.

goat's whiskers, grasshopper's knees, hen's eyebrows, kitten's ankles, leopard's stripes, monkey's eyebrows, pig's feet, pig's wings, puppy's tail, pussy cat's whiskers, sardine's whiskers, snake's ears, snake's hips, snugglepup's bow-bow, tiger's spots, and **turtle's neck**. The basic expressions persist to some extent today, largely among advertisement and headline writers. When astronaut Peter Conrad described the flight of Gemini 5 to *Life* magazine (September 24, 1965), he said, "We had an orbit. It was the cat's bandana."

The Flapper's animal references were not limited to these sometimes forced-sounding metaphors. A **good elk** was a kind and decent man, a **horse prancer** was an inept dancer, a **lounge lizard** a ladies' man, a **pastry snake** or simply a **snake** was a CAKE-EATER (see box on page 20), a **police dog** was a Flapper's fiancee, a **snugglepup** was a young man fond of petting, and a **tabby cat** was the person the Flapper hated the most.

Word History: Whence Flapper?

Lexicographers have advanced two general theories on the process by which the word "Flapper" came to signify, in the words of *The Flapper's Dictionary*, the "ultra-modern, young girl, full of pep and life, beautiful (naturally or artificially), blasé, imitative, and intelligent to a degree who is about to bloom into the period of womanhood and believes that her sex has been

and will continue to be, emancipated to a level higher than most mortals have been able to attain."[1]

The first school of thought tracks "Flapper" to the English dialect use of the term to mean a young bird of any kind only just able to fly, especially a young wild duck, a definition found in the *English Dialect Dictionary* dating to 1856 and traced by the *Oxford English Dictionary* to 1773. An anonymous reader wrote *The Evening News* of August 20, 1892, explaining the leap from duck to young girl:

Another correspondent points out that a "flapper" is a young wild duck which is unable to fly, hence a little duck of any description, human or otherwise. The answer seems at first sight frivolous enough, but it is probably the correct solution of this interesting problem all the same.

Stuart Berg Flexner agreed that the term's linguistic ancestor was probably flapper in the duck sense, while Robert Chapman, writing in 1986, suggested a further logical link between the meanings—"perhaps from the idea of an unfledged bird flapping its wings as one did while dancing the Charleston."

The second school traces flapper to the dialect word "flap," which Wright defined as "a young, giddy girl." The 18th and mid-19th century slang dictionaries do not treat "flapper" in this sense, although Farmer and Henley's *A*

Dictionary of Slang defines flapper as "a little girl" or "a very young prostitute."

These dual meanings were noted again by J. Redding Ware in 1909 in *Passing English of the Victorian Era*, where he defined flapper as "a very immoral young girl in her early 'teens.'" In *The Long Trail: What the British soldier Sang and Said in 1914-1918*, John Brophy and Eric Partridge identified *flapper* as pre-World War I "middle class slang" for a teenage girl, "from the pigtail of braided hair she wore and swung about on occasion." When he first published *A Dictionary of Slang and Unconventional English* in 1957, Eric Partridge retained the dual definitions of a young harlot or "any young girl with her hair not yet put up."

Flapper was thus established slang before the Flapper we know burst on the scene. Variations on *flapper* abounded even before the word was taken off the shelf in around 1920 and given new life, including *flapperhood, flapperdom, flapperism,* and *flapperish*. After the 1920s had passed, Maurice Weseen included several additional variants in his 1934 *Dictionary of American Slang*, including **flapperese** (the language of Flappers), **flapperitis** (the silliness of adolescence), **flapperocracy** (adolescent girls as a class), and **flapperology** (the attempt to understand the conduct of adolescent girls); one has to wonder if any of these words were actually used. One British adaptation that arose in 1928 after the grant of the franchise to women in the United Kingdom was **flapper-vote**.

In the 1920s, the Flapper also knew herself as a **barlow**, a **beasel**, a **chicken**, a **flap**, a **harmonica**, a **hot mama**, a **jazz baby**, a **jolappy**, a **mama**, or a **whoopee mama**. Special meanings were attached to **beaut** (a cute Flapper), **biscuit** (a pettable Flapper), **bookie** (a Flapper who was easy to date), **gerry flapper** (one who adored and imitated the American singer Geraldine Farrar), **hooker** (a Flapper who despised hard work), **jeweler** (a Flapper who collected fraternity pins), **no-soap** (a Flapper who refrained from petting parties), **pocket twister** (a Flapper with expensive tastes), **polly** (an effusive Flapper), **Princess Mary** (a Flapper who expected to marry soon), **sheba** (a sexy Flapper), **twister** (a Flapper taken to a dance by her GOOF), and **weed** (a risk-taking Flapper).

[1]In her *Dictionary of Word Phrase Origins*, Mary Morris suggested that perhaps the Flapper was known as such because of her "penchant for galoshes, worn...with buckles unfastened so as to create the greatest possible 'flap.'" This theory, however, has not found any following.

Sources

The primary sources for this chapter were "A Flapper's Dictionary" in *The Flapper*, Volume 1, No. 2 (July 1922): *The Flapper's Dictionary: As Compiled by One of Them* (Plattsburgh, New York: The Imperial Press, 1922); and "Flapper Filology—The New Language" in the *Philadelphia Evening Bulletin* of March 8, 1927. Shorter treatments of Flapper slang can be found in Stuart Berg Flexner's *I Hear America Talking* (New York: Van Nostrand Reinhold Company, 1976); *This Fabulous Century*, Volume III (1920-1930), edited by Ezra Bowen (New York: Time-Life Books, 1969); and Charles Panati's *Panati's Parade of Fads, Follies, and Manias* (New York: Harper Perennial, 1991).

CHAPTER 3
The 1930s: The Joe and the Jerk

▼

"They're mugging light, they're muggin' heavy, they're in the groove. They're goin' to town! They're SWINGIN'!"

The early 1930s were chaotic years in the United States. The national banking system collapsed, industrial output was drastically depressed, unemployment mounted without respite, and hourly wages plunged for those who were lucky enough to be working. Hunger, homelessness, desperation and dejection were epidemic. One third of the nation was, President Roosevelt said, "ill-housed, ill-clad, ill-nourished." Those who were not were ever conscious of the precipice over which they too could plummet.

Popular youth culture was in many ways undaunted by the nation's troubles. The entertainment industry knew an opportunity when it saw one, and the 1930s were glory years for the escapes of radio, movies, and music, all of which held no small appeal for America's young. Low-cost entertainment such as miniature golf, pinball, and jukeboxes swept the country, as did fads such as goldfish swallowing. As Grace Palladino observes in *Teenagers: An American History*, until the Great Depression most young Americans worked for a living and high school

Illustrations by Rick Meyerowitz

was the domain of the privileged few. The Depression forced young Americans out of the farm, factory, or the home into high school, and in the process of this shift they became for the first time a generational age-group, a separate teenage nation.

Popular youth culture of the early 1930s was defined as much by its revolt against the excesses of the Flapper era as it was by the exigencies of the Great Depression. Youth culture for a few years shied away from the subversive and daring ethic of the Flapper, with Joe College (according to Maurice Weseen "An imaginary typical college boy; a college student of the rah rah type") and the soda fountain worker (the jerk) epitomizing the cheerful, optimistic, wisecracking young. Especially in light of what hardships were to come, those who came of age in the early 1930s were a naive yet hopeful group, with a popular culture that reflected the small town, hometown, rural character of the country more than the urban values of Harlem and jive. While spurning the outlaw aspects of the Flapper years, popular youth culture of the early 1930s was nevertheless full of vitality, energy, and humor.

Youth Slang of the Early 1930s

Despite the basically conservative tilt of popular youth culture of the early 1930s, youth slang was remarkably clever and surprisingly modern. Many slang words and expressions which were popular in the early 1930s, before the infusion of jive later in the decade, either became fixtures of youth slang or after a dormant period emerged again towards the end of the century. *Bug, cheesy, cramp your style, fade, flick, get around, hot, juicy, large, mean, scrub, slam, slick, smooth, spiffy, spread, suck,* and *sweet* all sound quite

contemporary.

While the influence of jive that began to creep into wider youth vernacular in the late 1930s cannot be underestimated, considerable credit must be given to the pre-jive, Joe and Jerk idiom of the early 1930s. It had a decidedly innocent verve and vigor to it despite the conservative forces shaping it.

And Then Came Swing

After a staid first half-decade, the youth culture of the 1930s exploded with swing, big-band jazz that featured improvised melodies and rhythms developed around a given, rehearsed melody. In 1932, Duke Ellington released "It Don't Mean a Thing If It Ain't Got That Swing" (music by Ellington, words by Irving Mills); it was a catchy song but a few years ahead of its time. In 1935 swing took off for real with the hit song "Music Goes Round and Around" (a title with an uncanny resemblance to "The Rock Around the Clock" of rock and roll fame) which was worked out by Edward Farley and Michael Riley (words by Red Hodgson) at the Onyx Club on 52nd Street in New York. It was the biggest popular hit since "Yes We Have No Bananas" in the early 1920s. Peter Tamony recalled that "It spun interminably; it was seldom off the air. It fit the mood of the people at the time."

As America began slowly to pull out of the Depression, swing took off with a passion and ferocity not dissimilar to the Flapper frenzy of the early 1920s. In 1938 and 1939 the jitterbug craze swept the nation, leaving America's teenagers in large part enthralled and defined by Swing, Jitterbug, and Jive, gathering in hometown or neighborhood soda fountains with jukeboxes blasting Benny Goodman and Artie Shaw, the boys in their loose pants and letter sweaters, the girls in loose skirts, both in saddle shoes, dancing up a storm and talking about the musicians and last Saturday night's *Your Hit Parade* and wasn't life good!

And with it, Jive

With swing, the jive of urban black America (primarily New York, Chicago, and New Orleans) crept into the idiom of America's youth. The patois of jazz musicians had appeared in print and been used in the lyrics of popular recordings since the 1920s, but it did not begin to move out of the jazz world until the mid-1930s.

Most of the first wave of jive that stole out from the idiom of jazz into popular youth slang dealt with the music itself. Swing glossaries in *Downbeat* ("The Slanguage of Swing," November 1935), *The Delineator* ("It's Swing!" November 1936) and the *Baltimore Evening Sun* ("Swing Slang and the Argot of the Cats," December 19, 1938) were focused almost exclusively on music-specific jive vocabulary—"The cats are licking their chops, they're friskin' their whiskers,

they're getting off!!!! They're mugging light, they're muggin' heavy, they're in the groove. They're goin' to town! They're SWINGIN'! " In the early years, Walter Winchell stood out in his reporting of "Harlem Slanguage," bringing words other than musician-specific into the light in early 1935.

In 1938, Cab Calloway issued the first of his celebrated little masterpieces of jive lexicography, the *Cat-Alogue* (later the *Hepster's Dictionary: Language of Jive*), which he would revise on a semiregular basis until 1944. By the end of the decade, jive was on its way to defining the slang of American youth. In July 1941, the *Pictorial Review* reported that "The esoteric terms that were once intelligible only to musicians have become common colloquialisms, bandied about by swing aficionados from coast to coast." Jive reached its apex in the 1940s, but was revived by the hipsters of the 1950s, adjusted by the hippies of the 1960s, and revisited by the rappers of the 1980s. Jive, the lingua franca of the streets, is covered fully in Chapter Four.

A Joe's Word List	**all shot** Tired, exhausted	**Awgwan!** I don't believe you. "Oh, go on!"	**barge around** To walk slowly
	all to the mustard Excellent		**Be good!** Good-bye.
Abyssinia. I'll be seeing you.	**all wet** No good		**biff** A failure
aces up Excellent	**Ask me another!** I don't know!	**ball of fire** A bright and dynamic person	**Big It** An self-centered and conceited person

Child Tramps

As the Great Depression (the **big trouble** in the idiom of the child tramp) ravaged America, the ranks of hobos on the bum were swelled by thousands, if not hundreds of thousands, of homeless boys and girls. In their day-to-day conversations, they spoke a slang, separated by lifetimes from the carefree slang of middle-class youth.

Their main care and anxiety was traveling, usually riding freight trains (**on the rods**), if lucky inside a box car (**riding under cover**). The alternative to riding on a freight train was **legging** (walking). At the end of a day, a child tramp looked for a **jungle** (hobo camp); if very unfortunate, the child would **bunk on his ears** (sleep on the ground or floor without blankets). The police (**bulls**) were a major impediment to travel for child tramps.

To survive, a child tramp had to work, beg or resort to charity. There were not many jobs for homeless children, perhaps **pearl diving** (washing dishes), working **on the street** (soliciting for sex) or **pulling a job** (stealing). Begging involved either picking a **stand** (fixed spot with plenty of passing foot traffic) and panhandling there or **carrying the banner** (going door to door), **battering privates** (knocking on the doors of private homes) and **tooling ringers** (ringing doorbells); no matter where, **mush talk** (persuasiveness) was used to get the public to **shell out** (give money). If all else failed, one could go to **Sally's** (the Salvation Army), listen to the **Christers** and **accept the Lord** for a meal consisting of **days old** (stale baked goods), **mulligan** (a stew) or **swill** (food fed to hobos and hogs), and **misery** (bitter coffee).

Fights, quarrels, and sex—too often related—were also frequent subjects of child tramp conversation. Young boy tramps (**lambs**) had to be on the lookout for **wolves** or **fruiters** who would lure or force them into **that sin**. If a boy got involved with a **grill** (girl), he had to be careful or he would get **burned** (contact venereal disease).

The primary source for this sad little look at the slang of child tramps is *Boy and Girl Tramps of America* by Thomas Minehan (New York: Grossett and Dunlap, 1934).

bird
A noise made with the lips to indicate dissatisfaction with something. *An earlier, kinder, and gentler version of the bird as the profane middle finger. Why a bird?*

boil
To walk quickly, to hurry

bong
To catch on to a joke slowly

booshwash
Empty talk

bounce
To flatter

brodie
A mistake.
Steve Brodie claimed to have jumped off the Brooklyn Bridge on July 23, 1886, but having no witnesses, he was widely suspected of having faked the feat. Thomas Dorgan (TAD) first used the expression "do a brodie" on February 8, 1909, to mean "to leap." By the 1920's "brodie" had come to mean a failure or a mistake.

bug
Something that is hard to understand

cake
To eat

Can the twit!
Stop that idle talking!

cats, the
Too bad, as "That's the cats"

Chase yourself!
Go away and stop bothering me!

check *or* **checker**
A dollar

Check!
All right!

cheek it
To bluff

cheesy
Bad, repugnant

cheese it
To leave

cinch
A pushover

coffin nail
A cigarette

cords
Corduroy trousers

crack wise
To make sarcastic remarks

cramp one's style
To interfere with what one is doing

Crap!
I'm disgusted!

cush
money

desert horse
A Camel cigarette

dic
A dictionary

dilly
Foolish

dindy
Dandy

dingy
Silly

dirt
Gossip

dog it
To avoid work

doll up
To dress up

dope
1. Coca Cola
2. Flavoring put on ice cream

drag
Influence

drift
To leave

ducky
Good looking

Durham
Nonsense. *The association with Durham was undoubtedly Bull.*

eagers, the
Anxious desire, as "He has the eagers to meet her."

egg
A crude person

Idling

Slang of the young often reserves a special place in its heart for doing nothing, for idling. In the early 1930s, one finds the decidedly modern **jell** or the less modern **jelly** as a synonym for relax, with the disclaimer by *American Speech* that it was "Distinctively a University of Missouri Expression." Other candidates included **bean, cake, do the drag, horse around, louse around, mess around, phutz around,** and **sluff.**

A Ford by Any other Name

The automobile, still something of a luxury in the 1920s, became an integral part of the life of American youth in the 1930s. The Ford symbolized the automobile, and the slang idiom of the young provided a wide variety of terms for the humble Ford, including **a-merry-can, baby Lincoln, bone crusher, bouncing Betty, crate, Detroit disaster, flivver, Henry's rattle, Henry's go-cart, jitney, junk, leaping Lena, leaping Lizzie, Lincoln light four, Michigan mistake, puddle jumper, Rolls rough, Spirit of Detroit, tin can, Tin Lizzie,** and **tintype.**

fade
To leave

Fan my brow!
What a surprise! How exciting!

feed
A meal

flea
A pest

floss
To flirt

fog-bound
Inattentive

frog
To cheat

frog-skin
A dollar

full guy
A liberal spender

G

gasper
A cigarette

get around
To be popular. *Thirty years later, the Beach Boys released a hit single, "I Get Around," using the expression in this sense.*

ginned up
Dressed up

girk
To cheat

give the high sign
To wave and attract someone's attention

good egg
A popular person

Good Joe
An amiable person

good onion
A popular person

goof *or* **goofer**
A foolish person. *To the Flapper, a goof was a boyfriend. By the 1930s, the word had reassumed its earlier meaning.*

Got one?
Gimme one!
Kiss me!

goup
A stupid person

grounder
A cigarette butt picked up off the ground

half pint
A trifling person

hash
To gossip

heat
To criticize

Here I is!
Hello!

hit a flick
To go to a movie

honey, a
A person or thing that is pleasing or attractive

honey cooler
A kiss

honk
To cheat

hoot
Something that's funny

hops
Information

horsefeathers
Nonsense

hose
To flatter

hot stuff
The latest news or trend

H'roo
Hello

hump
A cigarette

Hurro
Hello

I mean and how!
That is so very true!

in the bushes
Despondent

In your hat!
I don't believe that!

invisible blue
A policeman

itty
Sexually appealing. *A probable allusion to the It Girl, Clara Bowe, the famous sex symbol of the 1920s.*

jack
money

jack up
To tutor

Joe
A term of address

joed
Tired

juicy
Enjoyable

kippy
neat

lacing
A thrashing

lalapaloosa
Anything out of the ordinary

large
Active and exciting

Lift it!
Move over!

lugg
A bulky young man

The Female

Youth slang of the 1920s was female-dominated, while the tone of slang of the 1930s reverted to the male. Within the body of slang was a wide assortment of words for girls, including a **baby, bag** (unattractive), **beetle, belle, bim** or **bimbo, blimp** (loose), **breigh, broad, buff, butter and egg fly** (popular), **buttermilk** (unattractive), **calico, canary, choice bit of calico** (attractive), **clinging vine** (delicate), **crock** (unattractive), **dame, darb** (popular; slightly altered from its "attractive" meaning in the 1920s), **doll, extra** (a girl whom nobody wants to date), **fem, filly, flame, flirt, frail, fuss** (frequent companion), **guinea, hairpin, heiferette** (young), **honey, hot mama** (attractive), **hot sketch, hotsy-totsy, keen number** (attractive), **lemonette** (unpopular), **lolleos** (popular), **Minnie, muddy plow** (unattractive), **muff, peach** (attractive), **petting skirt, piece** (loose), **piece of calico, pig, pot, powder puff** (frivolous), **queen** (attractive), **rib, S.Y.T.** (Sweet Young Thing, beating Michael Jackson's P.Y.T.—Pretty Young Thing—to the punch by more than 50 years), **sack** (unattractive), **sardine, sex-job** (loose), **sheba, skirt, smelt, snappy piece of work, squab, squaw, stuff, sweet mama** (attractive), **sweet patootie** (attractive), **tot,** or **wren.**

Marbles–Lost and Otherwise

With some exceptions, the acquisition of slang seems to begin as children approach adolescence. One notable exception is the slang and slangy jargon of marble-playing, a great Depression-era pastime for children. Games of marbles were played for centuries before the 1930s and are still played today, but the game's zenith was in the 1930s.

The equipment used in marbles was simplicity personified, marbles used for shooting (**aggies, alleys, bowlers, moonies, pimps, shooters,** or **taws**) and marbles used as targets (**baits, commies** as in "common," not "communist," **crockies, dibs, ducks, hoodles, immies, kimmies, mibs,** or **stickies**).

Technique was also described in slangy schoolboy terms. **Knuckling down** or **knucks** was to rest one's knuckles on the ground while shooting, **bowling** was rolling as opposed to shooting, **dive bombing** was shooting from your knee, **histing** was raising a hand from the ground while shooting, **lofting** was shooting in an arcing trajectory, and **fudging** was cheating. Hitting two or more of an opponent's marbles out of the ring was **dubs,** while a **snooger** was a close miss. To **clean the ring** was the marbles version of running the table in pool—to hit all of an opponent's marbles out of the ring.

Marbles as played in the 1930s was a game with a seemingly infinite variety of rules which could be shouted out by a player. These shouts themselves were rich in slang—**cow trail** (allowing you to dig a trench in front of your opponent's shooting marble), **drops** (allowing you to drop your shooter from above), **evers** (allowing the player to move around the ring), **fins** (a shout that suspends all other shouts while you plan your shot), **peaks and cleans in the ring** (allowing the player shooting to clear the path in front of the shooter), **slip** (shouted when your shooter slips from your hand; the shout allows you to shoot again) and **ups** (allowing the player to lift the shooting hand off the ground).

The primary sources for this look at marbles were "Technical Terms in the Games of Marbles" by John A. Zuger in *American Speech,* Vol. 9, No.1 (February 1934); "The Vocabulary of Marble Playing" by Kelsie B. Harder, *Publication of the American Dialect Society,* Number 23 (1955); and *The Mature Person's guide to Kites, Yo-Yo's, Frisbees and Other Childlike Diversions* by Paul Dickson (New York: Plume Books, 1977). Paul Dickson very generously turned over to me his entire file on marbles vocabulary, which includes several additional glossaries, including one produced by the National Marbles Tournament in 1940, and correspondence from marble-playing youth grown old.

The Toilet????

For reasons which are not at all clear from the cultural context, the young of the 1930s were extremely inventive when it came to devising slang words to describe the toilet. Examples of the art of naming the toilet, many of which were popular in the earlier part of the century, include **Chamber of commerce, crapper** or **crappery, domus, Egypt, honey house, Jake, Joe, John** or **Johnny, marble palace, may, old soldiers' home, poet's corner, prep chapel, Ruth** (for women), **shot tower, temple, Widow Jones**, and, simply, **X**.

lulu
Something that is very good

lung
To argue

mean
Attractive, excellent

Mitt me kid!
Congratulate me!

mope
An unclever person

muscle
To feign

muzzle
To kiss

niftic
Stylish

No soap!
That is not possible!

nobby
Stylish, fashionable

number
A partner

off the boat
Out-of-style, out-of-date

oil
Cajolery

Okey dokey.
Okay.

oodles
A large amount

paw
To caress

pill
A disagreeable person

pip
An attractive person

plenty rugged
Big and strong

plunk
A dollar

Dance–Party–Celebrate!

The Great Depression notwithstanding, the slang of the youth of the early 1930s was replete with words to describe parties, dances, and social gatherings. A dance or party was known as a **bat, bender, brawl, buzz, crawl, drag, egg harbor** (a free dance), **go, hop, jolly-up, march, pig fight, pounce, rag, romp, rub, shindig** (revived in the mainstream 1960s), **shuffle, struggle, tear, toddle, toot, trot, wingding, winger, wobble, work-out,** or **wrestle**. Most of these words could serve as verbs as well as nouns; to **drag a hoof** was to dance, while a **dead hoofer** was a poor dancer, also known as a **cement mixer**. As the music started, one would **tote** (escort) one's **frame** (dance partner) out onto the **scud track** (dance floor). Party on, Thirties!

plush
Stylish

put birdie
To vomit

R

razz
To ridicule.
A popular word in the 1920s that stays popular in the 1930s.

rib
To tease

S

samoa
Some more

Says which?
What did you just say?

scag
A cigarette

scram
To leave in a hurry

scream
Someone or something that is highly amusing

scrow, scrowl
To leave

scrub
1. A poor student
2. A member of the second team

shake a leg
To hurry

sho
Sure

shy
To cheat

skin
To defeat

slam
1. An insult
2. To criticize harshly

slay
To overcome with emotion

slick
Attractive, good

Slip me five!
Shake my hand!

snipe
A cigarette

spread
A banquet

spuzzed
Dressed up

suck
To curry favor.
One would not expect to find this seemingly '90s word in the slang lexicon of the 1930s, but there it was.

The Effeminate Male

The slang of the early 1930s saw a noticeable influx of words to describe the "effeminate male," many of them derisive terms which would persist through the end of the century. **Birdie, cup cake, fag, fairy, fluter, girlie, no bull fighter, pansy, pussy, queer, softie, thing,** and **weak sister** were all used as scornful slurs towards those who did not fit the bill of All Man.

suds
Money

T

that way
In love

That gripes my soul
That annoys me.
In the 1980s, this expression would resurface, reformatted as "that gripes my butt."

That's tough.
That's too bad.

tin
money

U

unconscious
A stupid person

W

wad
Money

What's hot?
What is new?

What's the score?
What are you talking about?

wheat
A hick

Wot a life!
How boring!

Y

Yo!
Yes

Who's milking this cow?
Mind your own business!

You and how many others? You and what army?
I doubt that you can accomplish what you just said

You and me both.
I agree

Yowsah!
Yes sir!

Winners & Losers

As with virtually any body of slang, the slang of the young of the early 1930s had a variety of words to describe both the good and the bad.

Something that was good was **aces up, hot, juicy, nifty, nobby, nugget, plush, smooth, snazzy, spiffy, sweet,** and **swell.**

In the other corner was the social misfit, known as a **cold shudder, cup cake, derail, greaseball, half portion, heel, hot blast, jelly bean, prune, sack** (a term which predates "Sad Sack" of World War II, both of which are derived from the country expression, "sad sack of shit"), **stick, wart, wet smack, wet sock,** or **worm.**

The Soda Jerk

The soda jerk of the 1930s was as charming and clever as any 20th century slinger of slang. The language of the young men who worked behind soda fountains—venerable social institutions that were important gathering places for the young—more closely resembled a jargon than slang, but it was a quick, warm, and funny vernacular that had a vibrant wise-guy ring to it.

The idiom of the soda jerk served several functions. It was a code that quickly and secretly conveyed an urgent message. Examples of between-us-jerks code are **eighty-six** (we're out of what was just ordered), **eight-seven and a half** (a pretty woman just walked in), **fix the pumps** (a girl with large breasts just walked in), **ninety-eight** (the manager just walked in), **ninety-five** (a customer is walking out without paying), **thirteen** (a boss just walked in), or **vanilla** (a pretty girl just walked in). Similarly, several orders invited a delicacy in handling— a **blue bottle** was Bromo-Seltzer, a **C.O. Highball** was castor oil, and an **M.G.** or **Mary Garden** was a dose of citrate of magnesia.

Intricate orders could be condensed into several words. Chocolate cake or chocolate fudge with chocolate ice cream was **all the way,** a glass of milk was a **baby,** a chocolate malted milk shake was a **burn,** a **cold spot** was a glass of iced tea, pies were **a-pie** (apple) or **c-pie** (cherry) or **coke-pie** (coconut pie), a **Dusty Miller** was a chocolate sundae with malted milk, spare ribs were a **first lady, in the hay** was a strawberry milk shake, a la mode was simply **L.A.,** and **tools** were table utensils. Quantities were reduced to clever coinages—a **pair** (2), a **crowd** (3), a **bridge** (4), a **handful** (5), a **load** of (plate of), or **long** (large).

Most importantly, the speech of the jerk established him as a singular individual who was in the know; it gave him the opportunity to show off. Rather than confront the complete boredom of a request for a glass of water, the jerk would call out for **Adam's ale, city juice, dog soup, eighty-one, eighty-two** (two glasses of water), **moisture,** or **one on the city, hold the hail** (without ice). There was an undeniably hip ring to the calls—**break it and shake it** (put eggs in it), **burn it and let it swim** (a float), **burn one all the way** (a chocolate malt with chocolate ice cream), **chase** (to pass or hand), **draw one** (a cup of coffee), **freeze one** (chocolate frosted), **hops** (malted milk extract), **ice the rice** (rice pudding with ice cream), **in the air** (a large glass), **java** (coffee), **natural** (7-Up, an allusion to craps where 5 and 2 are a natural 7), **on wheels** (to go), **shoot one** (a Coke), **spla** (whipped cream), **split one** (a banana split), **stretch one** (a large Coke), **through Georgia** (with chocolate syrup), or **twist it, choke it, and make it cackle** (a chocolate malt with egg).

In the late 1930s, the locally owned soda fountains began to lose ground to the national chains. Generally, the new owners took a dim view of the wise-guy element of the jerk's language, preferring the standard "hash" to **the gentleman will take a chance** or **clean up the kitchen,** ketchup to **hemorrhage,** frankfurter to **Coney Island chicken** or **ground hog,** prunes to **looseners,** cherries to **maiden's delight,** milk toast to **graveyard stew,** and cracker and cheese to **dog and maggot.** With the demise of the local soda fountain as a social institution, the idiom of the soda jerk began to slip into the past. Like its practitioners, it was a brash speech, full of life and humor.

Sources for this look at the speech of the jerk include W. Bentley's "Linguistic concoctions of the Soda Jerker," *American Speech,* Vol. 2, No. 1, (February 1936); "Soda Fountain Lingo," *California Folklore Quarterly,* Vol. 4, (1945); "Soda-Fountain, Restaurant and Tavern Calls" by Michael Owen Jones, *American Speech,* Vol. 42, No. 1, (February 1967); and the glossary compiled by Paul Dickson in *The Great American Ice Cream Book* (New York: Atheneum, 1982). No discussion of the language of the soda fountain is complete with a tip of the hat to Alexandra Day's children's book *Frank and Ernest* (New York: Scholastic Inc., 1988) which lovingly and carefully preserves a small sampling of the vocabulary of the diner and soda fountain.

Word History: Jitterbug

When the *jitterbug* dance craze swept the nation in the late 1930s, with it came the fanatic devotee who could not help but react to swing music with ardent athleticism, the jitterbug.[1] The origin of jitterbug may be understood by analyzing the word as a compound, consisting of *jitter + bug*.

After the stock market crash of 1929, *jitters* replaced *heebie-jeebies* as the slang expression of choice to convey extreme anxiety. Where *jitters* came from is anyone's guess, but the supposition that it resulted from a spoonerism of gin and bitters (thus bin and gitters) and was thus applied to a state of alcoholism is as good a theory as any, especially since **jittersauce** was an established euphemism for alcohol during the Prohibition. **Bug** meant anyone who was consumed with an idea or fervent about anything. Put together, one would have someone consumed with extreme anxiety, an apt description of the animated antics of the ardent swing fan known as the jitterbug.

The term existed in the early 1930s, before the jitterbug dance craze. Cab Calloway was the honorary president of a Jitterbug Society at an eastern college, where any student who could down six portions of jittersauce and then correctly pronounce "palsaddictinsomnidipsomatic" was a member. By 1938, jitterbug had attained commercialization status, with Macy's offering Jitterbug Jewelry, pins in shapes of different musical instruments. (*Life* May 16, 1938).

Sources: Peter Tamony's extensive files on jitterbug at the University of Missouri and his "Origin of Words: Jitterbugs" in the March 3, 1939 issue of the *News Letter and Wasp*.

Swing Jive

The first wave of jive to crest across popular youth culture was the vocabulary of swing music itself. The language used by the jazz musicians to describe their craft was quickly adopted by young swing fans, known as **cats** or **alligators** (probably derived from gate, the traditional term of address exchanged by jazz musicians). A **tin ear** did not like music.

Instruments were rarely called by their standard names. A clarinet was a **gob stick,** a string bass was a **doghouse,** a **tram** was a trombone, an **iron horn** a cornet, a **guinea's harp, gitbox** or **gitter** was a guitar, a **groanbox** was an accordion, a **wood pile** was a xylophone, drums were **skins,** a saxophone was a **gobble-pipe**.

There were two basic schools of jazz, **sweet** (conventional) or **hot** (swing). On the sweet side of the spectrum were **corn** (old-fashioned jazz), the **long underwear gang** (a sweet band), **salon** (restrained jazz), **lollypop** (cloying, sweet jazz) and **schmaltz** (overly sentimental music). On the hot side of the scales was **clam-bake** (wild swing), **dillinger** (very hot swing), **gut-bucket** (lowdown blues), **barrel-house** (free and easy jamming, or improvising), and in the center **collegiate** (extremely slow swing).

Musicians (all of whom except the band leader were **sidemen**) were known in large part by their instruments, such as **skin-tickler** for drummer, **squeaker** for violinist, **whanger** for guitarist, or **lip-splitter** for any wood instrumentalist. A female singer was a **canary;** a **paperman** was a musician who could only perform using written music, and to **fake** was to play by ear.

The techniques of swing were all described in slang terms known to most fans. The basics of music were covered by slang—**spots** were notes, **lay-outs** were rests, **frisking the whiskers** or **licking the chops** was warming up, to **jam** was to play without any arrangement, to **woodshed** was to work out and practice a new song in private, to improvise was to **kick out,** and a musical embellishment in an improvisation was a **break, get-off, lick, riff,** or **take-off**. To play with vigor and inspiration was to be **in the groove, break it down, get hot, give it a ride, go to town, send, swing out**. A hot passage or performance was a **solid sender** that would **chill ya**. Play louder? **Wang it!** Pick up the beat? **Quit mugging light and mug heavy!** After a **gang** (a medley of songs), the song worked into its **sock chorus** (final chorus of an arrangement), perhaps ending by **easing it in** (a soft finish).

GIT BOX

WOODPILE

GOB STICK

DOG HOUSE

GROANBOX

GOBBLE PIPE

SKINS

Word History: Swing

By the late 1930s, *swing* was one of the most important slang words in a young person's vocabulary, used to describe a style of jazz that swept the nation and held the rabid attention of young people for close to a decade.

The first highly public use of the word *swing* would have been in 1932, with Duke Ellington's "It Don't Mean a Thing, If It Ain't Got That Swing" (music by Ellington, words by Irving Mills). The words of the song ("It don't make no diff-rence if it's sweet or hot, just give that rhythm everything you've got") are an allusion to the then-existing differentiation between jazz bands. **Sweet** (or **straight**) bands played jazz scores as written, while **hot** bands included improvisation.

Although Ellington's 1932 title brought *swing* out into the open, it was by no means the earliest use of the word. Ellington himself had in 1928 recorded the "Saratoga Swing," and in the following year, Jack Teagarden sang in "I'm Gonna Stomp Mr. Henry Lee," "I've gotta stomp, honey, when they play that swing." Even earlier uses of *swing* are encountered, dating as far back as 1888 in conjunction with a dance step. In the 1930s sense of the word, its first use was probably in Jelly Roll Morton's "Georgia Swing," recorded in 1929 but named in 1907 (*Down Beat*, August 1938).

Peter Tamony associates swing hitting the big time both as a word and a craze with the release in 1935 of "The Music Goes 'Round and Around" by Riley and Farley; when you heard it, you knew what *swing* meant. Swing had arrived, and swing would stay.

Sources: Peter Tamony's files on Swing in the Tamony Collection, Western Historical Manuscript Collection, University of Missouri at Columbia, and his article "Swing: The Big Word" in *Jazz: A Quarterly of American Music*, Vol. 5 (Winter 1960).

* * *

[1]Jitterbug had several other minor slang meanings, including a type of lure used in fly fishing, a style of running in football, and a small industrial truck used for handling materials within a factory. None of these meanings, however, held a candle to the "swing enthusiast" meaning.

Sources and References

The primary sources of information for this chapter were found in the fertile files of the Tamony Collection, Western Historical Manuscript Center, University of Missouri, Columbia. This collection includes Tamony's clippings of newspaper and magazine articles, comic strips, and musical lyrics. With the exception of Cab Calloway's efforts in the late 1930s, the 1930s were lacking in the indigenous slang dictionaries found in every other decade. Because of that lack, the best sources for verifying slang of this era are Maurice Weseen's *Dictionary of American Slang* (New York: Thomas Y. Crowell, 1934) and *A Thesaurus of Slang* by Howard N. Rose (New York: MacMillan, 1934). From the pages of *American Speech* came Jason Almus Russell, "Colgate University Slang," Vol. 5, No. 3 (1930); J. Louis Kuethe, "John Hopkins Jargon," Vol. 7, No. 5 (1932); Hugh Sebastian, "Negro Slang in Lincoln University," Vol. 9, No. 4 (1934); Virginia Carter, "University of Missouri Slang," Vol. 6, No. 3 (1931), and John Ashton Shidler, "More Stanford Expressions," Vol. 7, No. 6 (1932).

CHAPTER 4
The 1940s: The Jive Generation

▼

"Hiya cat, wipe ya feet on the mat, let's slap on the fat and dish out some scat."

After the domestic turmoil of the 1930s, the 1940s offered a change of focus. Early in the decade, the United States was plunged into a world war which demanded a military and industrial mobilization of unprecedented proportions, both of which had far-reaching effects on the social fabric of the country. By the end of the decade, America was a world power at peace; as the country rushed into a newly defined normalcy, the Cold War descended.

With most men over 18 in the service early in the decade, the teenage boy assumed an unnatu-

rally important role in the family. Because of labor shortages, teenagers were often employed at least part-time, meaning that they had money to spend.

Where there's money, there's bound to be somebody to show you how to spend it, and this was the case with teenagers in the 1940s. Madison Avenue did its part in creating and sustaining clothing crazes, popular songs, and dances. Booming sales of phonograph records, the ascension of the jukebox, and the appearance of teen magazines and regular teen sections in newspapers all illustrate the rise of adolescents

Illustrations by Rick Meyerowitz

as a force (or market) that mainstream American began to notice and take seriously. Although the word "teenager" had been in use since the 1920s, it gained widespread acceptance for the first time in the 1940s.

The culture of the teenager in the 1940s was separate but not subversive, independent but not rebellious. While collegiate values dominated youth culture of the 1930s, through the middle of the 1940s, the jive/swing/jitterbug culture which began in the mid-1930s continued to define youth popular culture. In November 1942, Damon Runyon wrote a column entitled "The Jive Generation Goes to War" (*San Francisco Examiner*, November 17, 1942). While the tag never stuck to the extent that "Lost Generation," "Jazz Age," or "Beat Generation" did, it was fitting.

The end of the jive generation could be measured by the fact that in 1946 Hallmark cards issued a set of "Solid Sender" cards, "groovy as the movie MAKE MINE MUSIC," based on the "Disney hepcat scenes." When Hallmark sold cards wishing a "brutally reet" birthday, chirping "Sharp as a harp and neat as a pleat," or asking "What's tickin' chicken," one had a pretty fair idea that hep jive values had been co-opted by the mainstream.

By the end of the decade the influence of swing and jive was definitely on the wane, with youth casting about for something new. After a few years in the wilderness, they would be delivered.

The Language: Jive Comes of Age

Youth slang of the 1940s was influenced to an inestimable degree by jive, black street vernacular that began to migrate into broad popular youth culture with the swing music and jitterbug craze of the late 1930s.

The swing musicians themselves were the primary bearers of jive to mainstream youth. Although the golden era of AM radio disc jockeys was still some years away, several very influential disc jockeys in the 1940s also did their part to bring jive to youth with blasts such as— "Hiya cat, wipe ya feet on the mat, let's slap on the fat and dish out some scat. You're a prisoner of wov. W-O-V, 1280 on the dial, New York, and you're picking up the hard spiel and good deal of Fred Robbins, dispensing seven score and ten ticks of ecstatic static and spectacular vernacular from 6:30 to 9. We got stacks of lacquer crackers on the fire, so hang out your hearing flap while His Majesty salivates a neat reed."

The 1940s saw the publication of several jive and teenage slang dictionaries, most notably Cab Calloway's *Hepster's Dictionary: Language of Jive* (New York: Self-published, last edition in 1944), Dan Burley's *Original Handbook of Harlem Jive* (Chicago: Self-published, 1944), *The Slanguage Dictionary of Modern American Slang* ("Dictionary of Jive Jargon" at pp. 59-61) by L. B. Robison (Newton, Iowa: The L.B. Robison Company, 1944), and Lou Shelly's *Hepcats Jive Talk Dictionary* (Derby, Connecticut: T.W.O.

Charles Company, 1945). Although not first published until 1953, Lavada Durst's *The Jives of Dr. Hepcat* (Dallas, Texas: Self-published, 1953) dealt with jive as spoken in the 1940s.

In his introduction to the *Hepcats Jive Talk Dictionary*, Shelly described the degree to which young people had embraced jive: "A new language has been born and with its usual lustiness youth has made jive talk heard from one end of the land to the other."

Calling All Girls magazine got into the act, publishing a series of language and protocol guides for teenage girls. Entitled *Jabberwocky and Jive*, these small magazines rushed to report the latest heard (and most likely often quickly forgotten) slang. In 1943, the editors put their finger on the language of the young— "Jabberwocky is the jive talk, the slanguage of the 'Soda Fountain' crowd. It's a kind of whacky double-talk that brims over with teen age spirit and fun."

To be sure, there were cynics such as H.L. Mencken, who predicted that jive would live a short life and die an early death. In a 1947 letter to Peter Tamony, Mencken wrote of jive that "My opinion is that most of it is invented by New York press agents, and I am convinced that very little of it will live." In *The American Language: Supplement II* (New York: Alfred A. Knopf, 1962), which was written at about the same time as the letter to Tamony, Mencken wrote that "there is every indication that jive is not long for this life."

While Mencken was right about much, his dislike of jive may have clouded his predicting abilities when it came to assessing the staying power of jive slang. *Cap, fly chick, groovy, homey, hung up, icy, mellow, righteous, sharp, solid,* and *square* all endured quite nicely, playing major roles in the slang of the 1960s and the 1990s.

The jive-stimulated slang of the 1940s was based in large part on functional associations. Much of the expansive vocabulary dealing with clothing and body parts is derived from functionally driven metonymy, such as **blinkers** for eyes, **choppers** for teeth, **choker** for collar, or **kicks** for shoes. Likewise with a host of other words— **croaker** (doctor), **dreamers** (bed sheets), **drink** or **moist** (a body of water), **lamp** (to see), **lip** (an attorney), **slammer** (a door), or **stroll** (a street).

As is the case with the youth slang of every generation, youth slang of the 1940s was very status-oriented, with the **smooth** and **hep** to be envied and the **icky drip** to be pitied and avoided.

Most importantly, although much of the jive/youth slang of the 1940s would fade by the end of the decade, it would lay an important foundation for the slang of the hipster/beat movement of the late 1950s, the hippie movement of the late 1960s and early 1970s, and to some extent the hip-hop/rap phenomenon of the 1980s and 1990s.

Smooth

As is the case with almost every generation's slang, the young of the 1940s had many ways to describe something that was good. **Hep to the jive** and **smooth** were among the more visible, joined by **alreet, anxious, back, brutal, cagey, cheezle-peezle, darby, eager, elite, even, Fifth Avenue, frantic, geetchie, glassy, gone, groovy** (sometimes spelled **groovey** or even **grooby**), **hard, home-cooked, hot stuff, icy** (a 1990s word if there ever was one!), **in there, in the groove, killer-diller, kopasetic** (making a comeback from the 1920s, with a short-lived spelling variation), **luscious, lush, mad, mellow, messy** (extraodinary), **murder, neat, on fire, out of the oven, out of this world, potent, rare, reet, righteous, rugged, sharp, shiny, shrewd, snaky, snazzy, sock, spoony, super-duper, supersolid, supercolossal, the most, vanny,** and **wizard** (as an adjective).

A 1940s Word List

A

Abercrombie
A know-it-all.
Perhaps an allusion to the sporting goods store Abercrombie & Fitch, which had a reputation for being able to provide just the right kind of—and notably expensive— equipment and apparel

action
A proposition

advance the spark
Get ready

Ameche
A telephone.
For many years, Don Ameche was most clearly associated in people's minds with his role as the inventor of the telephone in the 1939 movie The Story of Alexander Graham Bell.

apron
A counterman or bartender

aquarium
An apartment or house

Are you kiddin'?
Wow!

artillery
Baked beans

B

backcap
A retort or response

bagpipe
Someone who talks too much

Boys

Girls of the 1940s were not without their slang vocabulary when it came to describe attractive or appealing boys, including a **B.T.O.** (a big-time operator, always on the prowl), **drooly,** a **glad lad,** a **go-giver, groovy, heaven sent, Jackson,** a **mellow man,** and **swoony.** She might describe her one and only as her **big moment, bunny boy, flutter, four-F, love light, P.C.** (Prince Charming, not "PC" by 1990s standards), **Pappy, Romeo,** or **S.P.** (Secret Passion). Boys who were less than attractive were a **dogface** (nice!), a **void coupon, too safe,** a **stupor man,** or a **sad Sam.**

bank
A toilet

bash
To eat to
excess

beagle
A frankfurter

beam
A great person

beans
Pocket change

beast
A gloomy
person

beat
Broke. *A word wait-
ing for its generation.*

beat to the socks
Very tired

**beat up one's gums
off time**
To talk out of turn

behind the grind
Behind in one's
studies

Bible
The true facts of a
situation

big talk
Boasting

birdwood
A cigarette

blip
A nickel

blow
1. To go away
2. To brag

blow your top
To become excited

blow your wig
To become very
excited

bondage
The state of being in
debt

boodle
A lot of money

boogieman
A jiving male

booper
A pop singer

boot
To inform fully

Boot me.
Introduce me

boy scout
An immature male

bright
Day

brightin'
Daybreak

brighty
Very smart

bring-down
Something that is
depressing

broom
A cigar

buffalo head
A nickel

bump the gums
To talk a great deal

burnt to a crisp
Up to the latest in
everything

bust loose
To escape one's
inhibitions

Girls

The slang that boys of the 1940s used to describe girls was in retrospective quite flat, with only **fly chick** having any staying power at all, and even it went into dormancy for 40 years until rediscovered by rappers. Among the slang words and expressions used to describe girls —**angel cake, battle** (unattractive), **bim, bobby socks, bree, butterfly, cattle, crate** (unattractive) **destroyer, dilly, drape shape** (attractive build), **filly, firm and round and fully packed, fly chick, pigeon, rare dish, scrag** (unattractive), **slick chick,** and **zazz girl.**

buzz
To kiss

Buzz me.
Call me on the telephone.

C

cap
To outdo.
Another big word of the 1990s that was not as new as it seemed.

cave
One's house or apartment

cello
A bass singer

charge
A marijuana cigarette

chime
The time

clicker
A jerk who talks too much

coffee-and-cake
Very poor pay

cogs
Sunglasses

collar
To catch on

college
Jail

colts
Youth

Come again?
Please repeat yourself.

conk
To strike

cookie
An effeminate young male

cooking on the front burner *or* **cooking with gas**
Doing very well

cop
To get

cream puff
An effeminate young male

croaker
A doctor

crunchy
The pavement

crust
To insult

cubes
Dice

cups
Sleep

curve
To disappoint

cut
To outclass

cut out
To leave

cuter
A quarter dollar

D

dead
Empty

dead president
Money

deece
A dime

deuce
A two-dollar bill

deuce of haircuts
Two weeks

dicty
High class

dig
To think hard or understand

Dig me?
Do you understand me?

dim
Twilight

dime note
A $10 bill

doss
To sleep

cabbage
Money

dotty
Insane

douse the glim
Turn out the light

down with it
Finished with it

drag
1. An effeminate party or dance
2. To deceive

drape
A suit

drape shape
A good figure

dreamers
Bed sheets

drill
To take a walk

drink
A body of water

drip
A social misfit

duchess
One's girlfriend

duck soup
A simple task

ducks
Admission tickets

dust
To leave

E

easy
Financially stable

evil
In a bad mood.
Boy, does this have a modern ring to it!

exodust
To flee

eye
A detective

F

face
A Caucasian

fade
To cover a bet

fall
To be convicted of a crime

fish
To lie

five spot
A $5 bill

fizz
A coke

flat
A boring person

fluff
To brush

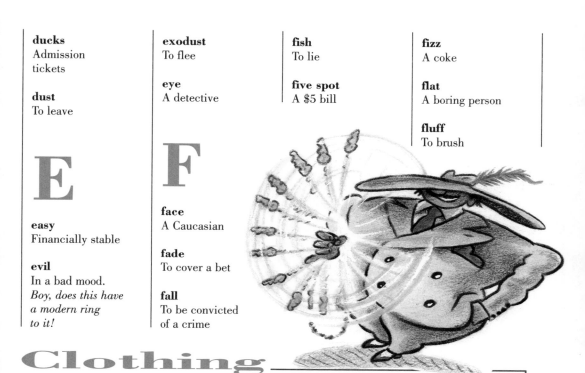

Clothing

Men's clothing played a decided role in the popular youth culture of the 1940s. The zoot suit with its wild colors, pants 30 inches in the knee and pegged down to 12 inches at the ankle, a hat with a four-inch brim and feather, and a long, gold-plated watch chain swinging down lower than the coat hem, took the fashion statement made by swing musicians such as Cab Calloway to an extreme; it was then copied by black and Mexican-American youth, and ultimately by some white youth.

As well should be the case with something so subversive as the zoot suit, it became a symbol of defiance of authority, and the War Production Board ruled in March 1942 that it was a material-wasting habiliment evidencing a lack of patriotism. After being glorified as ultimately hip in recordings by Kay Kyser, Benny Goodman, Art Kassel, Bing Crosby, and the Andrews Sisters, the zoot suit in 1943 became a symbol of cultural division, with police and servicemen attacking zoot suit youth in Los Angeles, Arizona, Texas, Detroit, Philadelphia, and New York. After the war, the zoot-suiter **togged to the bricks** in **bluff cuffs** was safely co-opted as an amusing if eccentric image.

Throughout the 1940s, there existed an unusually robust slang idiom dealing with men's clothing, many of it functionally derived. Taking the well-dressed youth from head to foot, one came across the following:

Hat: chimney (a top hat), dicer, sky piece.
Suit: racket jacket, vine.
Necktie or collar: choker.
Suspenders: pulleys, straps.
Belt: squeezer (tight).
Trousers: pegs, striders.
Pocket: coffee bag, hideaway, insider, kick, mouse.
Shoes: barkers, kicks, pinchers (tight shoes), stomps, stompers, treaders (boots), waders.

World War II Slang

What of the jive generation who went to war? In the first half of the decade, a large portion of the young population was in uniform. Its monumental tragedies not forgotten, World War II proved to be a most fertile breeding ground for slang, much of which was either brought from home or coined at war by young servicemen and servicewomen.

Entire books have been written on the subject of the slang of World War II, and no attempt at a thorough treatment is made here. It is possible, though, to glimpse the spirit of youth in some examples of the slang of the war.

Some expressions used by soldiers in World War II were direct transplants from the jive vocabulary they had learned at home—**all the aces** for excellent, **fish hooks** for fingers, **flap** for ear, **get-alongs** for legs, or **Jackson** as a term of address for another soldier. Other military expressions have a definite jive ring, such as **ankle chokers** (narrow-bottomed army-issue trousers) or **devil beater** (chaplain).

The slang idiom used to describe military food was in large part the same that the soldiers had learned as boys in diners and soda fountains at home. The mess hall was known as a **slop house,** a direct borrowing from home, or ironically as the **Waldorf**. Just as at the diner at home, the cook was a **hash burner** or **pan rattler** and the dishwasher was the **pearl diver**. Similarly, much of the slang used to describe the **gut-packin's** (food) was what the boys learned at diners at home—**bags of mystery** (sausages), **battery acid** (coffee), **black strap** (coffee), **blankets** (hotcakes), **blood** (catsup), **chicken berry** (egg), **cow juice** (milk), **fish eyes** (tapioca), **gasket** (pancake), **goldfish** (canned salmon), **grass** (salad), **ink** (black coffee), **looseners** (prunes), **mud** (coffee), **mystery** (hash), **red paint** (catsup), **shingles** (toast), and **SOS** (shit on a shingle, otherwise known as chipped beef on toast).

Youthful antiauthoritarianism is reflected in much of the military slang of the world war. The seemingly endless series of profane acronyms, such as **FUBAR** (fucked-up beyond all recognition), **JAAFU** (Joint Anglo-American fuck-up), **TUIFU** (the ultimate in fuck-ups), and the most famous of all **SNAFU** (situation normal—all fucked up) all reflect a youthful distrust of authority. To call a captain's silver bars **railroad tracks,** a group of military advisors a **brain gang,** a colorful collection of ribbons and medals a **fruit salad,** the gold braids on the caps of naval officers **scrambled eggs,** a nocturnal foray to steal something a **midnight requisition,** or a good night's sleep an **admiral's watch** is to defy authority, a wonderful quality of youth.

Likewise, young soldiers faced death with a certain ironic, flippant sense of humor. A **fatal pill, go-away kiss,** or **lead pill** was a bullet, a **meat wagon** an ambulance, and to die was to **check out**.

Other World War II slang with a definitely youthful ring to it include **badgy** (an underage enlistee), **blotto** (dead; before the war this simply meant drunk), **bug juice** (gasoline), **grease ape** (a mechanic), **in the drink** (downed at sea), **juice jerker** (an electrician), **little red wagon** (a portable toilet), **popsickle** (a motorcycle), **roller skate** (a tank), **rugged** (wonderful—a big word at home and overseas both), **snore rack** (a bed), **struggle** (a dance—a term from the 1930s), and **sugar report** (a letter from one's sweetheart at home).

One of the more interesting migrations of slang took place in *Yank* magazine, where in 1942 Sgt. George Baker created Private Sad Sack, the world's most inept soldier. Although many assume that **sad sack** was a World War II coinage by Baker, it was in fact a term in somewhat common usage in the 1930s to signify an incompetent person.

In the other direction, military slang expressions could be and were used at the homefront in slangy ways. **Coming in on a wing and a prayer,** a flying expression for a pilot trying to reach base and land when in distress, was used to mean coming home from a bad date. Instead of "let's

DO YOU TAKE COW JUICE WITH YOUR BATTERY ACID?

leave," you could allude to the Navy and say **Let's up anchor**. To cut in on somebody dancing, you could simply say **Shove off sailor, I'm convoying the ship**. When your partner is dancing up a storm, you might say **Now you're flyin' with Doolittle!** A **delayed action bomb,** no small thing in war, could be used to describe a girl who is always late for a date, with **zero hour** the time that the date is expected to arrive. Something that was **on target** was simply very good.

Sources: *Army Talk* by Elbridge Colby (Princeton: Princeton University Press, 1942); *The Slanguage Dictionary of Modern American Slang* by L.B. Robison (Newton, Iowa: The L.B. Robison Company, 1944); and *War Slang* by Paul Dickson (New York: Pocket Books, 1994).

fog
To kill

freeby *or* **freebie**
Something offered
without charge

fresh water
Good looking

front
One's appearance

fruit
To run around

fuss
To embarrass

gammin'
Strutting

gander
To examine

gas
To engage in idle
conversation

gasper
A cigarette

gasser
Something that is
sensational

Gimme some skin.
Shake my hand.

gory
Wonderful or
terrible

gravel
Gossip

green stuff
Paper money

Hand me that skin!
Let's shake hands.

happify
To make happy

hard
A person with
great taste

hardware
Ostentatious jewelry

headlights
Flashy diamonds

heater
A big cigar

heeled
Wealthy

hepcat
A swing musician,
or a fan of swing
music

hep gee
One in the know.
*When rap showed up
40 years later, "G"
was an allegedly
new term.
Not quite new.*

herd
A pack of Camel
cigarettes

high stepper
Someone who lives
above his means

hike
To hide

homey
Someone from your
hometown. *And here
we thought it was an
'80s word all along!*

hop
A dance

hot hose
A fast dancer

hung up
Bewildered. *There it
is again—a big word
from the 1960s here at
home in the 1940s.*

husk
To undress

in
An introduction

Jackson
A term of address

Jeff
A pest

jit
Five cents

jive bomber
The gossip
reporter for a

school newspaper

jump
To dance to swing
music

kill
To fascinate

killer
Hair grease

lamp
To see

lay out the racket
To explain something

Lincoln
A $5 bill

line
Cost, price

lip
An attorney

lob around
To idle around
together

make tracks
To leave in a hurry

Hello and Good-bye

Ritualistic slang expressions used on greeting and departing continued to do well in the 1940s. Instead of "hello," the young might call out **Greetings Gaits; Hello Joe, what d'ya know?; Hi ya chum; Hi gossip, what's news?; Hi sprout, what's growin'?; Hi there stuff; Hi Jackson; Hi Sugar, are you rationed?; Hi Cy; Salutations Hepper; Saludo amigo; What's buzzin' cousin?; What's steamin' demon?; What's the score?; What's perkin'?** or **What's knittin', kitten?**

Similarly, good-byes could be handled with any number of puns, false borrowings, and slang ceremonial expressions such as **Alcohol you; Au Reservoir; Be seein' ya; Be seein' you in the funnies; Bye-bye buy bonds; Good-bye gate, I must evaporate; Goom bye; Got to take a fast powder; I'm shoving off, Jasper; Let's fly the coop; Plant you now, dig you later; Saloon; So long chum; So long luscious; Swing you;** or **That's all for now Square.**

man-size
Difficult

mash
To give

mash me a fin
Loan me $5

meter
A $.25 piece

mezz
Perfection

moist
A body of water

money from home
Good news

moocher
Someone who sponges
off others

moola *or*
moolah
Money

mop
To dance

muggles
Marijuana

murder
To attain perfection

Murder!
Wow!

name
The most popular
band at the
moment

natch
Naturally

needle
A soft drink

nod
Night

off the cob
Corny

package
A girl

panic
To thrill

percolate
To do well

percolator
An automobile

piccolo
A juke box

platter
A record

play
A situation

poke
A large sum
of money or the
secret place
where it is
hidden

mud
Coffee

Pops
A term of address

rank
To criticize

ready
Perfectly

Reet, George!
I agree with you.

rink rat
A skating enthusiast.
*This sounds striking
modern, doesn't it?*

ripper
A no-account

rock
*Cab Calloway's
definition says it all—
"Send me, kill me,
move me with
rhythm."*

rolling
Very rich

roost
Your house

rubber
A car

ruff
A quarter

salty
Angry

scobo queen
A girl jitterbug

screwball
Crazy, wild

send
To excite or thrill

shin
A razor

shorts, the
The condition
of being without
money

signify
1. To brag or boast
2. To disparage

slammer
A door

slide your jive
To talk freely

smacker
One dollar

Social Outcasts— Icky Drips

Youth in the 1940s were not shy when it came to branding those whose looks, interests, or lack of social skills set them apart from the crowd, describing as outcasts as an **icky drip** or as **behind the ball, boonie, bump on the solid beat, cold cut, corpse, creep, cut-rate, dish rag, drizzle bag, drizzle puss, drooly, droop, drumb, dumb plumber, egg, fumb, garmy, gleep, goon bait, gooney drip, gruesome** (used as either an adjective or a noun), **herkle, ick, jerk, load, mangy, maroon, pork, prune, putrid, Sad Sam, sloop, specimen, spooky, square, square from Delaware, stooge, strictly stock, whack,** and **zombie.**

snapper
A match

snipe
A cigarette stub

sock
A lot of power

splash
To swim

square
A person who doesn't dance

static
Quarreling

stroll
A street

stud
An oaf

tab
A loan

tears
A pearl necklace

Tell me another while that one's still warm!
I don't believe what you just told me.

tick
A moment

timbers
Toothpicks

tin
Small change

togged to the bricks
Dressed up

Too much!
That's great!

track
A dance hall

truck
To dance

trucking
A dance introduced at the Cotton Club in 1933. *In the 1960s, R. Crumb would resurrect the expression in his underground comics, and the Grateful Dead would*

popularize it in the title of a song.

tumble
To dance

twister
A key

umcha
In bad taste

whacky
Crazy, discordant

Wham!
Great!

What's your story, morning glory?
What do you mean by what you just said?

whiffle
A crew cut

whip
To tell

yank
A dentist

yard
A $100 bill

yard dog
A loud and noisy person

You shred it, wheat.
You said it.
An obvious cultural allusion to Shredded Wheat cereal.

zeal girl
A hot girl dancer

Bebop Slang

After World War II, a new, innovative and experimental style of jazz began to emerge in the smaller clubs of Harlem, and to its practitioners and fans it—*bebop*—was musical freedom. By 1949, *Life* magazine had caught on, reporting the opening of Artie Shaw's club in New York, "Bop City," that boasted a menu including bop suey and bopana splits, and where the audience gave a nice round of "bopplause."

With the new music there emerged a new dress style; just as the big bands of the swing era gave way to smaller groups, so did dress styles evolve, hinging on eccentricity. Similarly, a variation on jive seeped out of this new musical subculture, influencing to some extent hipper youth.

Self-appointed lexicographer of "the be-bop language" was Babs Gonzales, a jazz musician who in the late 1940s wrote and distributed the *Be-Bop Dictionary* (New York: Arlain Publishing Company, 1949).

Some of what Gonzales recorded was certainly nonsense, such as **dil-ya-bla** (a phone call), **great-er-e-de** (to agree with someone), **Lop-Pow** (everything is okay), **Lu cu pu** (good night), **Lu-E-Pa** (What's your story?), **mop-shi-lu** (to be disappointed), and **Oop-pop-a-da** (hello).

Other entries are closer cousins of jive, such as **big eyes** (to like someone), **cooling** (unemployed), **crazy** (very good at what the person does), **geets** (money), **goof** (to daydream), **her future** (legs), **Hollywood eyes** (a pretty girl), **nab** (a policeman), **short** (car), **sing** (to play with one's best feelings), and **turkey** (a fool).

The importance of bop does not lie in its contribution to the language, although the movement did popularize the term *hipster* and it gives us early use of *cool* and early overuse of *dig*. Its mark was as a musical movement and as a cultural bridge from the swing and jive era of 1937-1945 to the hipsters of the 1950s, who in turn gave way to the Beats.

Word History: Bop and Bebop

As a movement within the jazz world, *bebop* or *bop* was relatively short-lived. The brevity of its tenure notwithstanding, the bop movement had a profound effect on jazz and on popular culture, defining the hipster (who gave way to the Beat who gave way to the hippie) and serving up to a hungry young world the term *cool*.

What, though of the terms *bebop* and *bop*? In the 20 years before 1945, the term *bebop* was used in jazz lyrics, generally as a nonsense sound. In an article appearing in *Jazz 2: A Quarterly of American Music* (Spring 1959), slang sleuth Peter Tamony exhaustively identified a number of pre-1945 songs that used the term *bebop*, including songs from 1928 ("Four or Five Times" by McKinney's Cotton Pickers: "Bebop one, bebop two, bebop three, De-daddle-do-de, four or five times"), 1936 ("I'se A-Muggin" by Teagarden Boys & Trumbauer Swing Band: "Be bop, be bop, be bop, be bo"), 1936 ("Don't 'Low" by Washboard Sam's Band: "Mama don't 'low no re-bop..."), 1939 ("Tain't What You Do" by Chick Webb and His Orchestra: ensemble intones "Bebop" at the end of the record), 1939 ("Wham" by Glen Miller and His Orchestra: "Re Bop Boom Bam"), 1940 ("Wham" covered by Jimmy Lunceford and His Orchestra), and 1940 ("Wham" covered by Doctor Sausage and his Five Pork Chops).

Despite the earlier appearances of *bebop*, it is generally recognized within the jazz and lexicography worlds that Dizzy Gillespie's 1945 release of "Be-Bop" on the flip side of "Salted Peanuts" launched the slang career of the word. Suddenly, there was a word to describe the new type of modern jazz that Gillespie and his cohorts were developing at Minton's in New York.

Slightly varying stories emerged on the coining of *bebop* almost immediately. Gilbert S. McKean, writing in *Esquire* in October 1947, offered this etymology:

Dizzy's manager explains the origin more or less lucidly. "You know when Diz started playing bebop with a group, all their stuff was head arrangements, memorized material that wasn't written down. Well, the pieces didn't have a name, so Diz would give them the first phrases something like this—bee-bobba-doe-bobba-doddle-dee-bebop! You know how many bebop choruses end in a clipped two-note phrase with the last note on the offbeat? It almost sounds like the instrument is saying "bebop!" And when Dizzy works with his group he tells the trumpets what to play, and the rhythm and the reeds what to play in that ah-boo-dle-dud-bebop talk.

Richard O. Boyer, basing his story on Dizzy Gillespie's claims, wrote in the *New Yorker* on July 3, 1948:

It was at Minton's that the word "bebop" came into being. Dizzy was trying to show a bass player how the last two notes of a phrase should sound. The bass player tried it again and again, but he couldn't get the two notes. "Be-bop! Be-bop!" Dizzy finally sang.

Kenny "Kloop" Clarke, the first bop drummer, offered yet another explanation which appeared in *Hear Me Talkin' to Ya*, edited by Nat Shapiro and Nat Netoff (New York: Rinehart, 1955):

Minton's lasted until and on through the war. I went into the Army in 1943, and Minton's was still going full blast when I left. The music wasn't called bop at Minton's. In fact, we had no name for the music. The bop label started during the war. I was in the Army then and I was surprised when I came out and found they'd given it a tag. That label did a lot of harm.

Lastly, Oran "Hot Lips" Page claimed that *bop* was coined by Fats Waller, who would lose his patience playing with the younger musicians at Minton's and shout at them, "Stop that crazy boppin' and a-stoppin' and play that jive like the rest of us guys" (Shapiro, *Hear Me Talkin' to Ya*).

In any event, *bebop* (at times spelled *be bop* or *bee-bop* and at times replaced by *rebop*) was widely used from 1945 until 1948, when it was almost completely replaced, first in the speech of jazzmen and later in the wider popular culture, by *bop*. The waning of *bebop* and waxing of *bop* can probably be measured by the release in 1947 of "Bongo" Bop by the Charlie Parker Sextet.

Bop continued to enjoy some popularity in the 1950s; however, its real staying power lay in the broader cultural context and its role in the hipster, New Bohemian, and Beat movements. Bop as a cool worldview expressed in cool, hip slang is wonderfully illustrated by Steve Allen's *Steve Allen's Bop Fables* (New York: Simon and Schuster, 1955).

Word History: Groovy

Although we tend to think of *groovy* as a quintessential if dopey 1960s word and find ourselves humming "A Groovy Kind of Love," "59th Street Bridge Song" ("Feelin' groovy..."), or "Wild Thing" ("You make everything—groovy") when contemplating its etymology, the popularity of *groovy* in the 1960s was a second incarnation for the word, which first came of age in the 1940s.

Groovy sprung from *in the groove*, another one of the many jazz musician terms that migrated into mainstream slang. The earliest written citations to *in the groove* which I have found are in *Down Beat*, including a December-January 1935-1936 story speaking of Benny Goodman's band laying "in the groove," again in a cartoon entitled In The Groove in November 1935, and again in a caption in March 1936 ("... a first class in-the-groove Bearer-Downer"). As was the case with many other jazz slang terms, *in the groove* was apparently used early by Louis Armstrong, who in 1936 defined it as "when carried away or inspired by the music, when playing in exalted spirit and to perfection" (Louis Armstrong, *Swing That Music* [New York: Longmans, Green & Co.]). *In the groove* soon made it into song titles (the 1939 release of "In the Groove at the Grove" by Chick Webb and His Orchestra with Ella Fitzgerald) and song lyrics ("Some folks say that swing won't stay and that it's dying out/But I can prove it's in the groove, and they don't know what they're talking about" in "Wham [Re Bop Boom Bam]" recorded by Mildred Bailey in 1940).

What did it mean? In a March 13, 1938 column in the *San Francisco Chronicle*, Herb Caen quoted Bing Crosby trying to define the term:

In the groove means just right, down the middle, riding lightly and politely, terrific, easy on

Body Parts

Jive-inspired youth slang of the 1940s had a prodigious vocabulary to describe parts of the body (the frame), many based on the function of the body part. No other decade can point to an anatomical slang anywhere even vaguely as extensive as that of the 1940s.

Starting from the head and working down to the toes:

Hair: brush (a mustache), face lace (whiskers), moss.

The head: biscuit, dome, idea pot, noggin and think-box.

The face: index, knob (an ugly face), map, phiz, puss.

Eyes: blinkers, lamps, pies, shutters (eye-lids), slanters, spotters.

Ears: flippers, flops, lugs (large ears), mikes, sails

The nose: handle (a large nose), horn, schnozz, sneezer.

The mouth and environs: bone box (mouth), chewers (teeth), chops (jaws), choppers (teeth), crumb crunchers (teeth), snags (tonsils).

The neck: stretcher.

Shoulders and arms: brace o' broads (shoulders), brace o' hookers (arms), floppers (arms), hinges (elbows).

Hands: dukes (fists), grabbers, meat hooks, paddlers, paws.

Fingers: feelers, fish hooks, forks, hooks, pickers, stealers, wigglers.

The chest, abdomen and contents: bread basket (stomach), clocker (heart), pail (stomach), pump (heart), ticker (heart).

Legs: drumsticks, pillars, prayer dukes (knees), splits, stems, stumps, uprights.

Feet: hocks, plates.

Toes: ten (as in—it's good to have ten).

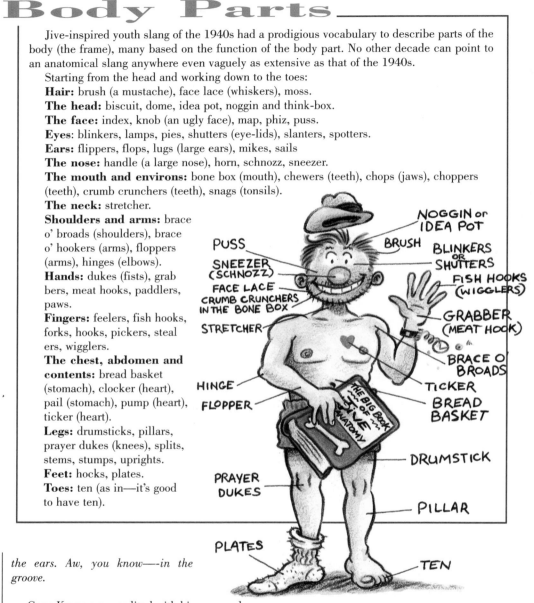

the ears. Aw, you know—-in the groove.

Gene Krupa was credited with his own explanation in the August, 1943, issue of *Correct English*:

"In the groove" came out of those back-room music sessions where each musician would play the theme according to his individual notions but keep within the bounds of harmony so he would blend with the other instruments. One was, or was not, *melodically in the groove, according to Krupa.*

Although *groovy* (then spelled *groovey*) was first reported in *American Speech* in 1937 as meaning "state of mind which is conducive to good playing," it was not widely used until the 1940s. Tommy Dorsey, quoted in the *San*

Francisco Call-Bulletin, February 25, 1942, placed the popular transition from *in the groove to groovy* as having taken place in 1941:

When the boys and I hear a good record nowadays we says it's "groovey." Last year that would have been "in the groove." The expression has nothing to do with the grooves on the record's surface, it just means we think it's a fine piece of music.

In the mid-1940s, *groovy* started popping up in a broader than musical sense all over, in Calling All Girls' 1943 publication *Jabberwocky and Jive* ("grooby" as synonymous with "smooth"), in the 1944 edition of Cab Calloway's *Hepster's Dictionary* (defined as "fine"), in Lou Shelly's 1945 *Hepcats Jive Talk Dictionary* (defining *groovey* simply as a superlative), in Hallmark Card's 1946 "Solid Sender Greeting cards on the teen beam" ("groovy as the movie"), in Mezz Mezzrow's glossary in *Really the Blues* (defined as "really good, in the groove, enjoyable"), in a Buick ad in the June 10, 1946, *Newsweek* ("Stand off and beam at Buick's years-ahead style—there's something not only favored by the old folks, but termed by the younger idea, definitely groovy!"), and in a reference to "groovy music on the juke" in Ralph Ellison's *Invisible Man* (New York: Random House, 1947).

By the 1950s, *groovy* was relegated to storage, occasionally making guest appearances such as in a 1957 Kraft Orange Drink advertisement ("Man this is the mostest! This groovy drink is real C-O-O-L. You'll flip over it!"). Oddly, despite *groovy's* decline in the 1950s, the quite hip Lord Buckley used it in his 1960 *Hiparama of the Classics,* translating Shakespeare's "the good men do is oft interred with their bones..." to "the groovey is often stashed with their frames..." By 1963, it was clearly a relic, as evidenced by the copy of an advertisement from Sears: "In times past a teenager might have called this Sears sweater 'super,' 'groovy' or 'the bee's knees.'"

Slang is economical, though, and not shy about recycling. In the mid-1960s, *groovy* came back for another visit, establishing itself as a mainstream youth slang word in about 1965. It was quickly marginalized and mocked, though, appearing in decidedly un-hip advertisements such as a 1967 newspaper advertisement for Roos/Atkins ("Grrrr....rrooviest jackets captured yet, ready to roar at Roos/Atkins today!").

Although *groovy* enjoyed limited hippie use, it had a corny ring to it and soon dropped from the idiom, showing up only in the hopelessly passé (such as Rick Springfield's 1988 release "[If you think you're] Groovy)" or openly derisive (such as "Groovy Times" by the Clash).

The degree to which it fell from grace is evidenced by the derisive term *groover* which slang-tracker Connie Eble reported first hearing at the University of North Carolina in the 1980s, referring to someone who is lost in the past, using obsolete words such as *groovy.*

Word History: Hep & Hip

Without doubt, the hardest working word in 20th century American youth slang is *hip.* Together with its twin *hep* and their cousins *hipster, hepster, hep-cat, hippie,* and *hip-hop, hip* has had a staggering run of success from generation to generation and from permutation to permutation.

Early in the century, *hep* and *hip* were used interchangeably to mean aware, world-wise, sophisticated, and up-to-date with trends in music, fashion, and speech. Not surprisingly, one finds a textbook case of lexical polygenesis, that is, a profusion of explanations for the etymologies of the terms.

The sense of hep and hip is derived from an old phrase used in wrestling, "to have on the hip." When a wrestler had his opponent on the hip he had complete and effective control of him, and was in position to drop to the floor on top of his man, ready to take the fall. (Peter Tamony, "Origin of Words: Hep," *News Letter and Wasp,* August 25, 1939)

Nowadays you have to call a gone character a hipster. That comes from the fact that a real gone musician is said to have his boots laced right up to his hips. (Cab Calloway, *Original Jive Dictionary,* 1942). [This theory is supported by the lyrics of "'Tain't What You Do (It's The Way That Cha Do It)" by Sy Oliver and James Young, recorded by Chick Webb and His Orchestra in 1939 ("This is something you don't learn in school / So get your hip boots on, and then you'll carry one...")]

"On the hip" used in the sense of a person who has a supply of liquor on his person. (Thomas Dorgan, *San Francisco Call and Post*, June 10, 1920 and April 21, 1927).

Actually "hep" and "hip" are doublets; both come directly from a much earlier phrase, "to be on the hip," to be a devotee of opium smoking, during which activity one lies on one's hip. (Ned Polsky, "The Village Beat Scene: Summer, 1960," *Dissent*, Summer, 1961).

Back in the 1890s, there was a saloon-keeper named Joe Hep who ran a saloon in Chicago that was frequented by the underworld. Joe was an honest fellow, but he liked to listen to underworld gossip. It reached a point where if somebody wanted to know the latest on some shifty character, he'd go to Joe Hep's place for the information. Today we still pay tribute to this eavesdropping Chicago saloon-keeper whenever we use the expression "get hep," or be in the know about something. (*Dell Crossword Puzzles*, January-February 1960).

Hep ... derived from the name of a fabulous detective who operated in Cincinnati, the legend has it, who knew so much about criminality and criminals that his patronymic became a byword for the last thing in wisdom of illicit possibilities. (*Vocabulary of Criminal Slang* by L.E. Jackson and C.R. Hillyer [Portland, Oregon, 1914]).

The expression was given its name from the characteristics of an old circus man who was famous. . . .He would always say that he knew just what to do or what was being said. . . . Finally, when anyone contemplated an act or expression around the show grounds, the gang would say, "Yes, you are the same as Joe Hept." (*How to be a Detective* by F.J. Tillotsen [Kansas City, Missouri, 1909]).

No doubt from the Army, where the sergeant or drill-master commands, "Step, step, step" to a squad of recruits until from sheer weariness the command becomes "Hep, hep, hep," meaning of course, "Keep in step, on the alert." (Godfrey Irwin, *American Tramp and Underworld Slang* [New York: Sears, 1931]). [To this, Robert L. Chapman adds in a *New Dictionary of American Slang* (New York: Harper & Row, 1986): Early jazz musicians often marched in parades, especially funeral parades.]

Perhaps a corruption of "hup" (aspirated up) and therefore ex English s. up to, "aware of." (Eric Partridge, *A Dictionary of The Underworld* [London: Routledge & Kegan, 1949]).

More prob. imm. ex hep! hep!, encouragement to a team of horses, the teamster calling hep and the horses getting hep. (Eric Partridge, *A Dictionary of the Underworld* [1949]).

Ultimately ex the ploughman's, or the driver's hep! to his team of horses (Get up!): the horses 'get hep'—lively, alert. (Eric Partridge, *Dictionary of Slang and Unconventional English*, 8th ed. [New York: Macmillan, 1961, 1984]).

In any event, *hep* and *hip* were used interchangeably for several decades. The earliest citation to *hep* which I have found is in a T. A. Dorgan cartoon which appeared on November 18, 1904, in which a guide suggests that a look-out be left behind so that "no one will get hep" (*A TAD Lexicon* by Leonard Zwilling [Rolla, Missouri: Gerald Cohen, 1993]). The *Oxford English Dictionary* finds *hip* first used in Jim Hickey by G. V. Hobart in the same year. In the mid-1940s, *hep* gave way complete-

HIP 'N' HEP

ly to *hip*. In the September 1945 issue of *Women's Digest*, Margery Lewis in "Jive Talk in One Easy Lesson" wrote that "Solid is still in use in some spheres, but has been replaced by great in the more hip circles (*Hip* is the word—not *hep*)." In *The Record Changer* of May 1946, Carlton Brown said:

...because like that I don't have to keep hep to the jive professionally, but can cultivate it as a hobby, like collecting shrunken heads. See, right in that sentence I've made a slip that shows how rusty I am at keeping up with the swift transitions of our times. If you say "hep," I read somewhere recently, you ain't hip.

In case we forgot, in 1955 Walter Winchell regaled us with the "Broadway Bop" by Jack Rael, which reminded us that "If you're hip—you're a cat/If you're hep—you're a square." In case we forgot again, *McCall's* magazine in August 1968 gave us a cartoon in which the wife asks her bong-smoking husband seated in a modern Danish chair, "Herbert, I keep forgetting. Are we hip or hep?"

Hip took over completely, leaving *hep* for the occasional self-conscious slang use by young people but fairly extensive use by advertisement copy-writers and headline-writers through 1965. The popularity of even *hip* declined in the 1960s, although the Beach Boys made strong use of it in "(I Wish They All Could Be) California Girls" ("East Coast girls are hip...."). Having carried the torch for several decades, the preeminent position of *hip* passed to *hippie* and then, in turn, to *hip-hop*. *Hip*, however, is still in use, as evidenced by its being featured in a 1980s song by Huey Lewis and the News, "Hip to Be Square."

Word History: Hepcat

Robert Gold dismisses *hep* entirely as never having been used by jazzmen. Be this as it may, this is not to say that *hep* was not used in popular youth slang, and by extension *hepcat*, which was synonymous with *hipster*. In fact, *hep-cat* seems to have enjoyed a decade or so of popularity, outliving even *hep* when *hep* turned into *hip*.

The earliest use of *hepcat* that I have found is in *Down Beat*, September 1937, in a caption over a picture showing three male musicians and a female singer: "3 'Hep Cats' and a 'Hep-Canary.'" In 1947, the *Encyclopaedia Britannica* defined hepcat as "a swing music addict" and attributed it to 1937. Subsequent usages include:

hep cat (N)—a guy who knows all the answers, understands jive. (Cab Calloway's Catalogue, 1938; Calloway's definition remains unchanged through 1944 edition)

A "hepcat," to narrow the case, is a person with decided tastes in both classical and modern music, and is considered slightly rarer than a "hep." (San Francisco Chronicle, March 13, 1938)

...the swing or "jive" performances which dazzle and delight New York "hep-cats" and "alligators"...(Life, April 4, 1938)

SEE Dick and the happy hep-cats do the Lambeth Walk! (Advertisement for *Going Places*, starring Ronald Reagan, in the *San Francisco Call-Bulletin*, January 9, 1939)

...the dances will be held in the San Francisco Building...where the "hep-cats" and "alligators" will give their all—for prizes. (San Francisco News, June 23, 1939)

Not only the hipsters (who were called hep-cats then) but the squares and even the older folks.... (The Capitol, May, 1946)

OPENING TONITE! TWO WEEKS ONLY! SLIM GAILLARD TRIO—M.G.M. Recording Star Voted "King of the Hep-Cats" (San Francisco Examiner, April 16, 1948)

Hepcat was popular enough to appear in the titles of two treatments of slang, Lou Shelly's *Hepcats Jive Talk Dictionary* (1945) and *The Jives of Dr. Hepcat* by Lavada "Dr. Hepcat" Durst (1953). In 1944, Harry Tobias and Al Sherman wrote a song entitled "Mr. Hepster's Dictionary" (Leads Music Corporation), in which the following definition was given by verse:

What's a hep cat?
A hep cat is a guy who knows all the answers,
And I'll tell you why,

He's a hi-falutin' student of the Calloway vocab,
Who's hep to Hepster's Dictionary.

The fact that *hepcat* was accepted—and well on its way to passé—was demonstrated in 1946 by the issuance by Hallmark Cards of a set of "Solid Sender" greeting cards "based on the Disney hepcat scenes." I have been unable to determine exactly what the Disney hepcat scenes were, but it is difficult to imagine that they were particularly hep or hip. All slang must pass, and hepcat was no exception.

Word History: Hipped

Despite a handful of other slang meanings, *hipped,* meaning aware of or knowledgeable about, has lived a life of its own, independent of its more famous cousins *hep* and *hip*.[1]

The earliest written use of *hipped* which I have encountered is in F. Scott Fitzgerald's *This Side of Paradise* (1920), in which a character speaks of being "hipped on Freud and all that." Other uses include "hipped on this prohibition racket" (*Hooch* by C.F. Coe, 1928), "hipped on the subject" (*Liberty,* May 31, 1930), "hipped on tunes" (*Night Clubs* by Jimmy Durante and Jack Kofoed, 1931), "thoroughly hipped, Kessel sent

out wires to every distributor within 24 hours..." (*San Francisco News,* July 4, 1936), "hipped ... on religion" (*Young Man with a Horn* by Dorothy Baker, 1938), "hipped on education" (*Gentleman's Agreement* by Laura Z. Hobson, 1947), "all you boys were hipped" (*The Amboy Dukes* by Irving Shulman, 1947), and "hipped on security" (*Life,* June 6, 1949).

By the 1950s *hipped* had done most of its work, although as late as 1965 one finds in the *San Francisco Examiner* an anonymous participant in a meeting at the White House saying, "The President is hipped on controlling the budget." You might think that if the President is hipped on anything, it's time to stick in the fork—*hipped* is done; but in fact, *hipped* continues to live on, as in this quote from John Hiatt in the January 16, 1993 issue of *Rolling Stone:* "He [his 15-year-old son] hipped me to Sonic Youth and Dinosaur Jr."

Word History: Jive

With the swing jazz craze of the 1930s, there came an equally impressive migration of language from the argot of jazzmen and the streets of Harlem and Chicago into popular youth slang. In the forefront of this language was the word *jive,* which first defined this new speech and then

Sub-Debs

During the 1940s, the teenage girl too began to assert herself as a distinct social being. Often called a "subdeb" or "subdebutante" by the mainstream press, she began to develop an intense and ironic, superlative-laced speech full of attitude.

Greetings were ritualistic and cute—**Hi there, playmate!, Hey devil, what say?** or **What are you featuring?** Conversations were adorned with exclamations which conveyed fervor—**Holy Joe!, Certainly has!, It's all too desperate!, Oh Bliss!, Oh nausea!, Oh Lord and butler!, Oolie droolie!, That's no lie!,** or **The hell you yell!**

If they **adored** something (said with verve), it was described with an intensifying adverb or adverbial phrase (**simply, too perfectly,** or **too positively**) and usually an understated (**adequate, cute, divine, genial, quaint,** or **smooth**) but sometimes extravagant (**luscious, marvelous,** or **priceless**) adjective. The very best? **Potent stuff!**

That which she did not like she described with a vocabulary and attitude that has to call to mind at least passingly the Valley Girl of the 1980s. Something disliked was **deadly, drear, foul, grim, loathsome, lousy, poisonous, repulsive, revolting, shattering, stark, stinky,** or **vile.** Again, she used intensifying phrases for effect, such as **definitely stark, actually.**

What was in the past known as petting or necking was known by the sub-deb as **boodling, gooing it, hacking, monking, mousing, mugging,** or **smooching.**

Time to leave? **Let's blow! Let's get on the ball! Let's get organized!**

Vout-o-Reenee

In 1946, jazz musician Slim Gaillard published *Slim Gaillard's Vout-O-Reenee Dictionary.* Gaillard had drawn attention to himself at Bill Berg's jazz club on Vine Street near Sunset Boulevard in Los Angeles for several years prior through his zany antics, creative bursts of language, and musicianship.

Gaillard was as hot as it got in the late 1940s, making a huge mark in Hollywood. On his radio show, Bob Hope asked guest Marlene Dietrich what she thought of Gaillard. Her answer? One word—"Vout!" Gaillard worked the celebrity hustle to the maximum, dating screen queens and becoming a fixture at the mansion of Howard Hughes.

More important from a cultural point of view, Gaillard was deeply admired by Jack Kerouac and Neal Cassady, the artistic and spiritual center of the Beat literary movement. Gaillard even makes a cameo appearance in Kerouac's *On The Road,* summed up by Kerouac as follows: "To Slim Gaillard the whole world was just one big orooni."

The extent to which Gaillard's dramatic stylistic flourishes and catchy use of the language caught the attention of young people in the United States is open to debate, but it was just the type of fad that popular magazines like *Time* and *Life* pounced on. In early 1947 both found evidence of a Gaillard fad at several American colleges, most notably at Tulane University in New Orleans; by later that year *Life* concluded that it had all but disappeared.

Gaillard's one-man brand of slang started with the then-known jazz slang *voot* (money) and expanded onward to either the quite predictable good-natured foolishness or the too obscure for most to understand.

In the predictable department words ending with *o-roony, o-ree-nee,* or *vout,* such as **blink-o-roony** (sleepy), **burn-o-vooty** (kitchen), **carosponee** (a letter), **color-vee-tee** (a butterfly), **digess-vouty** (book), **drug-o-ree-nee** (sad), **globe-o-vooty** (the world), **mello-ree-nee** (wonderful), **mug-o-vooty** (face), **rep-o-vouty** (answer), or **slim-o-ree-nee** (sharp).

Examples of the cryptic include **benny** (coat), **capa** (swallow), **cross-up** (ladder), **fiddler** (cat), **hurma** (year), or **lebes** (job). While some of the words were coined based on metonymy (*fiddler* from the nursery rhyme, "Hey diddle, diddle, the cat and the fiddle..."), and others (such as *benny* for coat) may have come from carnival slang, many simply appear to have been nonsense sounds to which were attached meanings to be guessed from context.

branched out itself to embrace a number of separate slang meanings.

Jive appears to have been derived from the standard English "gibe" or "jibe," meaning to tease in either a playful or disparaging manner. In the *Original Handbook of Harlem Jive,* Dan Burley in 1944 described jive's move into American slang:

...in the sense in which it came into use among Negroes in Chicago about the year 1921, it meant to taunt, scoff, to sneer—an expression of sarcastic comment. Like the tribal groups of Mohammedans and people of the Orient, Negroes of that period had developed a highly effective manner of talking about each other's ancestors and hereditary traits, a colorful and picturesque linguistic procedure which came to be known as "putting you in the dozens." *Later, this was simply called "jiving" someone. Subsequently ragtime musicians picked up the term and it soon came to mean "all things to all men."*

Jive's first widespread use outside black vernacular came with the popularity of swing as played by black jazzmen; taken with the music of the jazzmen, young Americans were equally fascinated with their speech, which quickly became known as jive. Cab Calloway in 1938 ("the lingo or speech of alligators and/or cats"), Dan Burley in 1944 (*The Original Handbook of Harlem Jive*), Lou Shelly in 1945 (*The Hepcats Jive Talk Dictionary*), and Lavada Durst in 1952 (*The Jives of Dr. Hepcat*) all use jive in this sense.

Secondly, *jive* retained its original Chicago meaning of to taunt, scoff, or to tease. This sense appears in Mezz Mezzrow's 1946 *Really the Blues:* "to kid, to talk insincerely or without meaning, to use an elaborate and misleading line." This meaning evolved from verb into both noun and adjective (as in the Bee Gees' number-one hit "Jive Talkin'"); meaning deceptive talk or nonsense, it was well-used slang in the hippie idiom, and it survives to some extent today.

Thirdly, *jive* was sometimes used to refer to swing music. Dan Burley wrote that "Since 1930 Jive has been accepted as the trade name for swing music." Illustrative of this meaning is an advertisement for the San Diego California Music Company which appeared in *Tempo* in February 1938, calling the store "Headquarters for Jivers and Jammers." To jazzmen themselves, *jive* had a more specific meaning: to improvise playfully with the melody. In "The Slang of Jazz" by H. Brook Webb, *American Speech* (October 1937), *jive* is identified as a synonym of "ride," which meant "The quality of intrinsic rhythmicity characterizing the melodic pattern of a lick." In March 1938, M. W. Stearns in his column "New Records" in *Tempo*, writes: "Without any fuss or feathers, Joe plays that piano with an iron left hand and plenty of jive in the right. It's bedrock copper-riveted swing."

Fourth, *jive* was used for several decades as a slang code for marijuana. In 1936, Pha Terrell's song "All the Jive is Gone" was an unambiguous reference to marijuana. From *Down Beat*, November 1937, comes this poetic reference to *jive* as weed: "So the cats continue to jive.... Torch up that roach, Jackson, it's meller as a cheller." In July 1938, Stuff Smith and his Onyx Club released "Here Comes the Man with the Jive," an obvious reference to marijuana; in 1940, Jimmy Dorsey and his Orchestra recorded "The Jumpin' Jive" ("... the jumping jive / makes you get your kicks on the mellow side . . . the solid jive / makes you nine foot tall when you're four foot five..."). *Jive* in the sense of cannabis faded in the 1940s, but was still used in a newspaper article about a youth attacking a doctor who had refused to give him some "jive" (*San Francisco Examiner*, December 9, 1956). To a limited degree, *jive* survived into the 1960s in this sense, with occasional use of **jive stick** to describe a marijuana cigarette.

Sources: Peter Tamony's file cards on jive and his article "Jive" in *News Letter and Wasp*, September 1, 1939; Dan Burley's *Original Handbook of Harlem Jive* (Chicago: Self-published, 1944); Robert Gold's *A Jazz Lexicon;* and, for *jive* as marijuana, Ernest L. Abel's *A Marihuana Dictionary* (Westport, Conn.: Greenwood Press, 1982).

Ball of Fire

The 1941 RKO movie *Ball of Fire* is every slang-lover's dream: Gary Cooper playing a Princeton professor in search of specimens of current slang for a new encyclopedia, Gary Cooper quoting Carl Sandburg ("Slang is language that takes off its coat, spits on its hands, and gets to work"), and Gary Cooper being courted by nightclub singer Sugarpuss O'Shea, played by Barbara Stanwyck.

In search of slang, Gary Cooper visits sporting events, night clubs, and colleges. He learns that **Dig me?** means "Do you understand me?" and that **blitz it** or **shove in your clutch** mean to hurry up and get moving. In the romance department, he learns that a **yum-yum type** is a kissable person, that **schmalzando** is sentiment, and that **squirrel fever** is a romantic desire.

Cut the menkenkes! What? Stop talking nonsense! **Off the beam,** Cooper learned, meant functioning poorly, while **pretty gestanko** was pretty bad, something you'd expect from a **loose tooth** (an incompetent person).

The glory of *Ball of Fire* is not just in its recordings of slang, but in its glorification of the study of slang. Gary Cooper with his note pad at the race track or college fraternity gathering samples of slang! Barbara Stanwyck and Gene Krupa showing Gary Cooper what *swing* means! What a dream!

Word History: Teenager

America discovered the teenager in the 1940s, or, perhaps more correctly, the American teenager invented herself and himself in the 1940s. In 1947, the *Encyclopaedia Britannica* identified *teen ager* as a new word that was coined in 1944, while *American Speech* included *teen-ager* in "Among the New Words" in its April 1945 issue, with an earliest citation of 1944.

In fact, *teenager* was a word waiting for a concept. In the *Boy Scouts of America Handbook for Boys*, 1926 edition, the Boy Scouts explained their position on militarism and in so doing were responsible for one of the first written uses of *teen-age*:

The boy scout movement neither promotes nor discourages military training, its chief concern being the development of character and personal efficiency of teen-age boys.

Teen was not new; several years earlier, Carl Ed has launched his highly successful comic strip *Harold Teen*, which was adapted for the movies in 1928.

While *teen-age* was used at times in the 1930s (*American Speech* in 1935 included a usage—"The dress is probably slinky and suitable for the teen-age group," while *Time* magazine of February 22, 1937, wrote of the concern of German parents for keeping "their teen-age son or daughter out of one of the Hitler camps for young people"), it did not gain momentum until the 1940s.

In the 1940s, the press caught on to teenagers as a class (exemplified by the *Archie* comic strip) and *teenager* as a word, with headlines blasting "Young Girls and Their Mothers Will Like Clothes Designed Just for the 'Teen-Agers" (*San Francisco News*, April 30, 1940), "Teen-Age Girls: They Live in a Wonderful World of Their Own" (*Life*, December 11, 1944), "Not our Teen-Agers" (*San Francisco News*, June 21, 1947), "Too Much Attention to Teens?" (*San Francisco News*, February 25, 1950), or "Ornery Teen-Agers" (*San Francisco News*, June 21, 1950).

Always on the prowl for a neologism, newspaper writers continued to suggest terms to replace teenager. In 1947, the *San Francisco Examiner* suggested **classroom crowd, subdebbers, skirt-and-sweater set, jive hound, coke 'n' soda set, soda set,** or **the junior edition** (*San Francisco Examiner,* February 9, 1947). None of these great new words caught on. In the *American Weekly* feature attached to the *San Francisco Examiner* of November 12, 1950, Ursula Throw noted that some young people wanted a new label because *teenager* "has become synonymous with delinquents, hoodlums, hot-rod road hogs and bad-mannered misfits." Trow suggested **bold ager, junior American, modernette,** or **teener**. None of these great new names caught hold either. *Teenager* stayed *teenager*, and so it remains today.

* * *

[1]In carnival slang of the late 19th century, *hipped* meant fond of, according to E.P. Conkle in the February, 1928 issue of *American Speech*. In *American Speech* of February, 1935, David Maurer in "The Lingo of the Good People" reported that *hipped* meant caught napping, whipped, or covered with a gun. It also meant taken at disadvantage, as reported in *Case and Comment*, March 1938.

Sources and References

The primary written sources for this chapter were as follows: Dan Burley's *Original Handbook of Harlem Jive* (Chicago: Self-published, 1944); Cab Calloway's *Hepster's Dictionary: Language of Jive* (New York: Self-published, first edition in 1938, last edition in 1944); Lavada Durst's *The Jives of Dr. Hepcat* (Self-published: Dallas, Texas, 1953); *The Slanguage Dictionary of Modern American Slang* by L. B. Robison (Newton, Iowa: The L.B. Robison Company, 1944); Lou Shelly's *Hepcats Jive Talk Dictionary* (Derby, Connecticut: T.W.O. Charles Company, 1945); *Jabberwocky and Jive,* Issues 1 through 5 (New York: Calling All Girls, Inc., 1943); and *Really the Blues* by Mezz Mezzrow (London: Secker & Warburg, 1946). The Tamony collection at the Western Manuscript Archives at the University of Missouri is a wonderful source for this decade, providing a full range of song lyrics, jazz magazines, daily newspapers, record industry promotions, ad copy, and comic strips that vividly illustrate the slang of the young.

CHAPTER 5
The Mainstream 1950s

▼

"COOL"

O n the one hand, the 1950s were a decade of tremendous promise and success in America. The economy prospered and the nation was on the ascent as a world power. After two decades defined by the Depression and World War Two, normalcy with a vengeance was the order of the day.

On the other hand, as suburban normalcy with its immense push for conformity and success defined in purely materialistic terms drove the country, there were certainly hints that all was not as well as it seemed. As Eisenhower beamed complacently in the White House, Joseph McCarthy terrorized the country (1950-1954), the Rosenbergs were convicted (1951) and executed (1953), and the Cold War grew colder. As Disneyland and the first indoor shopping mall opened (1955 and 1956 respectively), Rosa Parks made her place in history when the modern civil rights movement was born in Montgomery, Alabama, with a boycott of segregated buses (1955). As the Revised Standard Version of the Bible rested as the biggest-selling

Illustrations by Guy Billout

Around the Clock" by Bill Haley and the Comets, originally a country and western group who identified "Rock Around the Clock" on the record label as a "Fox Trot." The identification as fox trot notwithstanding, the music world exploded. Rock and roll had arrived.

In 1956, Elvis Presley, who had been billed as "the freshest, newest voice in Country Music" only the year before in his coming out announcement in *Billboard*, arose as the first superstar of rock and roll. Teenagers—the crew-cut/flattop boys in sports coats and charcoal gray flannel dress slacks and ties, perhaps a V-neck sweater under the jacket, penny loafers, and the girls in poodle skirts and saddle shoes and bobby socks, cardigan or crew-neck sweaters, and ponytails—were swept into the passion of rock and roll, singing along and dancing the steps they would learn watching Carol Scaldeferi, Jimmy Peatross, Justine Carrelli, Bob Clayton and the other kids from South Philadelphia on Dick Clark's *American Bandstand*, the *Your Hit Parade* of the 1950s.

Reaction to the initial burst of rock and roll was intense, as illustrated by the following quotations from startlingly disparate sources, all of whom believed that rock and roll was leading the youth of nation down a path of decline and depravity:

If we cannot stem the tide of rock 'n' roll with its waves of rhythmic narcosis and of future waves of vicarious craze, we are preparing our own downfall in the midst of pan-demonic funeral dances. (Milton Bracken, "Experts Propose Study of Craze," *New York Times*, February 23, 1957)

The entire moral structure of man, of Christianity, of spirituality in Holy Marriage ... of all that the white man has built in his devotion to God; all this, was crumbled and snatched away as the white girls and boys were turned to the level of the animal. As the sweating blacks lulled their heavy beat, the white children's conversation flowed around the auditorium replete with the coarse Negro phrases...(The Southerner, quoted by Douglas Cater, "Civil War in Alabama's White

nonfiction book in the country (1952-1954) and the hula hoop craze swept the country (1958), the John Birch Society was organized (1958).

Confronted with both the pressures of conformity and the early indications that all was not well, the young drifted, waiting for salvation. *The Catcher in the Rye* (1951), Brando in *The Wild One* (1954), and James Dean in *Rebel Without a Cause* (1954) all struck responsive chords in the young as rock and roll waited impatiently in the wings.

In 1952 and 1953, several pioneer disc jockeys began to promote music which in the past had been known as "race" music, the country blues, sepia music, or rhythm and blues. Most notable among these disc jockeys was Alan Freed at WJW in Cleveland, who promoted the music both on his radio show and at racially integrated concerts in the Cleveland area.

In 1954, Freed moved to New York and took his nightly "Rock 'n' Roll" party there, where he continued to promote live shows. Thanks to the efforts of Freed and a growing cadre of disc jockeys with their fingers on the pulse of the young, rock and roll began to enjoy a larger audience and to appear on popular song lists, even as the mambo dance and song craze raged.

If it is possible to identify a moment in which rock and roll emerged as a powerful movement, one would have to pick July 9, 1955. "Cherry Pink and Apple Blossoms White" slipped from the number one single, replaced by "Rock

Citizens Council," *The Reporter*, XIV, No. 10, May 17, 1956)

Rock 'n' roll is the martial music of sideburned delinquents all over the face of the earth. The music is sung, played and written for the most part by cretinous goons and the lyrics are sly, lewd and dirty. (Frank Sinatra, in the *San Francisco Examiner*, November 10, 1957)

Not to be outdone, East German leader Horst Sandermann, a candidate for the Communist Central Committee, accused the West of using Elvis Presley "to arouse a spirit of inhumanity among youth" in preparation for war. Among the factors which Sandermann pointed to was the fact that youths were encouraged "to use a language no sensible person could understand" (*San Francisco Examiner*, August 8, 1960).

By 1959, rock and roll was in need of a second wind. The charts were dominated by songs that sorely lacked the vitality and cutting-edge spirit of the first years of rock and roll. In a survey of rock and roll disc jockeys which writer Paul Dickson conducted in the late 1950s while a student at Wesleyan University, many of the disc jockeys predicted that rock and roll was on the wane ("it will revert to the limited popularity it enjoyed 10 to 15 years ago") or that it would soon be replaced by "a more acceptable type of music for young and old" or that jazz was "something good that may come out of the whole mess" or that there would be "a revival of the big band sound."

Youth Slang of the 1950s

Despite the undeniably potent effect of rock and roll and American youth culture, it was an off decade for youth slang. The decade began with a youth culture that was still dancing the dances of the late 1930s, casting around for new music, and recycling now tired jive and cleaned up Army lingo brought home by big brother.

Although rock and roll would ultimately prove to be a vital source of youth slang, it did not function as such in the 1950s. American youth sat up, listened, and sang along with Chuck Berry's "Maybelene," but their slang was not heavily influenced by rock and roll.

Towards the end of the decade, mainstream youth slang began to mimic in a modest way the caricatured speech of Beats, but from start of the decade to end it was a disappointing ten years for youth slang. *Cool* was and is a great word and *neat* has enjoyed a long if lackluster career. *Fat* (meaning cool, a precursor to *phat*), *hang* (meaning to relax), and *clue* (as a verb, meaning to inform) all have a pointedly modern ring to them. That said, most of the rest of the words and expressions that were near and dear to the lips of the young were colorless and flat, with the exception of the admittedly vibrant slang of hot-rodders and other car enthusiasts. With the rebirth of rock and roll in the 1960s there would come a new, hip and cool mainstream youth slang. For the 1950s, though, the creative and cultural energy of the young was directed towards music, not language.

A 1950s Word List

A

actor
A show-off

ad-lib
To play the field

agitate the gravel
To leave

Ain't that a bite?
That's too bad.

anti-frantic
Poised

apple butter
Smooth talk. *More than vaguely related to "applesauce" as flattery in the 1920s.*

Are you writing a book?
Why are you asking me so many questions?

argonaut
A boy with muscles

B

baby
A cute girl

bake biscuits
To make records

ballad
A love letter

bash
A wild party

bash ears
To talk

beard
A nice, smart guy

big tickle
Something that is very funny

binoculars
Glasses

bit
An act

Black time's here, termite.
I'll see you later.

blanket
A sandwich

blast *or* **blast and a half**
A good party

blow your jets
To become irritated

Bo-ing!
I approve

brew
A beer

bull
A big and strong athlete

bundie
A boy in need of a haircut

C

calf
An adolescent, usually a girl

cast an eyeball
To look

cheesecloth
A person whose motives are obvious

chili
A good deal

Cool Two Dozen Ways

Cool was the undisputed champion of approval-expressing slang in the 1950s, both in the mainstream and the beat youth. Other ways to express esteem for something that was cool included **bad, cobra** (a Washington State superlative derived from *snaky*), **crazy, creamy, fantabulous, fat** (yes—there it is—*Newsweek*, October 8, 1951—*fat!*), **feasty, frantastic, frantic, frozen, hairiest, hairy, in the know, kicky, mad, mean, neat, nervous, oogley, real basic, real George, rock** (a cool person), **shafty, snaky, the living end, the real Bikini,** and **the very end.**

chrome-plated
Dressed up.
An association with cars, carried into a broader social context.

circled
Married

clanked
Rejected

classy chassis
A nice body

closet case
Someone to be ashamed of

club, the
A group of several boys whom a girl dates, as in the phrase "in the club"

clutched
Rejected

Come on snake, let's rattle!
May I have the next dance?

committed
Engaged to be married

cool dad
A popular boy

cool it
To relax

cooties
An invisible affliction attached to social outcasts

cop a breeze
To leave

corral
A school yard

cruisin' for a bruisin'
Looking for trouble

cut the cheese
To fart

Cut the gas
Shut up!

D.D.T.
Drop dead twice.
To which one answered, "What, and look like you?"

dead head
An inept loser.
How about this seminal word of the 1960s through 1990s, here in an earlier and—some would argue—completely consistent sense.

deck of ready rolls
A pack of cigarettes

dictator
One's father

dis
A dissipated person.
How interesting! A major word from black street vernacular that jumps into the mainstream in the 1980s, but here with a completely different meaning.

dolly
A cute girl

Don't hand me any of that jazz!
You are talking nonsense!

Don't tense!
Take it easy!

double bubble
A very attractive girl

drag it
To hurry

drowning
Baffled

due backs
A pack of cigarettes

earthbound
Reliable

earth pads
Shoes

ends
Shoes

fade out
1. To disappear
2. Someone who broke a promise

fake out
A disappointing date

far out
Ahead of the times

fast
Sexually available

fat city
A good situation

flat-top
A crew cut in which the hair is cut flat across the top and rounded at the sides

flick
A movie

flip
To become extremely excited

flookie
A jerk

flutter bum
A good-looking boy

fracture
To amuse immensely

frail
Broke, without money

freak
A term of endearment

fringed
Left out

frosted
Angry

fuzzy duck
A girl with short hair

G

germ
A pest

Get bent!
I despise you!

Give me a bell.
Call me on the
telephone.

go ape
To get excited about
something

goof
To make a mistake

goopy
Very messy

grapes
Girls

gringles
Worries

ground-grabbers
Feet

grundy
Neither good nor
bad

H

hang
To loaf or idle. *How
about that! A big
word of the 1980s—
hangin'—here alive
and well and with its
1980s meaning in the
1950s!*

hard cat
A popular boy

heart
A good teacher

hefty
In the money

Hey beau!
Hello!

Hey, insect!
Hey, you loser!

Hey, nosebleed!
Hey, stupid!

hit the bottle
To bleach one's hair
blonde

hooker
A cigarette

hot spook
A good kid

hub cap
A boy who tries to
be a big wheel but
fails

I

ice it
To forget something

I'll clue ya
I'll tell you
about it

illuminations
Good ideas

in orbit
In the know

J

jacketed
Going steady

jets
Brains

Joe Roe *or*
Joe Doe
A boy involved in a
blind date

jolly tot
A young boy who
tries to act like
a big shot but
fails

K

Keep cool, fool!
Yes, that was
a pretty girl who
just walked by,
but keep your
poise!

keeper
A parent

kill
To impress
greatly

king
A good-looking,
popular boy

knuckle sandwich
A punch in the
mouth

kookie
Wild, offbeat

L

large charge
Something that is
exciting

Lay dead.
Wait a minute.

lighter
A crew cut

little monsters
Younger siblings

loose wig, a
An attitude that is
too wild

lover
A good-looking
boy

low hurdle
A cheap date

lump lips
To kiss

lumpy
Mediocre

lurp
A social outcast

M

made in the shade
Assured of success

Madison Avenue
Sharp, cunning

make it real big
To be very popular

make out
To kiss

make the scene
To attend an event or participate in an activity. *With the Beat movement and later in the 1960s, this expression took on a more status-oriented meaning and referred to being part of the in crowd.*

man
A prefatory word with no specific meaning

marble
A dope

mental case
A term of endearment

Mickey Mouse
Dumb

moldy
A bad teacher

monster
A term of endearment

mop
A person one is dating

most, the
Sexy

mush
Homework

My, how sanitary!
I approve!

N

negative perspiration
Easy. *Derived from "no sweat."*

nerd
A social outcast. *The word was first used by the young in the 1950s. It gained widespread usage in the mid-1960s and has stayed near the top of the pejorative pile since then.*

nest
A hair-do

night shift
A slumber party

no sweat
Easy

nuggets
Loose change. *A recycled piece of slang, which in the 1930s meant "excellent."*

O

odd ball
An eccentric

on pills
Dieting

on the hook
In love

on the stick
Prepared, alert

P

pale one
A dull person

panic and a half
A very funny joke

party pooper
A killjoy

pashpie
A good-looking boy

Percy
An effeminate boy

pile up the z's
To sleep

Pinky's out of jail.
Your slip is showing.

play dead
To keep quiet

pooper
A killjoy

passion pit
A drive-in movie

positive kill
A good joke

proof
Identification showing
that one is old enough
to buy liquor

**Put an egg in
your shoe and
beat it!**
Leave!

quaff a foamy
To drink a beer

queen
A popular girl

quote
To repeat oneself

radioactive
Very popular, all over
the place

raunchy
Messy

real gone
1. Madly in love
2. A little unstable

reds
An angry state, as in
the phrase "It gives
me the reds."

refuel
To eat

roach
An unpopular girl.
Nice word!

round-up time
The end of summer
vacation

royal shaft
Poor treatment

salty
Angry

scooch
A friend

scorch
Popular

scurve
A social outcast, not
as low as a NERD

sewer
Someone who is
incapable of keeping
a secret

shack up
To enter into a
sexual relationship
involving shared
living quarters

shoemaker
A boy who is not
too bright

sides
Records

skevee
A messy person

skinny
Broke, without
money

slodge
A friend

sluff
To cut classes

slurg
A milkshake

snowed
Infatuated

Sophie
One's girlfriend

sounds
Music

spades
Pointed shoes

squishy
Forgetful

**straighten up and
die**
To go away

strong
In the money

sucker
A good-looking boy
who is going steady

tapper
A boy who tries
repeatedly for a date

That vibrates me!
I approve!

That has it!
I approve!

slaughterhouse
School

Kookie Talk

The television show *77 Sunset Strip* was an enormous success in the late 1950s, and the idiom of its star, Edd "Kookie" Byrnes, was a distinctive element of the show.

Byrnes became a symbol of inventive youthful language.

The pinnacle of his impact on the language came with the publication in 1959, of *'Way Out with Kookie*, a joint production of Warner Brothers and Brylcreem. The introduction pointedly reveals the book's tone:

It's like this, Dad. A lot of the cats have been bugging me about the jive I make with in "77 Sunset Strip." Like where can we latch onto some of the words? So we decided to knock together a book, like fast.

Get with it, citizens. You've got to give with the "Kookie talk" or be from squaresville. There are more than 270 words and phrases to stash away in your noggin so you can beat your teeth on the beam with the other cats.

Kookie Talk consisted in part of authentic teen slang, in part of authentic adult slang, and in part of screenwriter fabrications. Among the more fanciful inventions were **beef with germsville** (an illness), **international intrigue dodge** (the private investigation business), **smog in the noggin** (lost memory), **you make with the king's jive** (your English is good), **stable the horses** (park the car), or **she's lighting up the tilt sign** (she's not telling the truth).

Despite the fame which this brand of slang brought him, Byrnes was quick to admit that it was all an artifice. "I never talk that way" he told *TV Guide*, "and the only way I can keep those speeches in my head is to learn them word by word."

The Kookie Talk phenomenon (repeated with less visibility by Vaseline Hair Tonic's *Flip-Talk Contest Booklet*) is illustrative of the near bankruptcy of mainstream youth slang by the end of the 1950s. No genuine or robust youth slang needs to be learned through commercially sponsored booklets.

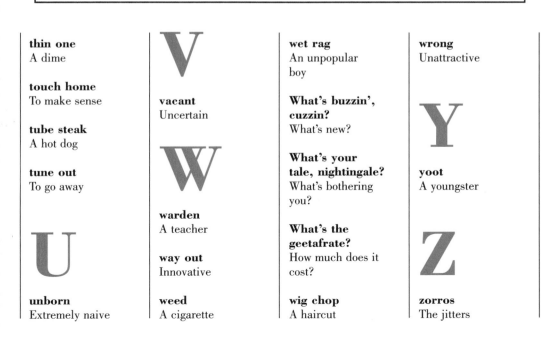

thin one
A dime

touch home
To make sense

tube steak
A hot dog

tune out
To go away

U

unborn
Extremely naive

V

vacant
Uncertain

W

warden
A teacher

way out
Innovative

weed
A cigarette

wet rag
An unpopular boy

What's buzzin', cuzzin?
What's new?

What's your tale, nightingale?
What's bothering you?

What's the geetafrate?
How much does it cost?

wig chop
A haircut

wrong
Unattractive

Y

yoot
A youngster

Z

zorros
The jitters

Hot Rods

The two major teenage trends to emerge in the 1950s were rock and roll and the culture of cars. Rock and roll, discussed above, did not produce a distinct idiom of any consequence in the 1950s, but the car culture most decidedly did.

Hot rods—usually older cars that were modified and improved for looks and/or speed—played a major part in the lives of many teenage boys in the 1950s. At least three magazines catered to hot-rod enthusiasts (*Hot Rod Magazine* which appeared in 1948, *Hop Up* which appeared in 1951, and *Honk* which appeared in 1953). The powerful role played by cars and hot rods well into the 1960s is illustrated by the popularity of the Beach Boys; after their first several hits dealing with surfing, they shifted themes and settled on cars and girls as the subject matter of their songs.

The language of hot-rodders was vivid, humorous, and considerable. In many ways, it was the most creative and inventive youth slang of the decade. Even excluding the most technical jargon of the hot-rodder, the following list of basic hot rod slang is impressively large.

A-bomb *or* **A-bone**
A hopped up Model A Ford

abortion
A poorly designed car

asphalt eater
A fast car

back off
To let up on the gas

bad news
A fast car

baldy
A worn tire

banzai
An all-out run

barrel
A cylinder

barrel ass
To drive fast

bash
A race or other car-oriented event

bathtub
A touring car

beast
A powerful car

bench racer
Someone who talks a good race

bent eight
A V-8 engine

big arm
A long piston stroke

big Merc
A bored and stroked Mercury engine

big rubber
Oversized rear tires for greater traction

binders
Brakes

bite
Traction

blinkey
The timing light at the finish line of a sanctioned drag race

blocks
Spaces placed between the rear axle and spring to lower a car

blow
To be damaged or ruined

blow off
To defeat in a race, usually a drag race

blower
A supercharger

blown
Supercharged

bobbed
Cut or shortened

bomb
A car

anchor
The brake on a car

boost
Manifold pressure supplied by a supercharger

boots
Tires

bore
To enlarge the cylinders

boss
Very good

box
The transmission

bucket
A car

bucket of bolts
An old car that rattles when driven

bug
car

bug catcher
A scoop around the injector system of a supercharged car

bull nose
A hood from which all ornaments have been removed

burn out, burn rubber, lay out, lay rubber, lay a strip, *or* **stripe out**
To lose rear wheel traction and produce a squealing sound

C

carp out
To misfire

channel
To lower the body by cutting out the floor and dropping the body over the frame rail

chatter
To vibrate

chauffeur
To drive

cherry
Attractive. *The term was originally applied to an unaltered, unrestored car; later came to mean a beautifully restored car.*

chizzler
A Chrysler engine

choose off
To challenge someone to race

chop
To remove a portion of a car

chop job
A car whose top has been removed

Christmas tree
An electronic countdown starter used in organized drag races

chrome
To add chrome trimmings and accessories

clock
To attain a speed that is verified by official timing

cough an engine
To experience extreme engine failure

crank up
To start a car by pushing it

cream
To dent a car fender

cut A
To leave

cut a fat one
To run at top speed

cut out
To leave

D

dago *or* **dago drop**
A lowered front end

daylight
To beat another car badly

deck job
A smoothed-off TURTLEDECK

deuce
A 1932 Ford

dig in
To accelerate a
car quickly, leaving
rubber patch
marks

dog clutch
A hand-operated
clutch

drag
A race between two
cars beginning at a
rest and covering a
relatively short
distance

draggin' wagon
A car

drop
To lower a car

drop the hammer
To engage the clutch
rapidly at the start of
a race

dump
To lower a car

dust off
To win a race

fadeaways
Front fenders that
blend into the side of
the body

fire up
To start an
engine

fireplace
A car's grille

five dollars a gear
A typical bet in a
drag race, where the
winner collects five
dollars for each gear
in which he is the
victor

flame-thrower
A highly modified
ignition system

flat out
Top speed

flip
To overturn

floor it
Depress the
accelerator
completely

four on the floor
Four-speed floor shift
transmission

freeze
To fail to function
because of some
parts expanding
more rapidly than
others

Frenched
Molded into fenders
(said of headlights
and tail lights)

full bore
Running at full
throttle

full house
An engine that
has been completely
modified for
racing

full Jimmie
A GMC engine that
has been completely
modified for racing

full mill
An engine that has
been completely
modified for racing

full race
An engine modified
and tuned specifically
for racing

garbage
An excess of acces-
sories

gasser
A hot rod that uses
gasoline as fuel

get a bite
To achieve traction
with tires

get on it
To give the engine
more throttle

glass-pack
A muffler specially
packed with fiberglass

go
1. A drag race
2. A car built for
speed as opposed to
looks, as in SHOW
OR GO

go-fast boys
Boys who strive for
top speeds

go for pinks
To compete in a drag
race in which the
stake is the pink slip
(certificate of owner-
ship)

go juice
Fuel

go off with
To drag race

goat
An old racing
car

goer
A fast car

gold
Trophies

gone
1. Good and
attractive
2. Beat up beyond
repair

goodies
Outside accessories
on a car

gook wagon
A stock car
with many
accessories

gooker
A reckless driver

goose it
To give the engine
full throttle

**Grind me off a
hunk!**
That was a
messy gear shift
that you just
made!

gut
To remove unnecessary body parts from the inside of a car

hack
A car

handler
A driver

Hang it easy!
See you later!

has-been
A modified car that has not been treated well

hat
A crash helmet

haul ass
To drive fast

hauler
A very fast car

Haulin' Henry
A fast Ford

have a go
To have a drag race

headers
Reworked exhaust pipes

heap
An old, junky car

Henry
A Ford

herd
To drive a car

hit the binders
To apply the brakes

Hollywood
A special exhaust system

honker
A very fast car, usually a very fast stock car

hop-up
A hot-rod enthusiast

hopped up
Modified with speed equipment for racing

horning
A GMC engine with a head manufactured by Wayne Horning

hose brakes
Hydraulic brakes

hot
Modified to produce faster speed

hot shoe
A very fast driver

hottie
A car with a very fast engine

hot to go
Ready to compete

huffer
A supercharger

iron
A heavy, newer car

jiggler
the rocker arm of an overhead valve

Jimmie
A GMC engine

Johnson Rod
A mythical engine part

jug
A carburetor

jump
To get a quick start in a race

kemp
A car

lakester
A hot rod used in competitions on dry lake beds

lay a cool shift
To execute a speed shift without any loss of speed or grinding gears

pooper
A car that fails to perform as expected

lead in
To fill in holes with lead as part of a BULL NOSE or DECK JOB

lead sled
A slow car

lid
A cylinder head

like a bomb
Very fast

little rubber
Small tires used on the front wheels

lower
To decrease the height of a car

lug it
To drive up a hill at low speed in high gear

lump
An engine

lunch
To scatter parts around during an extreme engine failure

M

machine
A car

mains
Main bearings

mashed-potato drive
Dynaflow

Mexican chrome
Silver paint

midnight auto supply
The source of stolen parts

mill
An engine

moons
Large, smooth hub caps

mother head
A fast car

move
To run rapidly

N

necker's knob
A spinner knob on the steering wheel that facilitates one-arm driving

nerf
To push another car

nerf bar
A bumper

nosed
Having the hood smoothed off by removing ornaments and plugging holes

O

off the line
The start of a drag race

on the piano
Not able to be found

P

pile
Anyone else's car

pipes
Exhaust pipes

plant it
To run at full throttle

pop the clutch
To release the clutch pedal suddenly, making for a quick start

pot
A carburetor

pot out
An engine breakdown

prune
To outrun another car

puffer
A supercharger

pull it down
To take an engine apart

pump
A supercharger

punch
To bore cylinders out

punch it
To step on the gas

put it to the wood
To run at full throttle

rag-top
A convertible

rail
A dragster

rail job
A hot rod stripped down the frame

rake
To lower the front end of a car

rappers
Short mufflers

rat
A badly running car

ripple discs
Large hub caps with a bar that creates a flickering effect

rocket
A car

rod
A hot rod

roll
To overturn

run
A drag race

run whatcha brung
A race with no rules

sauce
A mixed fuel

scat
To go fast

scream
To go fast

screamer
A hot rod

set of wheels
A car

shave
To remove chrome or insignia from a car's body

shot rod
A car

show or go
The two classic approaches to cars—restored for looks (show) or speed (go)

shut down
To defeat in a race

skin
To replace stock upholstery

skins
Tires

sleeper
A car that has been modified for speed but does not look it

slicks
Smooth tires used in racing

slingshot
A dragster in which the drivers seat is behind the rear wheels

slippery
Streamlined

slugs
Pistons

slush pump
Automatic transmission

Smitty
A muffler packed with Fiberglass

smoke out of the chute
To spin one's tires in a fast start of a drag race

smoothed
Stripped of ornamentation and hardware

snap shift
A very fast shift so that there is almost continuous power to the rear wheels

snowballs
White-wall tires

snowplow
A car with a dropped front end

solids
Solid valve lifters

soup
Racing fuel

souped up
Modified with speed equipment

spaghetti headers
Exhaust pipes made of flexible tubing

speed goodies
Speed accessories

speed shop
A parts house

spooking
Driving for the sake of driving

squirrel
A would-be hot-rodder

squirt brakes
Hydraulic brakes

stack up
To wreck a car

stand on it
To give a car full throttle

starved
Deprived of fuel (said of cylinders)

stick a foot in the pot
To accelerate to the maximum

stock
Original equipment

Uncle Daniel
A car that has been modified for speed but does not look it

storm
To accelerate fast

stormer
A hot rod

storming machine
A car that will go fast

stove bolt
A Chevrolet.
So called because many of the engine bolts were coarsely threaded and had a notched head—like a stove bolt.

strides
Old pants worn when working on a car

strip
A drag strip

stripped
Having all chrome removed

suicide front end
A lowered front end

that could cause an end-over-end roll if a plate broke during a race

taco wagon
A Mexican-American's hot rod

tails
Coon tails or fox tails used decoratively

take the torch to it
To lower a car by chopping the top

tear ass
To drive fast or recklessly

tight
Not yet completely broken in (said of an engine)

tip the gas
To fill the gas tank

tool
To drive

top end
A car's maximum speed

total
To completely demolish a car

traps
The start and finish of a race at a lake bed

tromp it
To give an engine full throttle

trumpets
Tailpipe extensions

turn
To attain a verified speed

turtledeck
The trunk of a roadster

typewriter
A Dodge. *So named because of the push-button automatic transmission.*

unglued
Blown (said of an engine)

unreal
Exceptional

virgin
A clean, sharp-looking stock car

J.D. Language

Along with its many successes, the 1950s saw a then-terrifying spread of juvenile delinquency and youth gangs. It is no accident that Leonard Bernstein's 1959 hit *West Side Story* involved warring gangs in Manhattan.

Within a gang, there was the **war counselor** (a top strategist or diplomat), the **ace men** (secondary leaders or top fighters), and the common **citizen** (a fellow gang member).

The territory controlled by a gang was known as its **turf,** and violation of a gang's turf could lead to **sounding** (hurling insults), a **fair fight** (a fight between designated representatives of each gang, no weapons allowed), or a **rumble** (an all-out mass gang fight with no restrictions on weapons). In an effort to negotiate their differences away, gangs might **declare a talk,** deferring to negotiations.

For a gang, a **fall in** was a group entrance designed to create an impression. To **punk out** was to back down from a fight, while **punk** or **chicken** as applied to a person were fighting words that could not be ignored.

W

works, the
Complete racing equipment

wail
To run very fast

wedge
A car

wheelie, do a
To lift the front wheels off the ground by rapid acceleration

wind
Good acceleration

windjammer
A supercharger

wind up or wind out
To run at maximum rpm

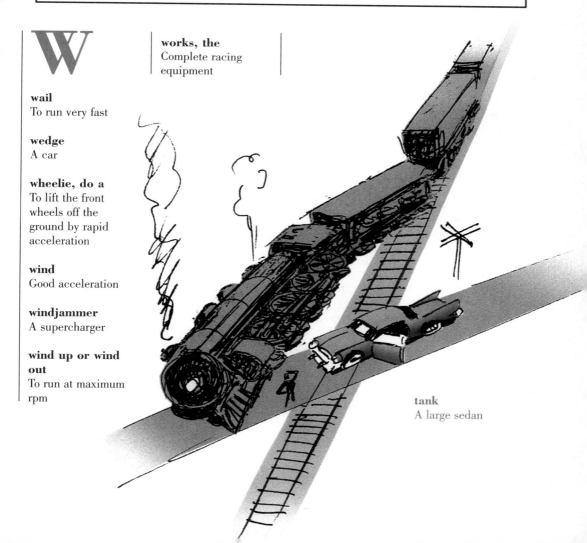

tank
A large sedan

Word History: Rock and Roll

Disc jockey Alan Freed is universally credited with applying an expression that had existed for decades to a music that had existed for years (known as rhythm and blues, sepia music, or race music) to give the young of the world rock and roll. Freed used the phrase as the theme of his popular radio show in Cleveland, "The Beat Beat," which he changed to "The Moon Dog House Rock-'n'-Roll Party." As Wes Smith wrote in *The Pied Pipers of Rock 'n' Roll* "while he may not have been the first to play the music, he was the first to put it all together in one package and peddle it to a big audience of both blacks and whites."

The phrase *rock and roll* was used prolifically in song lyrics for three decades before Alan Freed's inspirational appropriation of it, almost always as a euphemism from the black vernacular for sex. Examples include:

1922
Trixie Smith and the Jazz Masters: "My Man Rocks Me (With One Steady Roll)"

1932
Boswell Sisters: "Rock and Roll"

1934
From *Transatlantic Merry-Go-Round,* a Jack Benny movie: "Rock and Roll"

1938
Bunny Berigan and His Orchestra: "Rocking Rollers Jubilee"

1938

Hot Lips Page: "Rock it for Me"
("Rock and roll...")

1939

Buddy Jones: "Rockin', Rollin' Mama"

1947

Wild Bill Moore: "Rock and Roll"

1950

John Lee Hooker: "We're Gonna Rock,
We're Gonna Roll"

1951

Treniers: "It Rocks! It Rolls! It Swings!"

1951

Clyde McPlatter and the Dominoes:
"Sixty Minute Man" ("Rock and roll all
night long...")

1952

Lil' Son Jackson: "Rockin' and Rollin'"

1952

Nugerte: "Ting-A-Ling" ("All these girls 'bout
to drive me wild/The way they rock and roll and
call me angel child")

1952

M. Jackson: "Rockin' and Rollin' No. 2"

1952

Fats Gaines: "Gaines Boogie"
("We're gonna rock and roll and jump for a
long, long time")

1952

Wards-Marks: "Pedal Pushin' Poppa"
("I'll rock your soul and make you roll - a pedal
pushin' poppa I am")

From the start, rock and roll was often
referred to in the clipped form of simply *rock*,
which itself boasted two slang meanings. Like
the full expression, *rock* standing alone was a
euphemism for sex. Trixie Smith's "My Man
Rocks Me (With One Steady Roll)" left no doubt
as to its meaning in 1922, and neither did Laurie

Tate and Joe Morris's "Rock Me Daddy" in
1952—"They rock in the park, down in lover's
lane/Like it in the mornin' when it's pourin' down
rain." In the same year, P. Harris wrote "Rock,
Rock, Rock" with its explicit reference to sex—
"We rock on the sofa, we rock on the chair, we
rock on the table and we don't care."

Secondly, the term *rock* had been used for
years in connection with a band or song that con-
veys energy and passion, as illustrated by the
February 12, 1947, *Steve Canyon* comic strip,
which features our hero in a night club, telling
his date Miss Calhoon that "That band rocks
easy!"

Word History: The Suffix -ville

In the 1950s, it seems as if you could not turn
around without bumping into a something-*ville*.
In its simplest form, the suffix -*ville* served to
identify that the situation was characterized by
what was indicated in the base word. It did more
though, both intensifying the term or phrase and
signaling the hip status of the speaker.

The earliest use of the suffix -*ville* in a slangy
sense that I have uncovered is in the July 11,
1891, issue of *Sporting News:* "Then he was as
frisky as a young colt and a slugger from
Sluggersville." Several months later, on
November 14, 1891, *Sporting News* again resorted to -*ville*, writing that "Murnane is a hustler
from Hustlersville." In 1900, Williams and
Walker wrote the words and music to "The
Blackville Strutters' Ball," the next -*ville* that I
have found. In 1905, the diet book *The Road to
Wellville* was published, giving us a last -*ville* for
a few decades.

In the 1940s, there were a few -*ville's*. Damon
Runyon flirted with the suffix, coining **foldsville**
in 1942, while Tommy Dorsey came up with the
quite important **squaresville** also in 1942:
"Squaresville is the highly mythical place
squares come from, unless you say, 'He's a
square from Delaware—he ain't anywhere'" (*San
Francisco Call-Bulletin*, February 25, 1942).

The 1950s saw the huge boom in -*ville*, with
columnists such as Walter Winchell and Herb
Caen working overtime on concocting instant
slang-*villes*. Examples and the earliest citations
for them include **anti-squaresville** (1959),

antsville (1961), beatsville (1959), best-sell-erville (1958), bluesville (1960), boyville (1958), capital gainsville (1956), carville (1958), chillsville (1955), chumpsville (1957), closeville (1950), deadsville (no date), deathsville (1947), derbyville (1959), divasville (1961), dollsville (1961), Doodyville (1947), drabsville (1965), dreamsville (1960), duckville (1958), dullsville (1960), endsville (1959), fatsville (1961), filmville (1952), flatsville (1959), flipsville (1957), freesville (1957), funsville (1959), germsville (1957), girlville (1954), gloomsville (late 1950s), gonesville (1959), goonsville (1959), hangoversville (1955), happinessville (1959), hellsville (1962), hitville (1956), ho-humsville (1956), intriguesville (late 1950s), jumpville (1959), Kyneville (1950), lay-off-ville (1955), lone-lyville (1959), lootsville (1957), lootville (1957), Marilynville (1954), Monroeville (1954), moodsville (1960), movieville (1955), phoneyville (1952), pointville (1959), poundsville (1959), profanesville (1959), quaintsville (1960), quitsville (1953), riftsville (1952), rocksville (1954), rubesville (no date), ruthville (1954), sadsville (1956), samesville (1971), sausageville (1959), scamville (1955), Searsville (1963), sensationville (1955), shut-tersville (1957), sixville (1957), slickville (1959), sloggerville (1950), smashville (1959), soulville (1958), splitsville (1954), spookeville (1960), statisticville (1959), swapsville (1961), swimsville (early 1960s), swingville (1960), tagsville (1955), tapsville (1966), teensville (1959), tubesville (1961), ugsville (1957), weirdsville (1955), wigville (1955), yawnsville (1952), yuksville (1952), Zanuckville (1958), and zeroville (1958).

Whom do we have to thank for the prolifera-tion of -ville? In 1959, Henry (The Neem) Nemo, claimed responsibility in the San Francisco Examiner:

I brought the ville around and all those echo chambers that claim they put it down first are beachcombers and turnstilers. I did a thing called Jumpville, New York for Mildred Bailey in '37. Bingsville was the one who dug it. Only Bingsville said, "You're too far out, man, for the

common cats." (November 16, 1959)

Several years later, the San Francisco Examiner credited Frank Sinatra with the craze:

His habit of adding ville to words began with dullsville, which to him meant boring beyond endurance.

By the late 1950s, -ville was losing steam. Connie Francis, as straight as they came, spoke up against -ville in the San Francisco Examiner of September 7, 1959:

There's such a thing as being so hip you're square. All those words ending in 'ville' I don't use. Squaresville and Endsville, I don't like those.

Thankfully -ville faded back to Suffixville in the 1960s, although not before Stan and Jan Berenstain (authors in the 1980s of the child behavior modification books The Berenstain Bears) wrote Squaresville (The Teen's Guide to Adult Behavior)/Flipsville (The Adult's Guide to Teen-Age Behavior) (New York: Dell Publishing, 1965), as painful a use of the poor suffix -ville as was ever seen.

Sources and References

In considering the slang of mainstream youth in the 1950s, I did not rely on any single source to a significant degree. The only two full-length teen slang dictionaries from the decade that I have found are amusing but definitely suspect when it comes to their authenticity 'Way Out with Kookie (published by Warner Brothers and Brylcreem, 1959), and Vaseline Hair Tonic's Flip-Talk Contest Booklet.

A wide array of fan magazines, advertise-ments aimed at teenagers, music industry pro-motions, and clippings are housed at the Tamony Collection at the University of Missouri. Among the most helpful articles are "Jelly Tot, Square Bear-Man!" (Newsweek, October 9, 1951); "What are they saying?" by Robert Manry (The American Weekly, August 14, 1955); "Gator Gab" (Time, August 24, 1959); "English?" by Beulah Racklin (This Week magazine in the San

Francisco Chronicle, February 28, 1954); "For Women Only: American Teenagers and What They Are Made Of" (*Look,* August 10, 1954); "Dick Clark Talks to Teen-Agers" (*Look,* November 24, 1959); and "Teeners Orbit Around with Intercontinental Slang" by Gay Pauley (*San Francisco News,* March 25, 1958). In addition, *Who's Who in Rock 'n Roll,* edited by Vic Fredericks (New York: Frederick Fell, Inc., 1958), contains a brief "Rock 'N Roll Dictionary." Also of some help was "As We Used to Say in the '50s" by Howard Junker (*Esquire,* June, 1983). Finally, Paul Dickson kindly gave me access to his college research on rock and roll, including the deejay responses quoted in this chapter.

For the language of hot rodders, I relied on "Hot Rod Terms in the Pasadena Area" by Don Mansell and Joseph S. Hall, which appeared in the May 1954 issue of *American Speech* and glossaries contained in *The Hot Rod Handbook* (originally entitled *Hot Rod It—and Run for Fun*) by Fred Horsley (New York: J. Lowell Pratt and Company, 1957, 1965); *Hot Rod Handbook* (New York: Fawcett Books, n.d.); "Hot Rod Terms for Teen-age Girls" from *Good Housekeeping* (September 1958); and "Hot Rod Jargon," compiled by Tom Medley of *Hot Rod Magazine,* distributed by Capitol Records in 1963.

CHAPTER 6
The Beat Counterculture of the 1950s

▼

"Like we was up in this freak's pad, and she came off real lame, because we didn't dig the TV, you know?"

A long with rock and roll, the 1950s produced the first viable youth counterculture (a word not widely used until the late 1960s), a complex combination of four separate components which have come to be remembered collectively as the Beat movement or Beatnik movement, depending on perspective.

In its purest sense, the Beat movement was a serious literary movement involving a relatively small group of men who met each other while coming of age in New York in the 1940s, for whom World War II was a formative event, and who achieved their first degree of literary success before the Beat movement in its broader social sense developed. They included Jack Kerouac (*The Town and the City*, published in 1950, *On The Road* in 1957), John Clellon Holmes (*Go*, published in 1952), William S. Burroughs (*Junkie*, published in 1953), Lawrence Ferlinghetti (City Lights Bookstore, opened in 1953, first poetry published in 1955), and Allen Ginsberg (*Howl*, published in 1956). With their fellow writers they established a new

Illustrations by Guy Billout

genre of American literature, heavily influenced by French existentialism, Zen Buddhism, and the hipster's passion for jazz and life.

The second piece of the Beat puzzle is the hipster, the lover of bebop, sartorially stylish, jive-speaking, drug-experimenting, passionate about life, and something of a hustler, powerfully portrayed by Norman Mailer in *The White Negro* (*Dissent*, Summer, 1957): "In such places as Greenwich Village, a ménage-à-trois was completed—the bohemian and the juvenile delinquent came face-to-face with the Negro, and the hipster was a fact in American life." The hipster was a character type, not a movement, providing the social milieu in which the Beat artists—who for the most part shunned the affected dress and jive speech of the hipsters—operated. By the late 1950s the hipster gave way to the Beat.

The Beat movement in its social sense—piece number three—began to take hold in San Francisco, Venice (west of Los Angeles), Greenwich Village (where they were known as New Bohemians), and New Orleans in 1955. In San Francisco, the alienated young drifted to Grant Street and North Beach, gathering to listen to poetry and jazz at the Coexistence Bagel Shop, Gino and Carlo's Bar, The Place, Vesuvio's, The Cellar, and the Coffee Gallery. They dressed in sweatshirts or sweaters or boat-neck fisherman shirts, sandals, dungarees, dark glasses and berets, lived in garage apartments, North Beach walk-ups, little cottages, and storefronts, listened to jazz records, drank wine and smoked marijuana and ingested Benzedrine to stay up all night and be startled at their revelations, rejoiced in sex, painted and admired paintings, wrote poetry and admired poetry, and—most of all—they were young even if sometimes in a morose, bored but intense, and intellectual way.

In 1957, national attention was first drawn to this small countercultural movement by Kenneth Rexroth's article "San Francisco's Mature Bohemians" appearing in the *Nation* magazine on February 23, 1957. Later that year, Viking pub-

lished *On the Road,* prompting *San Francisco Chronicle* columnist Herb Caen to characterize the burgeoning Beat movement in San Francisco as the "Beat De-Generation"; also that fall, the *San Francisco Call-Bulletin* weighed in, branding the Beats as the "Get Lost Generation."

In 1958, San Francisco sat up and took full notice of the Beats in their midst. After John Clellon Holmes' thoughtful article "The Philosophy of the Beat Generation" appeared in *Esquire*, the *San Francisco Chronicle* ran a sensational two-part special on "Life and Love Among the Beatniks" while the afternoon paper, the *Examiner*, blared "Beat Generation Finds Mecca in San Francisco." Police cracked down on the Beats, and the murder of locally known Beat poet Connie Sublette (Dana Lewis) in June drew lurid headlines and speculation about the Beat lifestyle. National magazines such as *Esquire, Look, Playboy,* and *Time* all ran articles on the Beat movement.

By the fall of 1958, San Francisco newspapers were announcing the death of the Beats. After an August "Beatnik Party to Honor Debutantes," the *Chronicle* headlined "Good-by (sic) to the Beatniks" while the *Examiner* blared "The Old Beat Gang is Breaking Up: Kerouac and Hipsters Leave the Scene to the Tourists."

The end was not quite in sight though, for 1959 saw the launching by Allen Ginsberg, Bob Kaufman, and several others of *Beatitude* magazine. Never letting anything get by them for too long, the FBI and Vatican spoke up, with the FBI calling Lawrence Ferlinghetti a "beatnik rabble rouser" and Radio Vatican expressing alarm at the Beat generation's "moral and spiritual void."

By 1960 the Beat movement had lost its energy and drive, although that did not stop FBI Director J. Edgar Hoover from warning the Republican convention to beware of "Communist fronts and the beatniks and the eggheads." In April 1960, *Reader's Digest* ran an article entitled "Life Among the Beatniks," sure evidence that the movement must have been all but dead. In August, the *San Francisco Chronicle* trumpeted "Beatnik Land Goes Square"; a month later, the *News-Call Bulletin,* reporting on the Monterey Jazz Festival, boasted that the "Beatnik is as dead as hula hoops," confidently predicting that "Good sense prevailed with American youth." Not for long.

Just as the real thing was dying out, Hollywood and Madison Avenue created the fourth piece of the puzzle, a caricatured stereo-type—the beatnik—that eventually overshadowed the original, genuine article. In 1959, Albert Zugsmith produced for MGM *The Beat Generation,* a grossly inaccurate caricature of the Beat movement, and with it a glossary and novel which claimed to be a "shocking and revealing novel of a generation gone wild." Advertisements to "Rent a Genuine Beatnik" appeared in the *Village Voice.*

The clown prince of Beat caricatures, though, was Maynard G. Krebs, a "beatnik" character written into the television show *The Many Loves of Dobie Gillis.* Goateed and amiable, sweatshirt-ed and lazy, sandal-adorned and bongo-playing, Maynard became a national cultural symbol, probably more defining at the moment than Jack Kerouac, Neal Cassady, or any of the authentic product.

The speech, values, and manners of Beats were widely parodied in books, television skits, magazines, and comic strips, which collectively asked, "Who would want to be like them?" Strangely enough, to a new generation growing up within the confines of mainstream America, the answer was not as simple as those who posed it might have guessed. Strangely enough, the small, isolated pockets of Beats who had been influenced by the literary Beat movement (which had in turn been influenced by the hipsters) were made accessible to those tens of millions of American teenagers who did not live in Greenwich Village or North Beach. Although envisioned as a cultural torpedo, Maynard G. Krebs became in his own way a subversive, par-adigm-challenging figure, clearing the path for the hippie movement of the late 1960s.

Language of the Beats

In a spirited defense of the legitimacy of jive ("Is Jive Linguistic Jabberwocky?"), Peter Tamony recounted the following anecdote illus-trating the legacy of jive in the 1950s:

After the faint fumblings of the Beat Generation, amplified by a horrified press, gave Northern California and the North Beach-Telegraph Hill section of San Francisco national publicity, a few students from Cornell fell in to find out what was being put down. After a day or so, two of the more literate, Dick Farina and David Seidler, exclaimed, "What a town! Amazing! Everybody talks jive!"

Jive was the dominant influence of Beat speech.[1] Jack Kerouac described the patois of the late 1940s hipster as "a new language, actu-ally spade (Negro) jargon, but you soon learned it." By later in the 1950s, Kerouac noticed that "even college kids went around hep and cool and using terms I'd heard on Times Square in the early Forties" ("Beatific: On the Origins of a Generation," *Encounter,* August 1959).

Allen Ginsberg has written similarly in the *Prologue to Beat Culture and the New America: 1950—1965* by Lisa Phillips (New York: Whitney Museum of American Art, 1995), point-ing to Herbert Huncke, author of *The Evening Sun Turned Crimson,* as having been responsible for introducing the members of the Beat literary movement to "what was then known as 'hip lan-guage'...much used then in Times Square."

The language of the Beats—parodied and caricatured in the popular media images of the Beatnik—was, as Farina and Seidler observed, in large measure recycled Harlem jive. What distinguished the language of the Beats and made it so easy to parody was the heavy reliance on a handful of words—*cat, cool, dig, like, man,* and *square.* It did not take much screenwriting talent to string together a few "likes" and a few "digs" for hilarious beatnik dialogue. Forgotten in the mockery of Beat speech is the fact that it set the stage for the slang of the 1960s, both through the influence of the caricature on main-stream popular culture and through the influence of the counterculture of the 1950s on the coun-terculture of the 1960s. Looking even further ahead, the Beats were the first to butcher the word *like,* using it to de-intensify that which they were about to say, fattening the word for the kill of the 1980s.

Beat Words

A

action
A party, gathering, or something that is happening

ape
Frenzied, berserk

ax
Any musical instrument

B

baby
A term of address, used for male or female

bad news
A depressing person

ball
To engage in sexual intercourse

beat
1. To steal
2. Broke

behind
Under the influence of

bird
Airplane

bit
That which one does

or that which interests one. *A predecessor to the ubiquitous "thing" of the 1960s.*

blast
1. A good time
2. To smoke marijuana

blow
To perform

boost
To steal

boots
Any type of shoes

boxed
Intoxicated

buff
A jazz aficionado

bug
To annoy

bug out
To become psychotic

C

cat
A hip person

charge
Marijuana

chariot
A car

chassis
A body

chick
A woman or girl.

Chick was coined in the late 1940s in an effort to include women with men (cats) in the hip world.

chops
Lips

cloud 9
Euphoria

club crawling
Moving from night club to night club

clue
To apprise or advise

Clyde
A term of address, usually for a square

come on strong
To try to create a strong impression

cook
To do what you do well

cop out
To forsake Beat values

count
The amount

cranked
1. Excited
2. High

bring down
1. A depressing person or event
2. To depress

Beat for Good

Cool was the big word of the 1950s, both for mainstream youth and the counterculture Beats. Other Beat words to express approval included **bad, boss, crazy, the end, far out, gas, gone, groovy** or **groovey** ("coming back into use as a complimentary adjective" we are told in the *Hip Manual*), **hot, infinity, nutty, in orbit, out, rave, solid** (left over from the 1940s), **something else, swinging, too much, tough, uptown, way out, wild,** or **with it.**

cube
A person who is very out of tune, worse than a square

D

Daddy or **Daddy-O**
A term of address. *Originally black slang of the 1920s, brought to the beats through the bebop movement.*

deep end
The border between sanity and insanity

dents
Teeth

dig
To understand, to appreciate, to approve of, to enjoy

down with
To be with it

drag
A bore

dues
The hardships which you must endure to obtain success

E

epistle
A letter

eye ball
To look around

F

face
A clock

fall by
To visit

fall in
To arrive at an event

flaked out
Tired

flick
A movie

flip
To experience an extreme mood, from extreme enthusiasm to a complete break-down

foamer
A beer

four bars past ...
Very

frantic
Without poise or control

from in front
From the beginning

full, full-out
Absolutely

funky
Genuine, without pre-tensions

fuzz
The police. *"Fuzz" enjoyed wide use by criminal, hobos, and carnival workers for several decades before being discovered by hipsters and Beats in the 1950s.*

G

gay boy
A homosexual. *In the 1970's, homo-sexuality and the use of the word "gay" came out of the closet. The slang of young gays is addressed in Chapter 9.*

get with it
To understand

gig
Work

gimp, gimpy
Handicapped

Give me five!
Let's shake hands!

good people
A good person

goof
Someone who makes mistakes or wastes time. *Before the 1920s, "goof" was used in the sense of incompetence. In the 1920s, the Flapper appropriated "goof" in her slang to mean "boyfriend." In the 1930s, it reverted to its original slang sense, and here it is again in the Beat lexicon of the 1950s.*

grody
Dirty, sloppy. *There it is, a word generally associated with surfers and Valley Girls, used by Beats.*

groove
A good scene

H

handle
Name. *"Handle" was a venerable piece of tramp slang as early as the 1930s, and after its induction into the vocabulary of the Beats in the 1950s it had a major surge in popularity in the CB radio craze of the 1970s.*

hang-up
A fixed pattern of behavior

head
1. A marijuana user
2. Oral sex

heat
The police

hip
Up to date, informed, poised

hipster
Someone who is totally with it

Hit me.
Explain it to me.

horn
The telephone

hound
The bus

hummer
An arrest which leads to more serious charges

K

kick
A fad

L

Later!
Good-bye!

lay on
To give

lid
A hat

low
Depressed

lush
Alcohol

M

make the scene
To participate in Beat social life

man
An honorific term of address

man, the
The police

mark
One's signature

melt
To get lost, leave

Miss Green
Marijuana

N

nod
Sleep

nowhere
Incapable of understanding, the antithesis of HIP

O

off
To steal. *In the late 1960s, "off" would take on the more somber slang meaning of "to kill," with "rip off" taking over the former meaning of "to steal."*

P

pad
An apartment or home

pick up
To drink alcohol or use drugs

pond
Any large body of water

punk
A weak, useless person

put down
To disparage

R

rank on
To disparage

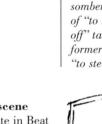

hippie
One who feels he or she is HIP when actually a SQUARE

parchment
Any paper

rap
To inform on someone

rock
A diamond

roust
An arrest

running lights
Eyes

S

scuffle
To live by one's wits, without a steady job

shuck
To deceive

sides
Phonograph records

sing
To inform on someone

slip me
Give me

sounds
Music

spade
An African-American.
There has been a tradition of claiming that "spade" could be used in some circles without giving offense and that this was especially the case among members of the jazz world, whose slang was being picked up by the Beats. There is some basis for this claim (and we will encounter it again in the 1960s); however, it is also true that "spade" was being used in a clearly derogatory way as far back as the 1930s and that for as long as this word has appeared in Merriam-Webster dictionaries, beginning in 1961, it has carried the warning note "usually taken to be offensive."

split
To leave

square
A conformist

squirrel
A SQUARE

straight
Reliable, honest

subterranean
A hipster.
The term was coined by Allen Ginsberg and popularized by Jack Kerouac's novel The Subterraneans.

swing with
To be friends

T

tapped
Arrested

That's close!
What you just said is completely wrong!

tick
A clock

tight
Close, friendly

tossed
Searched by the police

trim
Oral sex on a woman

turn on
1. To use drugs and become intoxicated
2. To introduce someone to something that one likes

V

viper
A marijuana user.
A term which would disappear by the 1960s and hippies.

W

wail
To perform superbly

What's happening?
Hello.

What's shaking?
Hello.

wig
1. The mind.
2. An eccentric

wig out
To become psychotic

word from the bird, the
The genuine truth

work
Sex

Word History: Beat

The term *Beat Generation* and the more popularly known *beatnik* were driven by the word *beat*, a distinguished piece of slang with several centuries of lineage before its adoption by jazz musicians in the 1930s, by hipsters in the 1940s, and by ultimately by Jack Kerouac and John Clellon Holmes in the 1950s.

Beat has been used to mean tired, exhausted, and impoverished since the early 1830s. It is found in *The Slang Dictionary* of John Camden Hotten (1860) and *Slang, Jargon and Cant* by Albert Barrère and Charles Leland (1889), with the derivative *beat-out* or *beaten out* used to mean exhausted as early as 1746. In his fine dictionary of jazz terms *A Jazz Lexicon* (New York: Alfred A. Knopf, 1964), Robert S. Gold reports that *beat* was "widely current among jazzmen since c. 1935" as meaning tired or lacking in spirit. As such, it is found in the slang dictionaries of Cab Calloway (1938) and the glossary to Mezz Mezzrow's *Really the Blues* (1946).

The term "Beat Generation" was coined by Jack Kerouac in a conversation with John Clellon Holmes in 1948. Discussing the character of different generations and specifically the "Lost Generation" of the 1920s, Kerouac pronounced his generation as the "Beat Generation." Allen Ginsberg, who certainly should know, wrote in the Prologue to *Beat Culture and the New America: 1950-1965* by Lisa Phillips (New York: Whitney Museum of American Art, 1995), that in so doing Kerouac was "not meaning to name the generation, but to unname it."[2]

The term first appeared in public on November 16, 1952 with an article by Holmes in *The New York Times Magazine* entitled "This is the Beat Generation," a catchy phrase to be sure. Holmes wrote:

It was John Kerouac...who finally came up with it [the expression "Beat Generation"]. Several years ago he said, "You know, this is really a beat generation." The origins of the word "beat" are obscure, but the meaning is only too clear to most Americans. More than mere weariness, it implies the feeling of having been used, of being raw. It invokes a sort of nakedness of mind, and ultimately of soul; a feeling of being reduced to the bedrock of consciousness. In short, it means being undramatically pushed up against the wall of oneself.

Shortly thereafter, Kerouac published in *New World Writing* (New York: New American Library, 1955) under the name of "Jean-Louis" a portion of what would later be known as *On The Road*, entitled "Jazz of the Beat Generation."

Kerouac's *On The Road*, published in 1957, became one of the several definitive articulations of the vision of the Beat movement. In it, Kerouac wrote, "They were like the man with the dungeon stone and the gloom, rising from the underground, the sordid hipsters of America, a beat generation that I was slowly joining." Peter Tamony of San Francisco identified 1957 as the year in which *beat* began to be used regularly to describe the new movement of hipsters.

In the February 1958 issue of *Esquire*, John Clellon Holmes took another stab at defining the elusive beat, as follows:

Now, with the word "beat," we may have their sobriquet at last. Everyone who has lived through a war, any sort of war, knows that beat means, not such much weariness, as rawness of the nerves; not so much being "filled up to here," as being emptied out. It describes a state of mind, from which all unessentials have been stripped, leaving it receptive to everything around it, but impatient with trivial obstructions. To be beat is to be the bottom of your personality, looking up; to be existential in the Kierkegaard, rather than the Jean-Paul Sartre, sense.

The next year, in identical articles appearing in *Playboy* (June 1959) and *Encounter* (August 1959), Kerouac himself revisited the meaning of *beat*. Acknowledging that he had originally picked up the term beat from Times Square hipster Herbert Huncke, who "perhaps brought [the word] from some midwest carnival or junk cafeteria," Kerouac went on with an attempt to rehabilitate the word:

...I went one afternoon to the church of my childhood (one of them), Ste. Jeanne d'Arc in Lowell, Mass., and suddenly with tears in my eyes and had a vision of what I must have really meant with "beat" anyhow when I heard the holy silence

Beat Money

Despite the decidedly antimaterialistic bent of the Beat culture, because of the strong reliance on the quite materialistic jive culture there was a surprisingly large idiom of slang dealing with money—**bread, geets, gold, grease,** or **green. Coins** meant a small amount of money, **short line** not enough money; **long green** meant a lot of money. Amounts of money included an **ace** ($1), a **deuce** ($2), a **nickel** ($5), a **dime** ($10), **twenty-five cents** ($25), and **a bill** ($100), all of which terms were used in the description of drug transactions.

in the church (I was the only one in there, it was five P.M., dogs were barking outside, children yelling, the fall leaves, the candles were flickering alone just for me), the vision of the word Beat as being to mean beatific...

Far from blatant revisionism, Kerouac's return to *beat* represented instead further evolution of the word's meaning in light of the journey that Kerouac and his fellow saints, angels, and hipsters had taken during the 1950s.

Word History: Beatnik

Beatnik must be considered one of the most successful intentionally coined slang terms in the realm of 20th century American English.

Herb Caen, a very popular columnist for the *San Francisco Chronicle,* found himself living in the midst of the Beat/hipster movement; while he did not dismiss the movement out of hand, he thought it took itself too seriously. Without much apparent premeditation, Caen wrote in his column on April 2, 1958:

Look magazine, preparing a picture spread on S.F.'s beat generation (oh, no, not AGAIN!), host-

ed a party in a No. Beach house for 50 beatniks, and by the time word got around the sour grapevine, over 250 bearded cats and kits were on hand, slopping up Mike Cowles' free booze. They're only beat, y'know, when it comes to work.

The term struck a responsive chord and was immediately pounced upon by the media who know a catchy label when they see one. "Beat" or "hipster" had no chance once the charismatic, clever *beatnik* made its appearance. With "Sputnik," "McNoodnik" (a character in the Li'l Abner comic strip), and "nudnik" (used in the column "Squirrel Cage" by Douglass Welch in

BEAT IT!

the *San Francisco Examiner* on the same day that Caen coined *beatnik*—"The man who does not wear a vest will be a nobody from Zeroville, a nudnik from Round Haircut City") paving the way for "-nik" as a suffix, "beatnik" soared, at first as a derisive term for members of the Beat counterculture, but later embraced by the Beats themselves.

Over the years, Caen has several times commented on the fabrication of the term in his *Chronicle* column:

"Beatnik," a term I coined four years ago, is in the new Merriam-Webster Unabridged Dictionary. I've never been particularly proud of the word, but it's nice to see it in such good company. (September 24, 1961)

I coined the word "beatnik" simply because Russia's Sputnik was aloft at the time and the word popped out; why the coinage earned worldwide currency is a minor and not very interesting mystery. (October 23, 1969)

In the same vein, Caen recently told the *San Francisco Focus* magazine (December 1995):

Kerouac was always at me because I invented the word beatnik, and they all resented that word. I didn't even know it was going to catch on. I just fell into the word writing a column one day about something happening in Grant Avenue! The next day it was used in headlines about beat-generation stuff.

While popular response to the term was enthusiastic, it was not without its critics. Caen recalls running into Jack Kerouac at El Matador the night that the term first appeared and that Kerouac was not at all happy: "You're putting us down and making us sound like jerks. I hate it. Stop using it" (*San Francisco Sunday Examiner and Chronicle*, November 26, 1995). In 1961, Kerouac formally petitioned that the term "beatnik" be stricken from his former wife's maintenance suit, arguing that "In conventional society, the term 'beatnik' is a term of disfavor, conjuring up images of unwashed, bearded persons" (*San Francisco News Call-Bulletin*, May 30, 1961). Similarly, in *Advertisements for Myself*, Norman Mailer identified "beatnik" as "A word coined by an idiot columnist in San Francisco."

Variations were abundant, with *Beatnikistan, Beatnikland,* and *Beatnikville* all finding some use, if only by headline writers. Self-styled neologists coined a number of derivative terms in this and succeeding decades, none of which had any of the appeal or draw of the original: **beardnik** (a bearded man), **beautnik** (applied in a headline to Kim Novak), **bikenik** (biker), **bleatnik** (someone who plays their radio loud in public), **causenik** (someone who wore buttons supporting different causes), **chicnik** (a girl), **creepnik** (a hipster), **draftnik** (someone who opposed the draft), **freezenik** (supporter of a freeze on nuclear weapons), **lovenik** (a futile attempt by Walter Winchell in 1967 to rename the hippie) **neatnik** (someone who is well dressed and well groomed), **nobnik** (a resident of Nob Hill in San Francisco), **rednik** (the child of Communist party members), **Vietnik** (someone opposed to the war in Vietnam), and **wobnik** (the child of a member of the International Workers of the World). Jack Kerouac himself toyed with **jazznik, bopnik,** and **bugnik** as descriptions of his peers. Advertisers got into the act, with steel office furniture that will "Beat...nicks," with a **bootnik** (a boot shoe), **beatknits** (underpants designed to be seen), and **Neatnik Notions** (a shoe polish).

Word History: Cat

In its several decades of popularity, *cat* underwent a generalization process, gradually over the years gaining a wider sense of meaning and evolving from meaning a jazz musician, to a devotee of jazz music and otherwise hip person, to simply a hip synonym for "guy."

In the late 19th century and early 20th century, *cat* in the slang and jargon of hobos meant an itinerant worker. According to Godfrey Irwin in *American Tramp and Underworld Slang* (New York: Sears Publishers, 1930), this was possibly because the migratory worker slunk about like a "homeless cat."

The word did not spring from the hobo community into mainstream youth slang, though, but rather seems to have been introduced into jazz slang in the 1920s. In his book *Swing That Music* (New York: Longmans, Green & Company, 1936), Louis Armstrong recounts his use of the word while playing on river boats on the Mississippi River in 1922:

> We "cats" (all jazz musicians from New Orleans called each other "cats" and still do) had got into our best clothes and were tuning up our instruments.

By the mid-1930s, cat was firmly established as meaning a jazz musician. Benny Goodman so explained in an article on swing in the April 17, 1937, issue of the *New Yorker*, and *Down Beat* magazine had included *cat* in a swing glossary in November 1935.

In the late 1930s and early 1940s, the first shift towards generalization began, with *cat* beginning to apply also to fans of swing jazz. Although *Down Beat's Yearbook of Swing 1939* included "people who like swing music" as a second definition of *cat*, Cab Calloway continued through the final edition of his *Hepster's Dictionary* in 1944 to define cat only as a "musician in swing band." In a similar vein, a year later, Lou Shelly in *Hepcats Jive Talk Dictionary* (Derby, Connecticut: T.W.O. Charles Company, 1945) defined *cat* as a "Jive musician."

By the mid-1940s, a final generalization took place, picking up on a secondary meaning of the word that had existed in the backwaters of the language, in which a cat is a regular fellow. For example, in the 1946 glossary of Mezz Mezzrow's *Really the Blues*, he defines *cat* as a "regular fellow, guy." While in the past a cat was by definition a hep cat, now there could be a square cat.

The hipsters and Beats and New Bohemians of the 1950s latched onto *cat* and the feminine *chick*, and it was one of the basic hipster words which made it into the media's parodied lexicon of the beatnik. It persists today to a limited degree, used either in a very studied fashion or by those who have embraced a new Beat identity.

Word History: Dig

Although *dig* has a certain anachronistic ring to it to the 1996 ear, Quentin Tarantino resurrected it with a startling degree of vibrancy in the 1994 movie *Pulp Fiction*, which had tremendous appeal to young people. Describing the quasilegal status of hashish in Amsterdam early in the

movie, Vincent Vega (played by John Travolta) tells Jules Winnfield (played by Samuel L. Jackson) that he would like Amsterdam: "You'll dig it the most." Late in the movie, as the two eat breakfast at a coffee shop, Jules tells Vincent that he does not eat pork. When Vincent asks if Jules is Jewish, Jules answers, "I ain't Jewish man, I just don't dig on swine."

Dig's history as youth slang is not atypical—a black vernacular word of the 1920s introduced via swing jazz in the late 1930s to the young, picked up by hipsters in the late 1940s and passed on to the Beats in the late 1950s and then picked up by hippies in the 1960s.

The roots of the modern slang meanings of *dig* (to understand, to appreciate, and to see) are found in the 1920s.[3] Robert S. Gold in *A Jazz Lexicon* (New York: Alfred A. Knopf, 1964) states that *dig* was "introduced into jazz speech by Louis Armstrong c. 1925, but widely current only since c. 1935." My review of past issues of *Down Beat* showed *dig* first used in March 1938, in a photograph caption that read "Max Baer was just a softie the other night at the Hotel New Yorker, where he dug Jimmy Dorsey's band and new singer, Helen O'Connell." Several months later, on June 21, 1938, *dig* appeared in an article on "Jitterbugs, Ickies and Cats" in the *San Francisco News*.

By the 1940s *dig* was on a roll. It is found in *The New Cab Calloway's Cat-ologue* in 1938 (as well as the subsequent editions of the *Hepster's Dictionary* ending in 1944), a "Glossary of

Harlem Slang" appended to a "Story in Harlem Slang" in the July 1942 issue of *American Mercury*, Dan Burley's *Handbook of Harlem Jive* (1944), Lou Shelly's *Hepcats Jive Talk Dictionary* (1945), and Mezz Mezzrow's *Really the Blues* (1946).

Dig was a staple word in the hipster/Beat movement of the 1950s, so much so that Dan Burley entitled his 1959 treatment of Beat speech *Diggeth Thou?* It was invariably included in any screenplay dialogue involving a Beatnik character, and was soon marginalized as slang; once the mainstream starts to parody a slang word, it loses some of its appeal to youth.

After several years in exile, *dig* sprang back into action in the 1960s. Mainstream disc jockeys picked up *dig*, as did hippies. *Dig* dug its way into a diverse assortment of musical lyrics of the 1960s, from the ultra-hip Jimi Hendrix ("Dig this, baby" and "Diggin' on everything") to the hokey Peter, Paul and Mary ("I Dig Rock and Roll Music"), from the self-conscious Beach Boys ("East Coast girls are hip, I really dig those styles they wear") to the self-indulgent Donovan ("Some guy diggin' on Joannie looking cool in a black lace fan...").

After a flourish of *dig* use by hippies, it was once again overused, marginalized, and discarded. *Dig* has now mostly dropped from the slang idiom of the young, although it is still occasionally used and is perhaps poised for another comeback.

Word History: Hipster

The hipster was a driving force within the Beat movement, helping shape both the world view of the handful of writers who were the artistic center of the movement and the counterculture which grew up around the Beats in the later 1950s and early 1960s.

The term *hipster*, a successor to *hep-cat*, had "some currency since c. 1940," says Robert Gold in *A Jazz Lexicon*. The earliest written use of *hipster* which I have uncovered is in Jack Smiley's self-published 1941 study of diner slang, *Hash House Lingo*, in which he defined hipster as "a know-it-all." It was not exactly the most flattering definition, but then again it was not exactly the least accurate.

The next written use was in *Down Beat* on September 1, 1945, mentioning that Harry "The Hipster" Gibson was playing in Hollywood. Over the next ten years, Gibson would provide a high-profile use of the word. Gibson, who was formally introduced to the listening public in the April 1946 edition of *The Capitol* (the house organ of Capitol Records) as "The Wolf of Vine Street," together with Slim Gaillard, was a regular at Bill Berg's club in Los Angeles. Nicknamed "The Hipster" by New York columnist Earl Wilson, Gibson went on to attract moderate fame with songs such as "Who Put the Benzedrine in Mrs. Murphy's Ovaltine" and "Hypo the Psycho," and with a well-publicized marijuana arrest.

While *hipster* was not included in even the last edition of Cab Calloway's *Hepster's Dictionary* (1944), it is found within the glossary of Mezz Mezzrow's 1946 *Really the Blues*, defined as a "man who's in the know, grasps everything, is alert."

The next year, the close reader of *Invisible Man* by Ralph Ellison (New York: Random House, 1947) would have picked up the use of *hipster* in one passage: "And this Brother Tod Clifton, the youth leader, looked somehow like a hipster...."

The word *hipster* and the character both began to garner serious attention in 1948. In June, Anatole Broyard published a thoughtful piece, "A Portrait of the Hipster," in *Partisan Review*. The San Francisco Chronicle took the time in its November 14, 1948, issue, to explain to its readers that "A hipster, in case you aren't one yourself, is a real gone guy in jazz parlance, a chap who's hep to what's happening."

In a UPI dispatch dated November 17, 1951, the original hep cat lexicographer Cab Calloway discussed his *Hepster's Dictionary* in light of the emergence of hipster:

"Even the title is out of date" Cab Calloway said. "Nowadays you have to call a gone character a 'hipster.' That comes from the fact that a real gone musician is said to have his boots laced right up to his hips."

In his self-published *The Jives of Dr. Hepcat* (1953), the late Lavada Durst (Dr. Hepcat) defined *hipster* as "one who is well schooled in the hep world." Four years later, Jack Kerouac breathed life into the word with his reference to "the sordid hipsters of America" in *On the Road*.

The year 1958 was a big one for the word. In January, Most Publications in New York launched *Cool: The Magazine for Hipsters (America's Coolest Teenage Magazine)*. The January and March issues included a "Hipster's Dictionary" for teens, marking for the first time a co-opting of the word. Hipsters, though, continued to receive serious attention in articles such as "The Innocent Nihilists Adrift in Squaresville" by Eugene Burdick in the April 3, 1958 issue of *The Reporter* ("The number of real hipsters, the boys who really hit the road and bummed from Denver to New York and back to San Francisco, the real pros of the movement, was always small") and "Hepcats to Hipsters" by William Raymond Smith in the April 21, 1958, *New Republic*.

Hipster was still used for the first several years of the 1960s, appearing in the ever-vigilant *Life* magazine as late as February 1, 1963 ("The Hipster's View of Washington"). The ever-so-catchy *beatnik* left little room, though, for competition, and *hippie* loomed on the horizon, anxious to take on all comers.

Word History: Like, Part 1

Well before its complete collapse into vague and undefined slang usage in the 1970s and 1980s, *like* had a somewhat risqué public life, beginning in the 1950s.

The first indignity came at the unlikely (or perhaps likely) hands of cigarette advertisers, who in the mid-1950s launched the "Winston Tastes Good/Like a Cigarette Should" campaign. Although *like* had been used in the place of "as" with some regularity for years, this open and notorious defiance of the rules of grammar actually left many critics aghast.

At the same time, *like* emerged as a verbal filler, a meaningless plug that often did not even intensify. In an article on Wayne University Slang in *American Speech*, Vol. 30, No. 4 (December 1955), William White described the use of *like* as follows:

A meaningless interjection used usually at the beginning of sentences but sometimes elsewhere; this same speech pattern has sentences ending with the word man. "Like we was up in this freak's

pad, and she came off real lame, because we didn't dig the TV, you know? She got hacked because we told her, like, that it interfered with our introspection, man—a real gas like."

Like became an annoying fixture of youth speech, both mainstream, Beat, and parodied Beat. By 1958 *like* was parodied; for example, columns by Paul Speegle in the *San Francisco Call-Bulletin* included "Like Wow!" and "Man, like who reads music?" in blasts at jazz experiments. The parodies aside, *like* persisted in the speech of mainstream 1960s youth and the hippie movement, perhaps not at the signature level of the Beats, but with a vengeance. But, like, the worst was like yet to come.

Word History: Square

Slang, particularly the slang of the young, often takes a word with a negative connotation in standard English (*bad, crazy, dope,* and *freak* all leap to mind) and attaches a positive connotation, a linguistic demonstration of the pride in defiance epitomized by the Jefferson Starship when they sang "Everything they say we are, we are/And we are very proud of ourselves!" Similarly, slang will at times appropriate a word with favorable connotations in standard English and throw it back in mainstream society's face as a negative.

Such certainly is the case with *square*. Since the 16th century, *square* and variations thereon (*on the square, square John, square haircut, squarehead, square game, square shooter,* and *square deal* all are examples) have been understood to mean honest, straightforward, upright, and free from duplicity—not at all bad.

Somewhere along the line, though, *square* was commandeered, converted to a belittling if not contemptuous rejection, and thrown back in society's face. While Robert Gold in *A Jazz Lexicon* pinpointed 1925 as when square first used to mean "nowhere, uncool, unhip," the earliest citation that I have found is from Cab Calloway's 1938 *Cat-alogue*.

Square hit its stride in the 1940s, showing up in the successive editions of Cab Calloway's *Hepster's Dictionary,* Lou Shelly's 1945 *Hepcats Jive Talk Dictionary* ("a hard-working, unromantic person"), and Mezz Mezzrow's 1946 *Really*

Classic Beat Language

Three of the great voices of the 1950s put their words to ink, offering glimpses of the creative use of the Beat brand of jive. In *Hiparama of the Classics*, Lord Buckley reworked Marc Antony's eulogy for Caesar as follows:

...The Roman Senate is jumpin' salty all over the place so Mark the Spark showed on the scene, faced all the studs, wild and other wise, and shook up the whole Scene as he BLEW:

Hipsters, Flipsters, and Finger-Poppin' Daddies
Knock me your lobes!
I came here to lay Caesar out,
Not to hip you to him.
The bad jazz that a cat blows,
Wails long after he's cut out.
The groovy, is often stashed with their frames,
So don't put Caesar down.

Dan Burley, author in 1944 of the *Original Handbook of Harlem Jive,* visited the language on "Beatnik, Bop, Cool and Jive Talk" with the self-publication in 1959 of *Diggeth Thou?* From "Was Red Riding Hood That Good?" in that book comes this passage:

She felt like a droop as she sat on her stoop and bemoaned her lack just as her Maw Squaw laid this shot on the rack: "Honeychile," she gummed as the Hi Fi hummed, "I got a basket that'll blow Ol' Granny's gasket. It's loaded with meat and lots of things sweet. There's an apple and mess of scrapple. I put in some eggs and fried frog legs; some jello real mellow and a brief bit of beef as a spell of relief. There's cake and a milk shake, like soda pop and a scallop; a drip of suds for her thirsty old buds; some wine from a dandelion vine. I want you to beat out a light trot to Granny's pad—and don't you dare to speak to nary a lad—while hitting the track to the Old Lady's shack."

The third voice was Steve Allen whose appreciation of jive and the art of the Beat movement were both great. In *Bop Fables*, Allen takes a stab at "Goldilocks and the Three Cool Bears:

Shortly thereafter the downstairs door banged open and in walked three bears. "I smell Arpege," said the mama bear to her mate. "Gus, you've had a broad here."
"You're out of your skull," said papa bear, "although it does look as if somebody had eyes for the soup over there."
"I'm hip," said the mama bear. "And dig! The upstairs bedroom door is open."
"Weirdsville," said the baby bear. "This whole thing is real nervous!"
"Let's fall upstairs," said the papa bear, "and find out what the skam is."

Are these guys cool or what?

Beat Drug Words

One of the more shocking and revolutionary aspects of the Hipster and Beat lifestyles was the widespread use of drugs. Accompanying the use of drugs was the embrace of the argot of earlier generations of drug users and drug addicts. In both the use of drugs and the reliance on drug argot, they paved the way for the excesses of the hippie movement to come.

The drugs themselves were known as **bennies** (Benzedrine), **leapers** (stimulants), **dollies** (dolophine, a narcotic), **dexies** (Dexedrine pills), **left wing Luckies,** and **pod** or **pot** (marijuana).

Drugs were bought from a **dealer, the man, the pusher,** or **the connection**. A small sample was known as a **taste;** good drugs were **boss, tough,** or **dynamite.**

To inhale a drug was **to blast,** so **blasting crap** was smoking marijuana. While on the subject of marijuana, it is interesting to note that Beats, like hippies, referred to short butts of marijuana cigarettes as **roaches.** To ingest through the nose was to **horn, sniff,** or **snort,** while to inject was to **skin pop, mainline, spear, spike,** or **point.** To fall asleep after using drugs was to **fall out.**

One who was under the influence of a drug was **high** or **strained out.** If one was **clean,** he or she was off drugs and not possessing (**holding**) drugs. To break a drug addiction was to **boot** the habit.

the Blues. In 1946, *square* made it into advertising for the *Record Changer,* a jazz magazine, with "WISE UP SQUARE FRIENDS AND RELATIVES—GIVE THEM A YEAR'S SUBSCRIPTION TO THE RECORD CHANGER FOR CHRISTMAS." Although the jazz world may have used *square* in a technical sense to mean someone who is unable to appreciate the finer points of experimental music, *square* did not linger long if at all in that jargon, leaping instead right into the mainstream. Tommy Dorsey, who coined **Squaresville** to mean the mythical place squares come from, in 1942 explained *square* lyrically—"He's a square from Delaware—he ain't anywhere" (*San Francisco Call-Bulletin,* February 25, 1942).

In 1953, *square* was bettered by *cube* (*San Francisco Call-Bulletin,* September 29, 1953), which despite its clever three-dimensional angle did not stick. In the mid-1950s, *square* was part

of mainstream youth slang, as epitomized by the song "You're So Square" by Lieber and Stoller and recorded by Buddy Holly, Elvis Presley, and later Joni Mitchell:

You don't like crazy music, you don't like rockin' bands
You just want to go to a movie show, and sit there holdin' hands
You're so square, baby, I don't care.

Square was a key word in the Beat movement, which drew the lines between us and them to a far starker degree than past youth subcultures had. In *Holy Barbarians* (1959), Lipton includes *square* in his glossary ("Conformist, organization man, solid citizen, anyone who doesn't swing and isn't with it. Also called creep and cornball. Man, if you still don't dig me, you'll never be anything but..."), as do Rigney and Smith in their

1961 *Real Bohemia*.

Square effortlessly made the transition to the hippie idiom, appearing in the early (Simmons and Winograd, 1966) and late (Landy, 1971) glossaries. With the easing in the mid-1970s of the youth counterculture and the reassertion of a youth subculture, though, square lost some of its usefulness and a great deal of its popularity after its 30-year run.

Although most modern youth would understand the use of *square*, it is not a word which is used with any great frequency. Its last big appearance until *Pulp Fiction* was in the mid-1980s, when Huey Lewis and the News recorded "Hip to be Square." *Square* was, though, used quite gracefully and effectively by Quentin Tarantino in *Pulp Fiction*. When Vincent Vega (played by John Travolta) balks at eating at a fifties-style diner, Mia Wallace (played by Uma Thurman) says, "You can get a steak here. Hey daddy-o, don't be a .... [Mia makes the international symbol for square, made popular by Pebbles Flintstone]" How exquisitely hip this use of *square*!

* * *

[1]The true Beats, the writers whose work galvanized the movement, had a vocabulary of their own. *Angel, saint,* and *holy* were prime value words for Kerouac and his cohorts, but this level of religious image did not filter out to popular youth speech.

[2]If this explanation fails to convince, there is a simpler one. In 1960 when City Lights in San Francisco anthologized the first 16 issues of *Beatitudes*, a Beat poetry magazine, it added a simple and playful suggestion of the origin of the term, fictitiously quoting Gertrude Stein as saying to Jack Kerouac, "You are all a Beat Generation."

[3]At least as early as 1827, American college students used *dig* in much the same way that 20th century students use grind, meaning to study diligently. This slang meaning has completely subsided.

Sources and References

Once again, the Tamony collection at the Western Historical Manuscript Collection at the University of Missouri at Columbia is a valuable source for primary and secondary materials on the 1950s counterculture.

In writing this chapter I relied on several general works on the Beat movement, including Lisa Phillips' *Beat Culture and the New America: 1950-1965* (New York: Whitney Museum of American Art, 1995); *The Birth of the Beat Generation:Visionaries, Rebels and Hipsters 1944-1960* by Steven Watson (New York: Pantheon Books, 1995); *Venice West: The Beat Generation in Southern California* by John Arthur Maynard (New Brunswick, New Jersey: Rutgers University Press, 1991); and Ronald Sukenik's *Down and In: Life in the Underground* (New York: Beech Tree Books, 1987).

Some books that give a real feel for the full force and effect of Beat/hipster speech include Steve Allen's *Bop Fables* (New York: Simon and Schuster, 1955); Lord Buckley's *Hiparama of the Classics* (San Francisco: City Lights Books, 1960); and Dan Burley's *Diggeth Thou?* (Chicago: self-published, 1959). Recordings by Lord Buckley and *How to Speak Hip* by Del Close and John Brent (Mecca Records OCM2205) are also quite helpful in giving a feel for this language.

Works that directly address the language of the Beats include *Swinging Syllables: Beatnik Dictionary* (Memphis, Tennessee: Kimbrough Publishing, 1959) and the nearly identical *Beat Talk* (Tulsa, Oklahoma: Studio Press, 1960); "A Square Digs Beatnik" in *A Charm of Words* by Eric Partridge (New York: MacMillan Company, 1960, 1961); a "Glossary of Beat Terms" in *The Real Bohemia* by Francis J. Rigney and L. Douglas Smith (New York: Basic Books, Inc., 1961); the glossary in *The Holy Barbarians* by Lawrence Lipton (New York: Julian Messner, Inc., 1959); and the "Glossary for Bods from Squaresville" in *Through Beatnik Eyeballs* by R. A. Norton (London: Pedigree Books, 1961).

Sources of information regarding the exploitation of the Beatnik include George Mandel's *Beatsville USA* (New York: Avon, 1961); Bob Reisner's *Beat Jokes, Bop Humor and Cool Cartoons* (New York: Citadel Press, n.d.); and *The Beat Generation Dictionary,* issued by MGM in conjunction with Albert Zugsmith's 1959 movie.

CHAPTER 7
The Mainstream 1960s

▼

"Hey you uptown groovers, knock me your lobes—are you ready for this?"

Along with producing the counterculture hippie movement, the 1960s sustained a healthy youth movement
within the friendly confines of the
predominant popular culture, at least for much of
the decade. With economic prosperity persisting
from the 1950s, popular culture too thrived in
the 1960s.

First and foremost, the decade was a golden
age for rock and roll. Many of the first generation
of rock and rollers faded away by the late 1950s.
With the first generation of rock musicians on

the ebb, second and third generations burst onto
the scene with tremendous vitality. Soul music,
girl groups, Italian-American groups, Motown,
and the surf sound all were major movements
within the domestic rock and roll scene. If that
weren't enough, between 1964 and 1966 along
came the several waves of the "British Invasion,"
rock and roll from Great Britain. While the raw,
rebellious edge of early rock and roll may have
been diminished, it was still a vital and robust
movement. Rock still had no pretensions of
being art—you certainly didn't need a lyric sheet

Illustrations by Istvan Banyai

Rockin' the Joint!

to figure
out "Duke of
Earl"—it was just music
that appealed to teenagers and did not appeal to
their parents.

Rock and roll was by no means the only man-
ifestation of popular culture. Television came of
age in the 1960s, with the programming of the
three major networks playing a central role in the
life of the American teenager. Looking at an
episode of the *Beverly Hillbillies*, *Get Smart*, or
My Favorite Martian today, it is difficult to
appreciate the hold that the medium had on the
nation, but it did. The 1960s were also the last
decade in which the automobile played a big part
in the drama of popular culture; the Mustang,
Barracuda, Corvette, and GTO were all to some
degree icons of popular culture. Movies and
clothing styles were both important outlets of the
popular youth culture.

The mainstream young of the 1960s had a
cool culture of their own. It was not rebellious in
a sweeping sense, but then again it was not without defiant and seditious qualities. Most importantly, it was a culture of the young. It may be
that adults did the twist and that the radio deejays and musicians were for the most part comfortably out of their teens, but the culture was a
teenage culture.

What started as a
cool mainstream youth
culture in 1960 had in large part withered by the end of the decade. The traumas of the
civil rights movement, urban riots, politics by
assassination, and the war in Vietnam took their
toll on the underlying optimistic assumptions of
mainstream culture. The allure of a wilder, bad-
der hippie counterculture that parents feared
and hated even more, combined with the commercialization, sanitizing, taming, and downright
trivialization of AM radio rock and roll, with deejays reduced to knock-knock jokes and sound
effects, doomed the predominant youth culture
movement. That which was cool in the beginning
of the decade was hopelessly square by the end.

The Language

The undisputed slang-shapers of the mainstream 1960s were the disc jockeys of AM radio.
Many of the first-epoch rock and roll deejays,
personified by Alan Freed, had passed from the
scene. Having brought rhythm and blues to white
America in the guise of rock and roll, they were
consumed either by the payola scandals of the
late 1950s or their live-fast-die-young lifestyles.

As was the case with rock and roll itself, a
second generation of deejays emerged. With

some rule-proving exceptions, these deejays were a tad less frantic and subversive than those of the first epoch. Their influence on teenagers, though, cannot be underestimated. They were advocates of teenagers—they brought teenagers their music, they defended teenagers from the criticisms of the older generation, they gave teenagers record hops and talents shows, and they guided teenagers in the protocols of cool.

Every city of any size had its share of fast-talking, personality deejays. Most were white, but many had adopted hepcat nicknames and black phrasing and jive vocabulary in their speech; they were unquestionably urban, and the decaying vitality of America's cities ricocheted in their speech.

In other generations, the musicians and music provided the slang. The music of the mainstream 1960s was not particularly slangy,

but the deejays were. Sitting down with his geometry homework in 1965, a teenager in Philadelphia could tune in to Hy Lit on WIBG, wailing cool: "Hey you uptown groovers, knock me your lobes—are you ready for this? When you hear that beat that can't be beat, get up off your feet and move, groove, romp and stomp with a musical treat. This tune is guaranteed to SNAP YOU off your feet...."

Nobody but a deejay would talk like that, but you could cull cues from the speech. Hy Lit could get away with saying "get off your heels and onto some wheels"; from that you might venture to use "wheels" when talking about your parents' station wagon.

Because the Beat movement of the 1950s had drawn so heavily on black jive, much of the slang used by the deejays sounded like slightly squared down slang of the 1950s counterculture.

The Word
of the Lord

Because slang moves so quickly, surreptitiously, and at times in clear defiance of linear expectations, it is usually virtually impossible to trace the path taken. Slang etymology is a difficult field, and tracing the spread of slang from generation to generation is even more difficult. Although the transmission of a particularly catchy fad phrase or fad word is sometimes possible to chart with some degree of precision, such cases are rare exceptions to the rule that the conduit for slang from one generation to another is usually not readily apparent.

One quite conspicuous carrier, though, was Lord Buckley, who provided a direct link from black English vernacular first to the youth slang of 1950s hipster and beats and then to the AM disc jockeys of the 1960s who in turn brought cool slang to mainstream youth.

Lord Buckley defies labels. Although he was known as a comedian in the 1950s, the term "comedian" is too confining a term. Born Richard Buckley in 1906, he cut his entertaining teeth in the free and loose clubs of gangster-controlled Chicago in the 1920s and 1930s and later as a master of ceremonies at dance marathons. He moved to New York in the 1940s, where he worked in jazz-oriented night clubs. The 1950s saw Buckley based in California and Nevada, while 1960 saw him die an early death.

From an association with black jazz musicians, Buckley developed a true love for and grasp of the black English vernacular. He took his love of black English to the stage, developing what he called "hipsemantics," a blend of traditional black colloquial speech, jive from the 1930s (playwright/poet Vaughn Marlowe, who was anointed "Prince Vaughn" by Buckley, believes that a great deal of Buckley's syntax and rhythm was directly derived from Louis Armstrong), and bop slang from the 1940s. Taking the title "Lord" onto the stage, Buckley's routines and records in the 1950s were based in large part on black vernacular, with renditions of stories from the Bible, Shakespeare, classic literature, and history told in a jazz voice toggle-switching between Shakespearean British and American black accents. (For a sample of Buckley's hipsemantics, see page 101.)

Although Buckley's fame was clandestine in the 1950s, his impact was not. Of particular interest is the impression which he made on the young men who in the 1960s taught mainstream

The hippie counterculture of the later 1960s also drew on the Beats and hence on jive. For this reason, many words used by hippies in the late 1960s had been used by the mainstream young in the early 1960s. This is not to say that the language was identical, for it was one thing for a well-groomed teenager with his thin tie, tab-collar shirt, black socks, and black shoes to say "groovy," and it was something else again for a hippie in her full peasant regalia, jewelry, and face paint to say it.

A major differentiation between mainstream youth slang of the 1960s and its hippie cousins was its all-consuming emphasis on one's station in the hierarchy of cool. The language of the mainstream 1960s was exceedingly status-oriented. The dominant theme was in/out,

cool/uncool, winners/losers, in crowd/all others. If you listened carefully and followed the advice of the deejay mentor, you too could be cool, in, a winner, a part of the in crowd.

They were the voices teenagers heard. In Philadelphia, it might be Jocko Henderson ("Greetings, salutations, oo-pappa-doo, and how do you do?"), or Jerry "The Geator with the Heater" Blavat ("Hey yon teenagers, hit that thing, hey hey ho ho..."), Hy Lit ("It's time to split the scene and leave it clean...")—whoever it was, they spoke a language that nourished a sense of unity. Whether you lived in the affluent suburbs, a lower middle class housing development, or a proud working class neighborhood in the city, they spoke to you, and you learned to speak from them.

American youth to speak cool—the future AM disc jockeys of America.

Robert Weston "Wolfman Jack" Smith, the quintessential hep disc jockey of the 1960s, was profoundly influenced by Buckley. Interviewed by Buckley's biographer Oliver Trager in February 1995, Wolfman Jack was reverent in his praise for Buckley, whom he first heard on record as a youth in Brooklyn. The Wolfman knew something about black music from listening to R&B on WLAC from Nashville, but he was simply stunned when he first heard Buckley: "Oh my God! He knows everything."

Wolfman told Trager that he "always thought Buckley was the man who created the slang, the very hip language we still use today. I thought he was the man who came up with the original statement." As he developed his own unique radio style, Wolfman Jack drew heavily on Buckley. "I actually created my style from Buckley, in a sense" he told Trager. "I'm a little bit of Buckley. I copied his style, I tried to get his voice down and everything. It was his hipness, it was his style, his timing."

The influence of Buckley on Hy Lit of WIBG in Philadelphia is also unmistakable. Lit's slang dictionary of the late 1960s contains several dozen words used by Buckley in his routines, while the entries of "Hipsters, flipsters, and finger popping daddies, knock me your lobes" and "jump salty" in the Lit dictionary can only have come from one place: Lord Buckley.

As disc jockeys pumped Buckley-transmitted slang to the mainstream youth of the 1960s, songwriters of the 1960s and 1970s also were paying homage to Buckley. Jimmy Buffett ("God's Own Drunk"), Bob Dylan ("Black Cross"), George Harrison ("Crackerbox Palace"), Joni Mitchell (a reference to "Willie the Shake"), and James Taylor (a reference to "jump salty") all used Buckley.

From Louis Armstrong and Dizzie Gillespie through Lord Buckley, then, to the voices who shaped the slang of 1960s youth, Lord Buckley was truly a missing linguistic link, a linguistic land bridge between generations and cultures.

Over the last ten years, Oliver Trager of New York has immersed himself in the life and work of Lord Buckley. Never losing sight of the Zen of Buckley, Trager has written the definitive, yet to be published, biography of Buckley. His generosity and enthusiasm were invaluable, particularly his interview with Wolfman Jack shortly before the Wolfman passed away.

A Mainstream Sixties Word List

a thing going
A close, understanding relationship, as in "We got a thing going."

about half
Relatively happy

ace
1. To do very well
2. Very good
3. A term of address used when greeting a best friend

all woke up
Well-informed on the latest styles and fashions

almost home
Near the end of a project

Are you ready for this?
A phrase used to gain attention before saying something

baby
A form of address used in an informal greeting

baby cakes
One's girlfriend

bad
1. Good
2. Bad

bad motorcycle
A person who is very cool but also a bit manipulative

bad news
The worst

bad pipes
A sore throat

bad scene
Any unpleasant experience

bad wheels
Homely legs, or a woman with homely legs

bad-head
An ugly face

bag
1. A job
2. To drink

Bag it!
Forget it!

bag some food for the brain
To study diligently

bananas
Upset

bang heads
To fight

bark
To brag

batshit
Anything that is not true or not important

Be's that way.
Nothing can change it.

Money, Honey

Unlike the hippie movement with its antimaterialistic focus and virtually no idiom for money, mainstream youth culture of the 1960s was decidedly materialistic; even the Beatles, who by the end of the decade sang that "All you need is love," in their early days sang about "Money—that's what I want." So it should be no surprise that the slang vocabulary of the 1960s was brimming with words dealing with money and things material.

Money itself was known as **bread, coins, geech, paper,** or **poke.** Your **game** was the way that you made money; **gravy** was profit, **ice** was a bribe or pay-off, and **in front** was money in advance. If you were **wrapped in trump** you had a lot of money; if you were a big spender, you were a **live one. Golden** meant assured of success, while **in the blue** was free of debt.

Slang recognized the absence of money no less than it recognized money's presence. To **take heat** was to lose a lot of money. **Traveling light** meant that you had little money; if you had **case money,** you were down to your last dollar. If you were broke, you were **hurtin', had short pants,** or were **skuffling.**

To borrow money you might ask a friend to **feel some bread,** or perhaps to **feel a ten.** If you owed someone money, the **mortgage was due** and they were **into you,** and if you had bad credit you had **sour scratch. Stormy Monday** was any day that bills were due.

Someone with **deep pockets** was very cheap; this meaning is quite different from the meaning the expression took on by the 1980s, when it was used largely to describe a wealthy or well-insured potential defendant in a lawsuit.

Be there or be square!
An expression suggesting that all the cool kids will be a certain dance or party. *This expression was popularized by Dick "Hug" Huggyboy in Los Angeles, advertising dances at the El Monte Legion Stadium. It eventually spread throughout the country as a slangy catch phrase.*

bearded
Tricked

B.F.D
Big fucking deal, usually meaning the opposite, of no consequence. *This is one of several slang expressions based on initials that was actually spoken in the 1960s. This particular expression was usually uttered with no small degree of sarcasm.*

big beat
Popular music

big cool
The state of being ostracized

big deal
Something of no consequence, as in "She had some big deal about not being late..."

big time
Someone who's self-esteem is excessive

bug
To bother

bird dog
1. To cut in on someone in the middle of a dance
2. To break up a romance

bit
Something of concern, as in "What is it with you and this turtleneck sweater bit?"

blade
A knife

blow
To miss an opportunity

blow your mind
To love a record, a thing, or a person. *As Hy Lit said in his dictionary, it happens when "any solid groove snaps you out." This expression had a decidedly drug-oriented meaning in the slang of hippies; in*

the survival of the fittest dynamic of slang, the drug-related meaning prevailed for several years, giving way eventually to the broader meaning here.

bod
Body, physique

Bogart
To injure or hurt. *As discussed in Chapter 8, in the slang of marijuana-using hippies, to "Bogart a joint" was to take longer than protocol dictated with a marijuana cigarette before passing it to the next person. This other, less-remembered meaning, recorded in Current Slang in the fall of 1966, plays*

upon the tough guy image projected by actor Humphrey Bogart in many of his movie roles.

bomb
A total failure

boob tube
Television

bookbusters
Students who study hard

Boot it, baby!
Way to go! (shouted to performers)

boots
Tires

boss hoss
A successful person

box
A record player

Less than Cool

Not everybody could be cool, and the slang of the predominant 1960s youth culture had words for the losers as well as the winners. **Square,** a vital word of the 1950s counterculture, became by the dialectic process of slang a vital word of the 1960s predominant youth culture; it is richly paradoxical that kids whom Beats would have found quite square used the word to vilify those who were out of touch with the latest mainstream fashions, styles, and trends.

Other slang words for the losers of the in-out mentality of the 1960s were **chaser** (a loser who will make every possible mistake), **clod, Clyde, dibble, dip** (emphasis on the dull), **doofus, dose, douche bag** (nice talk!), **farmer, nerd or nurd, seed, wimp** (passive, weak), and **winner** (lushly ironic). You did not associate with these people if you could help it; to escape their company, you at times had to **ditch** them.

In the adjective department, **gross** was the ultimate description of anything disgusting or offensive. It generated a small cottage industry of variations, including **288** (meaning "too gross," punning on gross as a dozen dozen, and two dozen dozen—288—as two gross), **gross out** (to disgust) and **grossery** (a crude act). Other disparaging adjectives in fashion included **clubby** (uncoordinated), **crusty** (dirty, unkempt), **groady** (also **groaty** and **grotty,** meaning unkempt, slovenly; precursors of the Valley Girl's *grody* in the 1980s), **grubby** (deliberately scruffy), **grungy** (dirty, messy), **out to lunch** (out of touch with current styles), **rank** (offensive), **raunchy** (disgusting), **scuzzy** (very dirty), **yesterday** (out of style), and **yicky** (dirty, unpleasant).

---

breeze
A term of address, as in "Hey Breeze, what's happening?"

brights
White socks

brodie
A very tight turn in a car. *Yes, there is a connection with the "brodie" of the 1930s. Both uses of "brodie" derive from the story of Steve Brodie, who claimed to have jumped off of the Brooklyn Bridge. The "brodie" of the 1930s meant "a mistake"; by the 1950s it had come to refer to a specific kind of mistake—the spin or turn made by a skidding or uncon- trolled vehicle, and by the 1960s it had developed the related sense recorded here.*

bumped
Fired, dismissed

burn
To continue doing something very well

burn one
To play a song

burn rubber
To leave quickly

burned
Cheated

burner
Someone who is doing well

bustin' concrete
Taking care of business

camp
Jail

cat
Any guy who is hip

cat bird
MAIN MAN

catch
To encounter or experience, as in "catch a flick" or "catch some rays"

chalk talk
A lecture in school

change the channel
To change the topic of conversation

chapped
Angry

check hat
To leave

check it out
To listen, to investigate

chicken head
A person who bothers you

chops
Teeth

Chuck it!
Shut up!

clue you in
To explain

college
Jail

come on strong
To try to start trouble

cooking
Doing something
well

cool your chops
To shut your mouth

cop
To take, earn, get, buy,
or steal

cop out
To let somebody
else down

cool it
To stop what you are
doing, to relax

cords
Corduroy pants, worn
tight in the 1960s

crack on
To tell on somebody

crib
Bed, apartment

cruisin'
Driving without a
destination, for the
joy of driving or
simply to see and
be seen

cut
To put someone
in his or her place
by a sharp remark

cut out
To leave

cut up
To make jokes or
pull pranks

Mod

In the late 1950s and early 1960s, a small group of young people in England rejected the prevalent highly affected Teddy Boy countercultural fad of the 1950s, which featured boys with a squeaky clean if odd and quirky look, including sweeping pompadours and elegant Edwardian clothing. Striking out on their own with a sharp, less-is-more style, the Modernist ("Mod") movement was in full swing in London, centered on Carnaby Street, by the time of the immense influx of British popular music to the United States in 1964.

The Mod movement had a moderate effect on American popular culture, most pointedly in the areas of music and fashion. Despite the fascination with all things from **across the pond,** Mod slang had only a limited impact in the United States.

The words that fared the best were **gear, fab,** and **tuff,** all of which could be used in place of *cool* as an adjective or exclamation voicing approval. **Carnabies** as a word describing Mods had some success in the United States, particularly on the East Coast.

Several Mod words describing girls were picked up to a limited degree in the United States —**luv** (any girl you like), **bird** (a young girl, the central focus of the enigmatic almost punk song "Surfer Bird" by the Trashmen), **pony** (your best girl), **shank** (cute but not bright), and **shadow** (your constant companion).

Other Mod slang words were used only infrequently in the United States, including several involving the telephone (**bell** for an incoming telephone call and **ring** for a telephone) and fashion (a **brim** was a stylish hat, a **skies** was an out-of-style hat, and **continentals** were low-belted slacks). A **cut-buddy** was your best friend, who might go to a **set** (a Saturday evening dance) with you; the dance might not be worth your time (**draggy**) or then again it might be very good (**dyno,** short for "dynamite"). For no apparent reason, **stingy** meant clever.

Slot Lingo

Miniature electric racing cars, or slot cars, were a fleeting but intense craze among young teenage boys for several years starting in 1965. You could race on a track built at home, but bigger fun and bigger tracks could be found at slot car centers, 3,000 of which could be found throughout the United States by 1965. By pooling their resources into the center's coffers, the boys could enjoy large racetrack layouts and the thrill of competition with their peers.

Slot cars generated their own slangy jargon.[1] Many words used for slot car racers were borrowed directly from the idiom of the racetrack. **Boots, donuts, meats, skins,** and **spongies** were all racetrack words for tires on loan to slot car racers. **Bite** (traction), **down the chute** (the straightaway), **glass** (fiberglass), **hauler** (a fast car), **mags** (magnesium wheels) and **shut down** (beaten) are all examples of adult/real car slang used by youth/slot car enthusiasts.

The world of slot car racing also produced its own particular language. A fast driver was known as a **heavy thumb** because he kept his thumb pressed to the control; a **flutter finger** was a racer who changed speeds regularly to manage his car's momentum, while a **trigger happy** racer was overly excited. A **powder puff** was that rare creature, a girl slot car racer. To engage in a **bench race** was to talk about a race and how well one's car would do.

An entire word-stock was dedicated to the cars themselves. A car bought from the store and not modified was simply a **ready to run**; given a modified, beefed-up motor it became a **full house**. A slow car was known as a **real raunch**, a **rock**, or a **stone**. Borrowing on **scarf** (to eat quickly), a **scarfer** was a car that goes around (eats up) the track fast.

The tiny electric motors had their own descriptive slang. A big and powerful tiny electric motor was a **big romper**, while a **juice sucker** drew too much amperage. If your motor armature unwound, you were looking at **cobwebs**.

A slot car race was a **bash**, so **bashin' wheels** was to engage in racing. A car that was going fast was said to be **honkin' on**; if it knocked another car off the track, it **nerfed** it.

D

dance holes in your soles
To dance energetically

dead wood
Tired hit records, stories, or complaints

deck
To knock someone down in a fight

Deuce and a quarter
A Buick Electra 225

dig
1. To understand
2. To appreciate, as in "I don't dig the drag you're putting on."

digger, the
The leader

do a number
To lose your temper

Don't go uptown on me!
Don't be arrogant

Don't sweat it.
Don't worry.

double clutchin'
In a hurry

double dipper
Someone who is making the same mistake twice

down to kill
Very handsome

drag
A boring situation or experience

drag and a half
Worse than bad

draggin' the main
Driving down any main street

drop a dime
To inform on someone

dues
The price to be paid for making a mistake

duke of the cat walk
Someone who has paid his dues and is now successful

E

eat dirt
To receive brutal criticism

eatin' the grapes right off the wallpaper
Very disturbed

Everything's everything.
The only answer to the question, "What's happening?"

F

fake out
To fool somebody

fall by
To stop by and talk

family, the
Your most loyal friends

fat city
A good situation. *Another carryover from the 1950s.*

finger poppin'
Snapping your fingers

fish eye
An evil look

five on five
A handshake

flack session
A big argument

Flake off!
Get lost!

flakey
Confounded

flap jaw
A garrulous person

Flash!
An exclamation denoting extreme disgust. *In the early 1990s, teenage boys shouted "Flash" when a member of the group said something foolish or believed something that was obviously a tease. They thought that they had come up with a new word. They were wrong.*

flee the scene
To leave

flick
A movie

flip side
The song on the reverse side of a record

flower
A pretty girl

flowered
Well groomed and smelling nice

fly
Well dressed. *"Fly" became a key word in the slang of rappers in the late 1980s and the 1990s, meaning something very close to this.*

fly right
To be honest

flyer
A fool

fox
A good looking woman. *Or, in the words of Hy Lit, "A boss-looking girl; out of sight, put together, stone cold, saying-something chick."*

freaky
crazy

freebie
Anything that is free

froggy-doos
Canvas shoes

frost
To anger

fun and games
Having a good time

G

gas
Something that is fun and amusing

gassed
Excited, satisfied

get into it
To get things going

get right
To fix a problem in your life

get your grits
To get enjoyment out of something

gig
A party

give it up
Let yourself go

Give me some sugar
Kiss me

Give me five.
Let's shake hands.

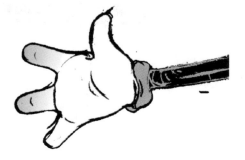

glad rags
Dress clothes

glued
Criticized, rebuked

go social
To stop fighting

God-size
Abnormally large

golden girl
One's main girlfriend

goof time
Time to relax

grab
To affect, as in "How does that grab ya?"

greaser
A teenage hoodlum

groove
1. A phonograph record
2. Something that you find satisfying or fun

groove yard
A record store

groovin'
Enjoying something

grub
To engage in sexual activity other than intercourse

grubs
Old, comfortable clothing

hack
To tolerate

hack off
To ignore one's homework or other duties and do nothing

hair
Courage. *To display courage was to show a lot of hair.*

hairy
Difficult

hang
To make a turn, as in "hang a Louie" (turn left), "hang a Ralph" (turn right), or "hang a U-ee" (make a U-turn). *There were endless variations on the theme, with families, groups of friends, and regions coming up with their own "hang a Larry," "hang a Ricky," and so forth.*

hang it up
To quit

happening
A good party. *A very tame, domestic meaning compared with the hippie appreciation of the word.*

harmless
Lackluster, tedious

He owns the lock.
He has control over the situation.

heavily conked to the bone
Well-groomed hair

hocker
Phlegm expelled from the throat

hog
A Cadillac

home free
Having completed a task

home plate
Where you live

hoss
A term used when greeting a close friend

Hot deal!
I approve.

hot wax
A very popular phonograph record

hype
To promise more than one can deliver

headlights
Eyes

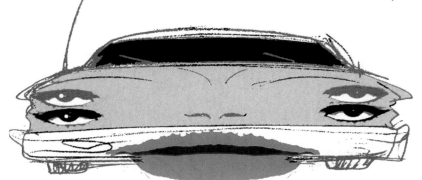

Intoxicated in the 1960s

As the last Beats and first Hippies expanded their consciousness with marijuana, LSD, and other drugs, the mainstream young people of the 1960s stayed with America's intoxicating drug of choice, alcohol.

Beer (**barley water, brewski,** or **suds**) was the drink of choice; **squaw piss** was beer with an alcohol level of 3.2%. As your older friend left the liquor store (the **happy shop**) with a six-pack of beer or as you enjoyed a beer at a **kegger** (a beer party), you might toast a friend and say, "Another Bud older, another Bud wiser," punning on a popular proverb and a popular beer, Budweiser. The pop-top was not prevalent on beer cans, and so you had to make sure that you had a can opener, which you called a **church key,** a slang term borrowed from your parents.

To drink was to **bag,** while to get drunk was to **amebiate**. If you were slightly intoxicated, you were **primed**. Fully intoxicated, you were **blimped, blitzed, crocked, decayed, dinged out, dusted, faced, flying high, in fifth gear, looped, out of it, plastered, plowed, shit-faced, slicked out, sloshed, smashed, soused, stewed, stoned, trashed, tubed out, wiped, wiped out,** or **zoned**.

If one drank too much, never fear—there was a rich slang vocabulary for the act of regurgitation. To vomit was to **barf, blow beets, blow lunch, boot, flash, flash the hash, heave, lose your lunch, ralph,** or **toss your cookies**.

in crowd
The group of popular people

in the groove
In the IN CROWD

jam
A party

jam the box
To play a phonograph record

Jim
A term of address for a close friend

jived
Duped

jock
1. An athlete
2. A disc jockey

Johnny Law
The police

jug, the
Jail

juice
Inside, confidential information

jump in with your hat in your hand
To enter a deal too quickly

jump salty
To become angry.
This expression is pure jive, passed on to 1960s teenagers by deejays who in their turn probably picked the expression up from the hip-talking Lord Buckley, who used the expression in his famous "Hipsters, flipsters, finger-poppin' daddy-o's" piece.

Keep up your front to make your game.
Don't quit; don't give up.

keyed
Excited

kickin' hard
Excelling

kicks
Shoes

kiss off
To dismiss

konk
The head

konk class
School

L

lame
Out of style, pathetic

moon
To drop one's trousers
and expose one's
naked buttocks

large charge
Big excitement

**large for
(something)**
Enthusiastic about
something

Later.
Good-bye.

Lay it on me!
Let me hear it!

lay out
To sunbathe

leaner
A freeloader

let it all out
To say what is on
your mind

Let it roll!
Start it up!

lift off big
To start a climb to
the top

lined
Popular, full of
people

little brother
A good and loyal
friend

looking glass time
Self-assessment

lunger
Phlegm expelled from
the throat

main man
1. Best male friend
2. A man who is
most admired

**maintain your
cool**
To stay calm, poised,
as in Hy Lit's sign-off,
"Maintain your cool
and don't be nobody's
fool. Solid, Ted. Nuff
said."

make out
To kiss in a sustained
and passionate
manner

make the scene
To visit, stop by

make tracks
To leave in a hurry

man, the
An important person

man's ace, the
The right-hand man

marvy-groovy
Bad. *Usually spoken
in a sarcastic, saccha-
rine tone.*

member
A good friend, mem-
ber of the IN CROWD

mess and a half
A situation which
has degenerated
beyond what you
can handle

messy attic
A mind which is very
confused, distracted

Mickey Mouse
Out of touch with
styles and trends

**midnight auto
service**
Car thieves

mileage
Wrinkles

moldy fig
A spoilsport. *In the
jazz world, a moldy
fig was a fan of tradi-
tional Dixieland jazz
who was not impressed
with the innovations
of the bebop pioneers.
It took on a more gen-*

eral meaning in the 1960s, although with limited popularity.

mover
A sexually aggressive person

Mr. Bad Face
One's competition or enemy

music machine
A radio, jukebox, or phonograph

my man
A term of greeting for a very good friend

nitty-gritty
The core of truth

no sweat
No problem

No way!
No possibility of success. *This expression was popularized by actors Mike Meyers and Dana Carvey in their "Wayne's World" sketch on* Saturday Night Live *in the late 1980s. It was recorded in* Current Slang *as having been in vogue at the University of California at Davis as early as 1968.*

not too cool
Devious, unfair

on Broadway in a fast trolley
Living for big stakes. *A precursor to "life in the fast lane."*

on the hook
Responsible for the outcome of something

on the turf
Looking for work

out of his tree
Crazy

over the wall
Past a bad situation and moving on

P.D.A.
Public display of affection

pack it in
To get rid of someone or something

partner
A very good friend

party face
The appearance of being happy

Pay it no mind.
Don't worry about it.

pay one's dues
To pay for making a mistake

peel
To hurry

Percolate!
Let it happen!

pisser
A disappointing experience

pit guard
Underarm deodorant

pits
1. Armpits
2. Anything unpleasant

play room
A diaphragm, as in "Before you go all the way, you better find out if she added a play room to the house..."

pluck
Wine

pokey
Jail

poop
The latest information, as in "What's the poop on the movie Friday night?" *This use of "poop" enjoyed wide use during World War II. It persisted through the 1950s in the slang of those in or associated with the military and was picked up by a younger generation in the 1960s.*

program
Promoting something for one's personal benefit

pull a train
To engage in serial sex with different male partners

put away
To please. *Hy Lit explained this expression as referring to "A groovy thing that snaps you off your feet."*

put on your happy feet
To prepare to dance up a storm

put on the sham
To carry out a lie or hoax

put the hurt on
To reject in love

put together
Well-built, usually said of a woman

rack
To sleep

rags
Clothes

rainin'
Characterized by hard times

rainin' all over
Characterized by harder times

rat
1. Someone who

Shades of Cool

Cool reigned as the 1960s word of approval, admiration, and approbation. Matchless as *cool* was, it was not peerless. **Bad, bat, beautiful, bold, boss, casual** (very cool), **cat's ass** (a nice allusion to the *cat's meow* of the Flapper era), **chaud** (a forced use of the French for warm, hot), **flippin', freak, golden, groovy, hip, in, nitty, out of sight** or **outasite, peachy** or **peachy keen** (usually said sarcastically), **sharp, solid, something else, suave, swingin', the end, together, tough** or **tuff** (the intentionally incorrect spelling was favored by teenage fan magazines and was a direct spelling ancestor of *phat* in the 1990s), **uptown, wailin', wild,** and **zero cool** (as cool as possible), were all common terms of praise for someone or something that deserved the stamp of the champ.

Fat was another word used to describe that which was good or pleasant; Hy Lit outdid himself in his definition—"Cool; you dig it; boss; likable; nice; ultra-hip." *Phat* would emerge as one of the big slang words of the early 1990s, meaning roughly what "fat" meant in the 1960s.

Uptight was another term meaning "very good," a very different connotation than that attached to the word in the hippie slang (inhibited) which survived at the expense of this mainstream meaning. The mainstream meaning was exemplified in the lyrics of a hit song by Little Stevie Wonder: "Baby, everything is all right, uptight, clean out of sight..."

informs on you **2.** A greaser **rat around** To lounge around doing nothing in particular **rat fink** Someone who informs on you	**rat fuck, R.F.** A practical joke. *The term "rat fuck" enjoyed brief fame during the Watergate scandal, when several of President Nixon's advisors described their dirty tricks in the political arena as nothing more than*	*extensions of their college rat fucking pranks at the University of Southern California.* **ratty** Sick **rays** Sunshine, as in	the phrases "catch some rays" and "soak up some rays" **read** To understand completely **real people** An honest, sincere, candid person

rents
Parents

**ring on the
ting-a-ling**
Call on the telephone

rinky-dink
Trivial

rude
Ugly

rule
To be the leader of a group, as in "Tony's word is law—he rules..."

rumble
A fight

run for the hoses
To talk your way out of a touchy situation

S.W.A.K.
Sealed with a kiss. *This acronym was known for years before the 1960s and was often scrawled on the back of envelopes bearing love letters. It took on special meaning in the early 1960s, though, thanks to the popular if trite song by Brian Hyland.*

sack out
To go to sleep. *"Sack out" appears to have started as*

military slang in the 1940s and to have had some limited general use in the 1950s before becoming part of mainstream youth slang of the 1960s.

salty
bitter

say something
To make an agreeable statement, as in "Now you're saying something."

scarf *or* **snarf**
To eat quickly and rudely

scene
The place where what's happening is happening

score
1. A victory
2. To attain sexual relations with a date

scratch
A beard or whiskers

screamer
A party girl

send you south
To end a romance or friendship

seven-ply gasser
Fantastic, better than a GASSER

shades
Sunglasses

shaft
An unfair arrangement

shake loose
To get rid of inhibitions and start to enjoy yourself

shank
A knife

sharpen up your game
Be vigilant

shoot down
To terminate a dating relationship

short
A car

shot down *or* **shut down**
To be rejected, depressed

shut your face
To stop talking

skate
To hurry through something

skinny
The latest information, as in "What's the skinny on Archie and Veronica?"

snap case
A bizarre person

snuff
To ignore or to break a date

soak up some rays
To sunbathe

soc *or* **soch** *or* **sosh**
A socially oriented party girl

sock it to me
1. Let me have it
2. Say what it is you have to say

sounds
Music, good music

split the scene *or* **split the scene and leave it clean**
To leave

stay loose
To remain poised, calm

stiffin' and jivin'
Showing off

stoked
Excited, enthusiastic

straight
Honest, on the level

straight goods
The complete truth

strung out
Disturbed, worried. *In drug argot and the slang of hippies, "strung out" very specifically meant addicted. This is another case of a word's meaning being softened.*

submarine races
Lover's lane

swave and blaze
Intentional and ironic mispronunciation of "suave and blasé," used to denote sarcasm

switched on
Animated

tagged
To be caught doing
something

**take care of
business (T.C.B.)**
To do something well

talkin' trash
Gossiping, lying,
exaggerating.
*At the time, "talkin'
trash" was a common*

*expression used by
African-Americans as
a synonym for "signi-
fying," a game of
verbal jousting and
ritualistic insult. In
the late 1980s, "talk-
ing trash" took on a
very specific meaning
associated with the
banter exchanged
between basketball
players.*

taste
A sample, your share
of something. *Again,
this word had a very
specific meaning in
drug argot and hippie
slang—a sample of a
drug that one was*

*considering buying—
and again it had a
kinder and gentler
meaning in the slang
of the mainstream
1960s.*

tear it up
To come on strong

**tell 'em where
it's at**
To let somebody
know what is
happening

tell it like it is
To speak the whole
truth

tennies
Tennis shoes

That's down!
That is not good!

That's no blast!
That's the truth!

That's up!
That is good!

throw a seven
To have bad luck,
to lose one's poise.
*An obvious gambling
allusion, specifically
to the game of craps
where a roller loses if
he rolls a seven before
his designated
number.*

ticked off
Angry

The Conflict Overseas

For many young people, the 1960s meant a tour of duty, voluntary or involuntary, in the armed forces in Vietnam. As most of us came of age safely ensconced in the mainstream youth culture or hippie counterculture, others came of age or died in Vietnam.

As is the case with every war, Vietnam begot an ample idiom of its own, drawing on military slang of the past, the unique features of the war in Vietnam, and the influences of the counterculture at home (drugs and sex). It was a war fought by young people, and its slang reflects their youth. The vernacular of the young soldiers fighting in Vietnam could be, and has been, the subject of a book in and of itself.[2]

The business of war is to kill, and young soldiers in Vietnam used several new slang expressions in place of kill, including **cap, dust, grease, pop, waste, wax,** and **zap**. The cynicism of the young soldiers was illustrated by their describing a dead enemy soldier as a **believer,** while their antiauthoritarian ardor was illustrated by the practice of **fragging**—killing one's commanding officer. Typically, a fragmentation grenade (hence the clipped "frag") was thrown into the sleeping quarters of an overzealous or brutal officer. Another form of defying authority was to go **M.O.P.** (missing on purpose).

Several racist slang terms for the Vietnamese were widely used, including **dink, gook, little people, slant, slope,** and **zip**. More clever terms for the enemy were based upon derivations from Viet Cong, V.C., or Victor Charlie; the evolved forms included **Charlie, Mr. Charles, Mr. Charlie,** and **Chuck**.

Fellow soldiers were not immune from the acerbic wit of slang. Soldiers assigned away from combat were known as **Betty Crockers** (because of their domesticity), **clerks 'n jerks,** or **REMF's** (rear-echelon motherfuckers). An infantryman was known as a **grunt,** a term which was

tight
Very friendly

tight chops
The condition of
being tight-lipped

tighten up your game
To change your ways, focus

tones
Phonograph records

tooling
In search of something to do, often "tooling around"

toothy
Intentionally out of style

torn up *or* **all torn up**
Hurt, depressed

town talk
Speech using big words

treads
Sneakers, shoes

brought back to the United States and transplanted into the vernacular of labor to mean an unskilled worker. Because both are known to fall from the sky, paratroopers came to be known as **bird shit**. A **boonie rat** was a soldier who had spent an extended period in the jungle, the **boonies** being an old slang term for the hinterlands.

Drawn from the vernacular of the streets, a **blood** was a black soldier. Continuing the long military tradition of contempt for military authority, a monumental foul-up was known as a **clusterfuck,** again a graphic term which came home with the boys.

In the drugs and sex department, several new terms were coined for sex, including **boom-boom** and **fucky-sucky,** both of which are fairly self-explanatory. Drug use was widespread among American troops, and the drug vernacular was very much like that at home. Several terms were unique to young soldiers in Vietnam, including **as loud** (heroin mixed and smoked with tobacco, which was not "as loud"—as smelly—as marijuana), **Buddha grass** (marijuana, hashish, and/or heroin mixed with tobacco and smoked), **dew** (marijuana), and **O.J.** (a marijuana cigarette soaked in an opium solution—the perfect way to start a day).

The standard tour of duty for a soldier in Vietnam was 12 months, 13 months for Marines. When he first arrived, he was known as a **cherry** (an obvious sexual allusion), an **FNG** (fucking new guy), **newby, puke,** or **turtle.** As he neared his expected date to leave Vietnam (got **short**), he became a **short-timer.** His last day in Vietnam was a **wake-up;** he would speak of "ten days and a wake-up" until leaving. The United States and home were known simply as **the world,** a reflection on the view of young soldiers that life in Vietnam (in-country) was not life in the world as we know it.

tube
To do poorly

Tuesday
Later, never

tuna, big tuna
A fat person

tuned in
Attentive, listening

tunes
Songs

U

unglued
Distraught

unreal
Very difficult

unscrewed
Mentally ill

uptown groovers
The IN CROWD.
As Hy Lit wrote in his definition, "they ARE

W

walk heavy
To be in charge

walk that rope
To do your job as well as you can

warden
A parent or adult authority figure

wash out
To fail completely

wax
A phonograph record

What a gas!
What fun!

nifying that a man has been dominated in a relationship by a woman.

whippy
Clever, astute

whole bit, the
Everything

womp
To defeat soundly

woofer
Someone who talks, complains, and brags too much

work out
1. To dance furiously
2. To engage in sexual intercourse

turn on
To arouse someone's interest in something.
In the slang of the mainstream 1960s, this expression existed without drug or sexual overtones.

tusker
A heavy, unattractive girl

the scene because without them whatever is happening ain't gonna happen."

V

vine or **vines**
A sharp-looking suit

What's happening?
A greeting, answered by "Everything's everything."

What's the deal?
What is happening?

wheels
A car

whipped
Obedient.
This appears to be a euphemized version of "pussy-whipped," sig-

Y

You ain't front page news.
You're not as cool as you think you are.

You ain't too cool.
You don't know what is happening.

Yo-Yos

No discussion of American youth slang of the 1960s would be complete without at least a mention of yo-yos. Yo-yos had been around for decades, but the early 1960s saw a crest and boom in 1962, followed by a bust and the filing for bankruptcy in 1965 by the Duncan Company.

Yo-yos did not produce a slang per se, but both the names of the yo-yos and the names of the tricks had a very slangy ring to them. Slangy names included Cheerios, Chicos, Royal Tops, Good Filipino Twirlers, Dell Big D's, Butterfly, Gold Award, and Be-A-Sport. In regard to technique, one first had to learn to **sleep** the yo-yo, letting it spin at the end of the string before jerking the string and getting the yo-yo to return. Slangy-sounding tricks include **walking the dog** (letting the yo-yo roll on the ground while sleeping), the **buzz saw** (letting the yo-yo roll across a piece of newspaper while sleeping, producing a buzzing sound), the **forward pass** (a horizontal throw), **over the falls** (adding a drop to the forward pass after it returns to you), **around the world** (sending the yo-yo into an orbit, a 360-degree circle), the **creeper** (letting the yo-yo walk on the ground and retrieving it horizontally along the ground), and many others—**around the corner, rock-the-baby, bite the dog, the rocket, sleeping beauty, eating spaghetti, taffy pull, rattlesnake, elephant's trunk, double or nothing, skin the cat, man on the flying trapeze, the machine gun,** and **crazy cradle**.

You take care of the hot dogs and I'll take care of the orange drinks
You do your part and I'll do mine, mind your own business

You got it
You understand the situation fully

Z's
Sleep. *The term was derived from the comic page device of denoting sleep by a stream of Z's trailing up from the sleeping character.* *Variations on the theme included Z'ing it, bagging Z's, copping some Z's, cutting some Z's, knocking out Z's, and snagging some Z's.*

za
Pizza

zilch
Nothing. *There may be a connection between this word and* the "Joe Zilsch" of 1920s college slang, but no one is sure. "Zilch" has had some use in almost every decade of the century, although only on a limited basis until its flowering in the 1960s.

zit
A facial blemish

zot
Nothing

Word History: Cool

Cool is one of the more amorphous and ubiquitous of slang words used by American youth in the latter half of the century. Its several meanings are vague and overlapping, and analyses on historical principles are particularly difficult. For example, in *This Side of Paradise* (1920), F. Scott Fitzgerald wrote of his protagonist: "In his search for cool people, he remembered Mrs. Lawrence, a very intelligent, very dignified lady, a convert to the church, and a great devotee of Monsignor's." Especially given the later meanings attached to *cool,* it is difficult to know exactly what Fitzgerald had in mind when he spoke of Mrs. Lawrence.

Used in a metaphorical sense to denote one who is marked by steady dispassionate calmness, *cool* has been around the block a time or two.

Chaucer, Shakespeare, and Ralph Waldo Emerson all employed *cool* in this metaphorical, if slangy, sense.

The general spread of *cool* into the mainstream slang vernacular, though, was the work of bop musicians who in the late 1940s embraced *cool* as an adjective to describe the jazz they were playing, in contrast to the hot jazz then in vogue. The July 3, 1948, *New Yorker* and the July 28, 1948, issue of *Down Beat* acknowledged cool in its bebop sense. Cab Calloway, slang-master of the swing era, told United Press in November 1951, "If you want to compliment an artist, you now say he's cool." *Cool* retained that specialized meaning for the next decade, culminating in the release in 1954 of *The Birth of the Cool* by Miles Davis.

At the same time, *cool* began to take on a different, quite specific meaning, applied to

Surfing in the Sixties

Thanks first to the hip yet clean-cut surfers portrayed in *Gidget* in 1959 and then the powerful evocation of the surf culture by the Beach Boys starting in 1961, surfing—or the idea of surfing—captured the fancy of American youth in the 1960s. The Beach Boys, Dick Dale, The Ventures, and Jan and Dean all provided the steady soundtrack for young people across the country who imagined California as portrayed in the songs, an endless summer of outdoor fun.

The surf culture, a small but fiercely devoted group of young people, developed over the years a full vernacular, small parts of which seeped out to mainstream youth in the 1960s. **Surf's up** (an exclamation meaning that the waves are good enough to ride, let's go) became an all-purpose exclamation with a more general meaning of "let's get going." Mainstream youth hundreds of miles from the nearest wave understood that to **hang ten** was to surf with ten toes over the nose of the board and that a **wipe out** was a complete loss of control and fall off the board. Two surf adjectives that found their way into mainstream youth slang in the 1960s were **stoked** (excited) and **bitchin'** (cool). In *Surfin'ary,* Trevor Cralle recounts the claim by surfer Dale Velzy that he coined *bitchin'* as a classic bad-as-good slang word while surfing with the Manhattan Beach Surf Club in 1949. Thanks to the Beach Boys, teenagers in Illinois and Montana knew that **baggies** were loose-fitting, large swim trunks, and that a **woody** was a wood-paneled station wagon favored by surfers. **Bro, brah,** and **dude** were all core surfer words, and all made a run at mainstream slang. **Dude** made more than just a run.

Only a tiny portion of the surfer's rich idiom reached mainstream youth. Within the surf culture, a **gremmie** was a neutral term for a beginner surfer (which would evolve in the next decade to **grommet**), a **kook** was a derogatory term for a beginner, a **hodad** was a derogatory term for a non-surfer, and a **surf nazi** was a young surfer who embraced Nazi symbols as an act of social defiance.

A surfer probably had several surf boards, collectively referred to as a **quiver**. Structurally, the **skeg** was the fin of the board, the **stringer** was the piece of wood running the length of the bottom

detached, cerebral, stylish hipsters, jazzmen, and rebels. To be cool was to be intuitively aware of and in touch with the latest, a world view that embraced jazz, fashion, drink, drugs, and relationships. Perhaps the earliest use of *cool* in this sense is found in Marcus Boulware's *Jive and Slang* (Hampton, Virginia: M. Boulware, 1947), where cool is defined as "neatly dressed."

Cool, though, was too good a word to stay pigeon-holed with a specific subculture or meaning, and it quickly began its surge towards a mainstream slang term of approval. There is some evidence of the use of *cool* as a general accolade in black vernacular in the 1930s, and of use at the turn of the century

of the very closely related *cooler* at Rensselaer Polytechnic Institute in Troy, New York, and Western Reserve University in Cleveland to mean "Sharp, witty." In any event, *cool* did not enter the main river of Harlem jive which flowed in

of the board, a **ding** was any damage to the board short of a full break, and the **rocker** was the curvature of the board from nose to tail.

Ocean and wave conditions were fertile grounds for surfer slang. Several examples are **glassy** (smooth and calm), to **peel** (to break—as does a fast curling wave—perfectly from one side to the other), a **pipeline** (a large and long tube wave), **point break** (a type of surf condition where waves wrap around a point of land and peel as they break), and **tube** (the hollow part of a curling wave). Staying with tube for a moment, while surfers used the word *tubular* to describe the shape of a wave, for the most part, they did not use it as a general superlative; it was the Valley Girls who transformed *tubular* from technical adjective to all-purpose praise.

Lastly, surfers had a wide range of slang to describe surfing technique, including **goofy foot** (riding with the right foot forward), **Quasimodo** (a show-off stance where the surfer is up on the nose of the board, crouched, hunched down with one arm forward and one to the rear), to **shoot the curl** (to ride a wave into the shore without falling), and **walking the nose** (stepping to the forward part of the board while surfing).

As much as its vocabulary, the surf culture of the 1960s provided American youth with a cool attitude. Hang loose, dude.

Sources: Trevor Cralle, author of *The Surfin'ary: A Dictionary of Surfing Terms and Surfspeak* (Berkeley, California: Ten Speed Press, 1991), helped me develop this collection of surfing words. There are a number of surfing glossaries available, but *Surfin'ary* is in a league of its own. It is a vibrant and caring look at the surfing culture, and in my opinion stands as one of the greatest slang books ever written.

youth slang, and was in no edition of Cab Calloway's *Hepster's Dictionary* (1938 through 1944) or Mezz Mezzrow's *Really the Blues* (1946).

The next, quite unlikely appearance of *cool* comes in the September 1945 issue of *Women's Digest,* which reported that "Cool, daddy" meant "okay," and that "Cool also means diplomatic or smooth." An anonymous teenager told *Newsweek* in October 1951, "If you like a guy or gal, they're cool." *Life* magazine caught on, reporting in its September 29, 1952, issue in a short list of "Bop Vocabulary" that *cool* meant "tasty, pretty." *Time* magazine got into the act on June 22, 1953, quoting a teenager describing a "really cool cat..." In a syndicated comic strip appearing on October 18, 1953, Donald Duck's three nephews approve of a couch he has just bought with an enthusiastic "Cool, absolutely cool." Dorothy Parker in the *New Yorker* of January 15, 1955, noted that the young now used *cool* "for reasons possibly known in some department of Heaven...to express approbation."

By the mid-1950s, *cool* was firmly identified as slang used by hipsters/Bohemians/beats. Every glossary or dictionary of the Beat movement includes *cool;* it was a prime value slang word of great currency in everyday speech, to such an extent that it was included in most parodies of Beat/Beatnik speech. In June 1956, Greyhound Bus Lines advertised their air-conditioned coaches with the headline "Cool, Man, Cool." In June 1957, a clothing store in San Francisco which appealed to mainstream youth blared in an advertisement in the *San Francisco Call-Bulletin:* "Man, they're really cool." In 1958, a teen exploitation movie *The Cool and the Crazy* was released, almost a certain sign that *cool* had indeed arrived.

Cool entered the flow of youth slang in full force in the 1960s, effortlessly bridging the gap between mainstream and hippie youth, finding appeal with surfers, Deadheads, skaters, and even rappers (if only in the name "Coolio," reminiscent of the 1970s funk group "Kool and the Gang"). It survives today with only brief rest stops along the way, including one to devolve into a clipped *coo'* in the early 1990s. In the process it has evolved to the most general of terms of approval or assent, a yeoman jack of all trades of youth slang.

[1] An indispensable written source for slot car lingo, which complemented contributions by Criswell Davis who in 1965 and 1966 tore up the slot car center across Lancaster Pike from the Berwyn station of the Pennsylvania Railroad, was the glossary printed on the record jacket of "The Exciting Sounds of Model Road Racing!" featuring music by the Phantom Surfers (Hobby Hut Inc., San Francisco).

[2] In addition to the glossaries contained in the many books written about the war in Vietnam, several thorough books on the vernacular of the war have been written, including *Soldier Talk* by Frank A. Hailey (Irving Publishing Company, 1982); *A Dictionary of Soldier Talk* by Col. John R. Elting, Sgt. Maj. Dan Cragg, and Sgt. Ernest Deal (New York: Charles Scribners, 1984); Gregory Clark's *Words of the Vietnam War* (Jefferson, North Carolina: McFarland & Company, 1990); *In the Field: The Language of the Vietnam War* by Linda Reinberg (New York: Facts on File, 1991); and the less slangy *Dictionary of the Vietnam War* edited by James S. Olson (New York: Greenwood Press, 1988). Further, Paul Dickson's *War Slang* (New York: Pocket Books, 1994) contains a careful treatment of slang from the conflict in Vietnam.

Sources and References

Mike Connell, Criswell Davis, Paul Dickson, Cres Fraley, Dick Gleason, Dick Grossboll, Jeanne Liberatore, John Morse, and Richard Perlman all helped me with their memories of the slang we spoke coming of age.

For written sources, the Tamony collection is a powerful and valuable resource. Another excellent source is *Current Slang,* a quarterly edited by Stephen H. Dill and Clyde Burkholder and published by the Department of English of the University of South Dakota from summer 1966 until winter 1971. It accepted contributions from any source; most offerings came from college and high school teachers. While the production values were a bit rough, it served as an invaluable road map of the slang of the mid and late 1960s. Another major source for the decade is the *College Undergraduate Slang Study Conducted at Brown University, Semester II, 1967-1968* by Collin F. Baker III, D. Robert Ladd Jr., and

Thomas N. Robb (Copyright 1968 by College Undergraduate Slang Study).

Also very helpful, and liberally quoted in this chapter, is *The Hy Lit Dictionary* by Philadelphia disc jockey Hy Lit (Philadelphia: Hyski Press, 1968). I grew up listening to Hy Lit, and the discovery of his self-published dictionary in the stacks at the University of California at Irvine was a true delight.

Other valuable sources of information for this decade include *English in the Mod Manner* by "Key Man," a brochure published by Mogol's Mens and Boys Wear in the mid 1960s and kindly provided to me by The Associates, book dealers in Falls Church, Virginia; a "Glossary of Teenage Terms" published by Macy's Hi-Set in 1964 and found for me by Bibliomania in Oakland, California; and an eight-page dictionary of slang in use at Washougal (Washington) High School by Lola W. Phipps entitled "English for Elementary Teachers" (December 3, 1968).

Lastly, Tom Konrad of the Aircheck Factory in Wild Rose, Wisconsin, provided me with a number of tapes of deejays from the 1960s; they served as a most constructive guide back to the real voices of the decade.

CHAPTER 8
The Hippie Counterculture of the 1960s

▼

"Far Out!"

The 1960s are often remembered as the decade of the hippies, a dramatic if historically oversimplified focus on just one of several youth movements that were alive and well in the decade.

Who were the first hippies? Writer Ken Kesey traveled across the United States in the summer of 1964 in a converted school bus with a band of young people who called themselves the Merry Pranksters, voyaging for a large part of the journey under the influence of the then-legal, then-fledgling drug LSD. Photographs of that bus journey show a group of well-scrubbed, short-haired young people, perhaps zonked out of their gourds on LSD but still a far cry from the flamboyant image of the hippie that America came to love and fear. Straight America didn't know what to call Kesey and his band, resorting to "beatnik" when all else failed. In spirit and substance they had made the leap from Beat to hippie, if not in fashion and style.

The word "hippie" was first attached to young people in the fall of 1965, and by 1966 the hippie movement had moved out of its hometowns of the Haight-Ashbury neighborhood of San Francisco and the East Village in New York and was in full blossom throughout the country. The mass media caught onto the movement in early 1967, just as it began to splinter and disperse.

The hippie movement can be seen as an explicit reply to the conventional culture of the time. All that made the United States a great country in which to be a white, middle-class-or-better male in the 1950s was coming apart at the seams. The price of the Cold War, centuries of slavery and institutionalized racism, and the constricted restraints of social and cultural conformity were taking their toll. Televised war in southeast Asia and assassination as a brutal way of life at home shocked the young and called into question conventional cultural values.

Equally true, and more interesting, is the fact that the hippie movement was in large part a direct reaction against the Beat movement. There

Illustrations by Istvan Banyai

were obvious links between the movements, such as Allen Ginsberg and Neal Cassady, but an oppositional process was also at work. The music of the hippies (raucous rock and roll) could not have been more different than the music favored by the Beats (cool jazz). While intellectual Beats intently listened to poetry readings, sensualist hippies chose to dance the night away. Beats favored black clothing, while hippies reveled in bright, clashing colors. Beats prided themselves on staying cool, within themselves, the antithesis of the hippie creed of public exposure of the soul.

Add to the mix of rebellion against the conventional culture and rebellion against the Beats several seeming random developments (the proliferation of use of the birth control pill and government experiments with LSD), and it is possible to see where the hippie movement came from. It did not come from nowhere, and it was not a godless, flag-hating, family-hating, everything-good-hating Communist conspiracy.

Images of hippies draw on all the senses—the patchouli oil and sandalwood and Krishna musk incense mingling with the smell of marijuana and cat litter boxes and burned stir-fry and mildewed fruit, strobe lights and amoeba lights and black lights and fluorescent pastels, Robin Hood felt hats and medals from the King of Norway and vests and ribbons and buttons and reflectors, tuxedo shirts with billowing sleeves and sashes and World War I leather aviator helmets, tunics and capes and soap bubbles, granny glasses and wizard hats and rainbows and prisms, dashikis and peasant blouses and lace with ruffles and feathers and face paint, long India print skirts and no underwear and earrings and jangling jewelry, Jesus Christ strung-out hair and Afros and gnome beards and hippie girls with hair down their backs, pouches and boots and paisley patches and scarves and beads, jumpsuits and buckskin shirts and jackets and fringe all over, Afghan coats and top hats and peasant shirts and torn jeans and sandals or bare feet, tie-dye and headbands and buttons and Native American and Asian symbols everywhere, acid rock and sitar music and the Whole Earth Catalogue sitting on the chair covered with an American flag next to the bowl of brown rice, leftover Buddhism and Hinduism plus Blake and Huxley and Bucky Fuller and Jung's theory of

synchronicity and Hesse and Kerouac and mysticism from anywhere.

To hippies, "Sex, Drugs, and Rock and Roll" was not just a catch phrase, or even just a workable lifestyle, but a religion/political party/central organizing principle of life. Jane and Michael Stern, exceptional students of popular culture, call hippies "the last American innocents," and there was an undeniable wide-eyed enchantment with life, at times excusably naive and at times truly dopey.

Some say that the 1960s ended with the violent and death-marred free concert by the Rolling Stones at the Altamont Speedway east of San Francisco in December 1969 or with the National Guard shootings at Kent State University and Jackson State College in May 1970; others point to Richard Nixon's resignation in August 1974, as the true end of the sixties. In any event, the hippie movement defined popular culture well into the 1970s. Because of its broad base in popular culture, particularly music, it was a far more influential movement than its fringe quality and excesses would have predicted.

The Language of Hippies

In a note housed in the Western Historical Manuscript Collection at the University of Missouri, Columbia, the San Francisco word scholar Peter Tamony wrote: "The Hippies did not bring in a word, or add to the vocabulary in any way."

While this may not be completely correct (*doobie, ginchi, grok, munchies, psychedelic, sopors,* and *teenybopper* are all candidates for hippie neologisms), the language of hippies was in large part either derivative of other cultures or consisted of standard English used in a new, unforeseen sense.

Despite their rebellion against Beat values and style, the speech of hippies drew heavily from Beat and jazz slang. *Ax, baby, cat, chick, cool, dig, fox, gig, groove, hip, pad, shades,* and *threads* were all words borrowed from the Beats and used with some frequency by hippies. Slang spread largely by word of mouth within the hippie subculture, aided by "underground" deejays on FM radio stations whose roles cannot be underestimated when analyzing the spread of hippie slang.

As was the case with many other aspects of hippie culture, hippies took words (largely from drug argot) that were discarded or even ostracized by their parents' culture and made them useful, valuable, and at times artistic parts of their speech.

Cap, crazy, dope, and *dealer* are only several examples of outlaw words embraced and embellished by hippies, not to mention the warm welcome given to such heretofore taboo words as *fuck* and *shit.*

A special colloquial vocabulary sprung up around LSD, and many words which in 1965 were drug-specific had by the end of the decade migrated into broader metaphorical meaning; words like *freak out, head, trip,* and *bummer* started as LSD vocabulary and worked their way into a broader social usage.

A small body of language from Eastern religious systems found its way into hippie speech. While not slang, there were about a dozen words from the mélange of Asian culture and religion adopted by hippies that enjoyed popularity, and several that have endured in less-than-pristine condition, most notably *guru, zen* and *karma*.[1]

Lastly, the surfer culture of Southern California made a modest contribution to the hedonistic philosophy of hippies and to their language, with words such as *bitchin', dude, dynamite, killer, outrageous, primo,* and *righteous.*

In retrospect, the language of hippies was less interesting and colorful than other manifestations of hippie culture. A striking feature of hippie speech was its vague nature. The hippie culture was inclusive, unlike many subcultures which in their own way were exclusive and elitist. The vocabulary of the hippie movement was almost intentionally ambiguous, facilitating conversation if impeding communication; heavy reliance was placed on equivocal words such as *thing, they,* or *there.* Words could and did change meaning in a single conversation, depending upon the context in which they were used and to a lesser degree the intonation. *Shit* could be good or bad, *motherfucker* could be an insult or term of endearment, and so on.

Steve Salaets, who wrote a caring and clever dictionary of hippie slang in 1970, illustrated the inherently blurry character of hippie speech with his treatment of the word *jive,* which he chose to not define as follows: "Means a whole lot of weird things. Best you should just kind of vibe it out as you go."

With this type of nebulous language, it was easy to suppose that people agreed with each other for the simple reason that everyone attached his or her own meaning to words and phrases. This type of language also made it possible to descend into what from a distance seems like brainless palaver, a meaningless pastiche of fillers and intensifiers, resulting in "Man, like I mean, you know, really..." The following passage from *Changing My Mind, Among Others* by Timothy Leary, an early and ardent advocate of LSD, epitomizes the illogical extension of hippie speech:

Do not "drop out" until you have "tuned in." Do not "turn on" unless you know how to "tune in," or you will get "hung up!" Every "bad trip" is caused by failure to "tune in."

While hippie speech is today the subject of not inconsiderable parody or caricature, it survives to a surprising degree in mainstream conversational standard English, in words and expressions such as *bad scene, bent out of shape, blow your mind, bummer, burn out, cop out, flip out, freak out, hang-up, rip off, sell out, space out, trip,* or *uptight.* Further, to the extent that hippie speech contributed to the weakening of taboos regarding profanity, its influence on the language is still very much with us today.

A Hippie Word List

ace
1. Superior
2. A marijuana cigarette

acid
LSD-25, Lysergic acid diethylamide

acid head
A regular user of LSD

acid rock
A type of rock and roll played by and geared towards LSD users. *Acid rock was long on improvisation (often self-indulgent and inaccessible), echo, and LSD-inspired lyrical images.*

acid test
A concert or "experience" designed to enhance the effects of LSD. *The word-playful term was coined by Ken Kesey and his Merry Pranksters; if one could last the entire night of intensely interesting and intensely boring experiences, one passed the acid test. Kesey and the Pranksters staged a number of acid tests in California in 1966; the acid tests evolved into Trips Festivals staged by Stewart Brand and then by Bill Graham. The audience was "invited to wear ecstatic dress and bring their own gadgets."*

Afro or **'fro**
A bushy hair style favored by black nationalists and black hippies, long and frizzy

baby
An informal term of address

bad
Tough, mean

bad scene
Circumstances apt to present unpleasant experiences, distress, and/or trouble

bad trip
A negative reaction during drug intoxication, usually LSD, including panic, fear, depression, or anxiety

bag
A person's interests, vocation, avocation, or situation. *Salaets defined it as "Something you dig on. Place where you carry your head."*

bail out
To leave

ball
To engage in sexual intercourse

bang his head
To disparage

be aware
1. To have experienced LSD, as in "We're Not Gonna Take It" from the rock opera *Tommy,* by the Who, where the protagonist tells campers "My name is Tommy, I became aware this year."
2. A catch phrase urging attention to one's surroundings

be-in
A planned gathering where spontaneous activities take place. *An early, if not the first, widespread use of the word was on October 7, 1966, with a Love Festival and be-in in San Francisco to observe the effective date of a new law making LSD illegal in California; it was conceived by Oracle editor Allen Cohen as an "ecstatic union of love and activism" between Berkeley radicals and San Francisco hippies. Ann Mathers defined it as "a people assemblage of celebration, where anything may happen with the acceptance of all that is and all that is not." In Do It!, Jerry Rubin recounted first hearing about the San Francisco be-in and having no idea what it would be like. Rubin attended the be-in and described it as follows: "A magnet drawing together all the freaky, hip, unhappy, young, happy, curious, criminal, gentle, alienated, weird, frustrated, far-out artistic, lonely, lovely people to the same place at the same time."*

beat
To cheat someone

beautiful
Good, wonderful. *An all-purpose, overused hippie superlative denoting a wide range of approval, sometimes as an exclamation—Beautiful!*

beautiful people
Kindred hippie spirits, as in "Dear Mom and Dad, Don't worry about me. School got to be too much so I came to Mexico where I am staying with some really beautiful people...."

Beautiful People
Rich, fashionable, trendy hippies. *John Lennon was talking about Beautiful People, not beautiful*

people, when he sang, "How does it feel to be one of the Beautiful People?"

bent
Slightly annoyed

bent out of shape
Upset, agitated. *In explaining the expression, Ann Mathers cautioned that it is "a bad time for tripping."*

bit
An activity

bitchin'
Very good. *Generally a surfer word that migrated to the Valley Girls, but it was occasionally used by hippies*

black box
A home-made electronic device which when connected to a telephone circumvented the charge for all incoming calls. *A* **blue box** *did the same thing but for outgoing calls.*

black light
Ultraviolet light used to enhance Day-Glo colors

blast
1. A prolonged, deep puff of a marijuana cigarette
2. A very good time

blissed out
In a euphoric state

blood
An African-American. *The late 1960s saw a shift in standard English from the term "Negro" to "black." As "black" took root, the student New Left and black nationalists briefly flirted with "Afro-American," while hippies took up "blood" as the hip noun of choice for African-Americans.*

blow
1. To leave
2. To destroy or ruin
3. To smoke marijuana
4. Marijuana

blow your cool
To lose your self-control

blow your mind
To be confronted with any astonishing, strange, or stimulating mental experience. *Donovan Leitch's "Sunshine Superman" spoke of "blow your little mind off...," the Beatles in "Day in the Life" sang, "He blew his mind out in a car...," while the Rolling Stones in "Honky Tonk Women" punned, "She blew my nose and then she blew my mind."*

boogie
To go somewhere, as in "boogie on down to the park"

bug out
To leave

boss
Very good. *This word has a distinctly unhip ring to it 30 years later, and it definitely was used outside hippie circles. It was, however, used by hippies, at least until the late 1960s.*

bread
Money. *Good, old-fashioned hip slang imported into the hippie lexicon.*

bring down
To depress another's feelings, as in Neil Young's "Don't let it bring you down, it's only castles burning..."

brother
1. An African-American
2. A black-to-black term of address

browned off
Exasperated, frustrated

bug
To bother

bum
To borrow without expectation of returning, as in "bum a smoke"

bum rap
False criminal charges or accusations of wrongdoing

bum trip *or* **bummer**
A bad LSD experience. *This expression was used in the earliest hippie days and quickly evolved to mean any bad or depressing experience. Tom Wolfe wrote in* Electric Kool-Aid Acid Test *that "bummer" was a term used by members of the Hells Angels motorcycle gang for a bad trip on a motorcycle, and that it was quickly adopted to describe a bad LSD experience.*

burn
To cheat

burned out
Exhausted, unable to cope

bust
1. To arrest
2. To catch someone in the act of doing something wrong
3. To inform on someone

4. An arrest. *This expression was popular in Harlem in the 1930s, making its way to hippies via Beats.*

busted
1. Arrested
2. Caught in the act
3. Without money

Captain Crunch
A whistle from a cereal box which when blown into a

A Pot Potpourri

Marijuana and LSD were the drugs of choice for hippies. Unlike LSD, a drug which came without a lexicon, marijuana had been used in the United States for decades and when it was discovered by the hippies it came with a ready-made idiom. Hippies borrowed from the argot of the past, at times seriously and at times mockingly; just as Flappers had an abundant slang vocabulary dealing with alcohol, so did hippies surround themselves with a surfeit of marijuana slang.

Marijuana itself was called **banji, bhang, boo** (shortened in the 1950s from "jabooby," a term used in the 1930s), **buds, bush, dew, dope** (a great scare-word of the 1920s), **gage** or **gauge** (a term from the 1940s, used occasionally by hippies, especially in the rhyme "the gage that's the rage"), **grass** (probably the most popular word for marijuana in the 1960s), **hay, hemp, herb, hooch, loco weed, mary** or **mary jane, pot** (probably the most common word for marijuana in the 1950s; Salaets created a good pun in his definition: "What you put a lid on"), **scuz, shit, smoke, spliff, tea** (a good, old-time slang expression from the 1920s, used with some affection by hippies), and **weed** (recorded as early as 1928). Special terms for special types of marijuana included **Acapulco gold** (a fine grade of marijuana from Mexico), **Colombian gold** (high grade marijuana from Colombia), **ganja** (excellent Indian marijuana), **gold** (very high quality marijuana), **kief** (marijuana from the Middle East, not particularly potent and often mixed with tobacco), and **Panama Red** (reddish-yellow marijuana grown in Panama and memorialized in the song *Panama Red* by New Riders of the Purple Sage).

Different amounts of marijuana had special slang names, including a **baggie** (an unspecified amount of marijuana, enough to fill a plastic sandwich bag), a **brick** (a block of marijuana or hashish, at times a kilogram), a **key** (a kilogram), a **lid** (one ounce of marijuana), and a **matchbox** (a small amount of marijuana, enough to fill a matchbox). A **stash** was a hidden supply of drugs, usually marijuana; derived from the verb, it was recorded as a noun in this sense as early as 1955.

Before rolling a marijuana cigarette in **papers** (commercially available cigarette papers) one

telephone would clear the phone line and permit free long distance calls

cat
1. An accepted, HIP man
2. Any male. *A decidedly hip and then Beat term which endured into hippie days. Salaets' definition shows how far the term came: "Digs on just cooking it and scoping out the action. Likes high places."*

change
Money

check out
To examine or investigate. *Once daring slang, this expression is fixed in standard colloquial speech today.*

chick
A woman. *This word has migrated from black to hip to beat to hippie to sexist to hopelessly dated; in the 1960s, hippies used it without a second thought.*

chill
1. To ignore
2. To refuse to sell drugs to someone. *Landy recorded this word in 1971. It certainly became much more widely used to mean "calm down" in the 1980s.*

first manicured the marijuana, removing the seeds and stems from the smokable leaf. A marijuana cigarette was known as an **ace** (a term from the 1930s), **bomb, bomber** (Salaets defined the term colorfully, as "Captain Hooboy's super joint"), **doobie, jay** (short for *joint*), **joint** (the term of choice in the 1960s), **number, reefer** (the most popular street name for marijuana used in the 1930s, used by hippies with some glee), and **stick**. Instead of rolling a cigarette, marijuana could be smoked using a **bong** (a water pipe introduced to America by soldiers returning from Vietnam in the late 1960s) or **hookah**. If no pipe was available, one could always fashion a **doobie tubie** out of a paper towel or toilet paper cylinder, punching a hole in the tube to hold the joint while puffing on one end and covering the other with the hand, thereby creating a vacuum; when the hand is removed, one inhales a rush of built-up marijuana smoke.

Once the cigarette was rolled, one would **fire up** (a Beat expression recorded as early as 1960) the joint. To **do** or **use** marijuana was to smoke it; to inhale was to take a **hit** or a **toke,** while to take longer than necessary to pass the joint was to **Bogart** the joint. The short remainder of a marijuana cigarette was known as a **roach** (a term recorded as early as 1938 but glorified by hippies). It could be placed in the tip of a regular cigarette for smoking (a **cocktail**) or smoked pinched in a **clip, roach clip** (known sometimes as an **RC**) or **roach holder**. A regular smoker of marijuana (a **pot head** or a **doper**) might finish the roach with a **Jefferson Airplane,** named after the rock group, a split paper match used as a clip to hold the roach.

Rock Talk

Rock and roll was a third of the hippie religious trilogy, and within its ranks there grew a distinctive slang, some of which transcended its rock roots to be used in a broader social sense.

Starting with the players—a **guitar hero** was a legendary, expert rock guitarist, while to **front** a band was to be the main vocalist. A band or performer's equipment staff was known as the **crew,** with individual members known as **roadies;** a roadie sent to do menial errands was the **gofer.** A **groupie** was a woman, usually a young woman, who pursued short-term sexual relationships with rock and roll stars; a **plaster caster** was a groupie who made plaster casts of the penises of rock stars with whom she had sexual relations.

Equipment drew some slang nomenclature. The jazz term for guitar, **ax,** was adopted by rock musicians, and at times was used as a metaphor to mean the tools of anyone's trade, from typewriter to piano to guitar. **Amps** were amplifiers, and **cans** were headphones used in a recording studio.

When it came to playing in the band, a **break** was a solo instrumental passage; like much of the slang favored by rock musicians of the 1960s, *break* had been used in this sense since the 1930s, but hippie music had extended breaks and extended use for the word. Similarly, the term **jam** was first used in the 1930s to mean to improvise or play without rehearsing, but with the free-wheeling, extemporized nature of much of hippie music, it gained a new life in the 1960s.

Chops referred to one's expertise on the guitar; to **cook** was to perform well, which might draw the adjectives **demon** (superb, amazing, as in "demon guitar work") or **tasty.** A series of notes on a guitar forming a musical phrase was known as a **lick** or a **riff,** a jazz term coined decades before hippies (as early as 1917), but which was used by hippies as a metaphor for improvised speech.

Several slang words were used to describe types of music. **Bubblegum** as an adjective meant silly, shallow, appealing to young adolescents; the word was most commonly applied with some condescension and condemnation to music marketed for preteens, which was also labeled as **saccharine.** On the opposite end of the spectrum was **heavy rock,** ponderous, loud, testosterone-laden music, which in the 1970s evolved into what was then called *heavy metal.*

At a concert, the **bouncer** was a security guard hired by concert promoters to eject troublemakers. **Insies and outsies** referred to permission to leave a concert hall and return after refreshing oneself outside. At the Fillmore Auditorium in San Francisco, as you picked up a free apple from a barrel on the way up the stairs you passed the sign saying "No insies and outsies." A song was a **number,** and the group of songs played in a live musical performance was a **set.** Again, *set* was a term from the 1920s, revived and popularized by hippies because of the dominant role of live music in hippie culture.

In a recording studio, a musician would **lay down** a song, or **cut. Charts** could mean sheet music, which was used by few rock musicians, most of whom played by ear, or could refer to listings of best-selling records. A **sleeper** was a song or record album that became popular long after its release.

chopper
A modified motorcycle characterized by a low body and high handle-bars

chucks
The intense craving for sweet food that a drug addict experiences shortly after withdrawing from an addictive drug

clean
1. Not HOLDING any drugs (See box on page 151.)
2. Free from HASSLE, as a "clean scene"

cold turkey
1. Withdrawal from drugs suddenly, completely, and without the aid of medication
2. Sudden and complete cessation of any activity. *Used with respect to drug addicts, this was not a new hippie term; hippies simply expanded its drug-specific use and applied it to a broader range of situations.*

color head
A hippie who became consumed with the beauty of colors. *I have found this expression only in Lay and Orban, suggesting that it was a short-lived local San Francisco expression at best. It illustrates, though, the endless possibilities for expressions including* HEAD.

come on
1. To begin to experience the effects of a drug
2. To flirt
3. To put oneself forward in a certain manner, as "He came on like Genghis Kahn..." *A good example of the vague nature of hippie speech, where one bland expression could mean several very different things.*

consciousness-expanding
The effect of meditation or drugs on the ego. *This expression and others of its psychological ilk were bandied about by hippies quite freely.*

cool
Good. *An old word that hippies embraced in their own way. Salaets wrote that cool is "measured in ergs and vibes on a scale of 10." Get it?*

cool it
1. To calm down
2. To stop doing what one is doing

cop
To acquire or obtain something, often drugs, often by illegal means

cop out
1. To evade an issue or make an excuse
2. To return to a

conventional lifestyle

cop to
To admit

cosmic
Very difficult to understand but very good

crabs
Body lice, especially in the pubic region. *Crabs were glorified by Frank Zappa, who wrote in "Hey Punk" of teenage runaways living on Owsley's floor and getting crabs.*

crash
To sleep. *According to* Time *magazine's correspondents, the term was derived from the Hells Angels' use of the word to mean "to die."*

crash pad
Temporary sleeping quarters

crazy
Very good. *To use "crazy" as a term of approval, often for something that conventional society would consider odd or unacceptable, illustrates the way that hippie language often directly confronted convention. The term was first used in this sense as early as 1946, but first found wide use with hippies.*

cut out
To leave

dig
1. To appreciate or like something
2. To understand
A Beat word appropriated by hippies.

Digger
A San Francisco-based hippie collective founded by Emmet Grogan with the goal of making hippies self-sufficient and free from relying on the ESTABLISHMENT. *The name was borrowed from 17th century English farmers who raised food at Walton-on-Thames to feed the poor.*

Do it!
A hippie credo, long before the Nike advertising campaign of the late 1980s.

do your thing
Follow your inner voice and do what makes you happy. *Ralph Waldo Emerson coined the phrase "do your own thing" in 1841. It became a classic, vague if not meaningless hippie phrase.*

dork
A person who is hopelessly out of touch with the present

down
1. Negative, depressed
2. A central nervous system depressant
3. To take or swallow

downer
1. A central nervous system depressant
2. Any depressing experience. *Like* BUMMER *and* BAD TRIP, *downer migrated from drug-specific jargon to general use fairly quickly.*

down on, to be
To dislike

down trip
An insipid or dispiriting drug experience

drag
1. To inhale a cigarette
2. Something or someone that is undesirable. *As the Rolling Stones sang in "Mother's Little Helper," "What a drag it is getting old..."*

drop out
To withdraw from or quit an activity, such as college

duds
Clothes. *Actually a very old word, going back to the 1500s.*

dude
A male

dynamite
Extraordinarily good

edge city
The status of living dangerously. *This expression has a distinct literary ring to it, and was used extensively by Tom Wolfe in* Electric Kool-Aid Acid Test. *Nevertheless, it was an authentic, if not widely used, hippie expression.*

ego game
The placing of one's own needs as the most meaningful with no concern for others. *A term coined and used extensively by Dr. Timothy Leary.*

ego trip
An activity that bolsters the ego

Establishment, the
The powers that be. *In Great Britain, "the Establishment" had long been used as a synonym for the established churches (of England and of Scotland) when the term seeped into more general usage in the 1950s as a label for the power elite. The*

expression crossed the Atlantic about ten years later and soon became a fixture of counterculture youth speech. Salaets defined the word with no pretense of objectivity as "Ground zero." In a late 1960s Columbia Records advertisement collected by Peter Tamony (Western Historical Manuscript Collection, University of Missouri, Columbia), young people were asked, "If you won't listen to your parents, the Man, or the Establishment... Why should you listen to us?" This is a wonderful example of the Establishment trying to co-opt the language of those who spoke about the Establishment with contempt and distrust.

fall by
To visit

far out
1. Extraordinarily good
2. Bizarre

flash
1. To understand something, usually intuitively and suddenly

2. To hallucinate
3. The abrupt first feeling after taking a drug

flash paper
Highly combustible paper which came in handy for making lists that could be easily destroyed

flashback
Feelings or sensations reminiscent of an LSD trip experienced while not under the influence of the drug

flip *or* **flip out**
To have a negative emotional experience, usually drug-induced, ranging from anxiety to an emotional breakdown to full-blown psychosis. *This cheerful word was coined very early in the hippie experience to describe one unfortunate result of drug use.*

flower children *or* **flower people**
Hippies. *This hapless expression was actually used by hippies for several years before it was abandoned by them and seized upon by the media.*

flower power
The ability of the hippie philosophy to transcend the status quo. *This truly dopey concept actually held some sway in its day.*

Ann Mathers described the meaning—"en-flower everyone, including the fuzz...it may not keep them from busting you, but it will surely blow their minds." Okay!

fox
An attractive woman.

freak *or* **freek**
1. A hippie
2. A devotee of something, often a specific type of drug, as in a "speed freak"
3. To lose control.
Freek was an affected spelling (much like "Amerika") advanced by Jerry Rubin, who used the term to refer to street radicals.

freak flag
The different ways in which a hippie told the world that he or she was a hippie. *In "Almost Cut My Hair" by Crosby, Stills, Nash, & Young, David Crosby sings of being glad that he decided not to cut his hair and of "letting my freak flag fly..."*

freak out
To lose control

freaky
Bizarre, weird

free
Uninhibited, natural. *Free meant more than free, it meant* ***free.***

funky
Down to earth, acceptable. *Salaets provides a definition for funky that is a model of murkiness: "A grundged norb that resembles a Salvatore Dali hemalstadt rusting in a reign of tears..."*

Further!
A general rallying cry, derived from the word appearing in the destination sign on the Merry Pranksters bus. *On the back of the bus was a sign, "Caution. Weird Load." Mathers includes "further" in her dictionary, defining it simply if enigmatically as "a possibility."*

fuzz
Police. *A holdover from the 1950s with roots going back to the 1930s.*

groovy
Fun, acceptable, good. *As we remember from Chapter 4, "groovy" first appeared in 1937, and it enjoyed a fair degree of success in the slang world in the 1940s. Seemingly vanquished to obsolescence by the early 1960s, it was taken off the scrap heap and given new life later in the decade.*

G

gas
Something that is highly entertaining or amusing

get into
To become engaged in an activity

get it on
To have sexual relations

get off
1. To achieve drug intoxication
2. To achieve sexual climax

get off on
To enjoy greatly

get one's shit together
To organize oneself in a general sense

gig
A job. *A jazz musician term for a musical engagement, adopted and broadened by hippies to refer to any job.*

ginchy *or* **ginchi**
Bad

go
To participate in something in an ardent and eager fashion

go down
To happen

goof
To take delight in something

green
Money. *The expression "long green" was used as a slang synonym for "money" at least as early as 1891, and*

An Acidic Vocabulary

The substance d-lysergic acid diethylamide tartrate 25, shortened to LSD-25, more commonly shortened to LSD, was first developed by Dr. Albert Hofmann at the Sandoz Laboratories in Switzerland in the late 1930s. Colorless and tasteless, LSD is a powerful synthetic hallucinogenic drug.

Before the 1960s, LSD was virtually unknown to the American public. In the 1950s, the federal government introduced LSD in experiments to test its usefulness as either a truth serum or a way to disable and subdue an enemy population. Use spread from the government experiments, thanks in large part to several early LSD zealots, including Dr. Timothy Leary and Richard Alpert (now Baba Ram Dass) at Harvard and Ken Kesey in California.

As LSD use spread through the growing hippie movement, a vocabulary sprang up around it. While some words used in talking about LSD were drawn from existing drug argot, for the most part the vocabulary of LSD was freshly minted, often involving the metaphor of a voyage.

LSD was known nearly universally simply as **acid**. Other slang names for it included a **cap** (a word directly imported from drug argot, where it usually referred to a capsule of heroin; it is a good example of how hippies chose to flaunt and ridicule the risks and dangers of drugs by using hard-drug argot), **'cid, the chief, hits, liquid, sheets** (100 doses on perforated blotter paper), a **tab**, and a **ticket** (if the drug experience is a trip, then the drug that makes the trip possible would be the ticket). Sold as a drop absorbed on a piece of paper, LSD was known as **blots, blotter acid,** or **blotter**. To **dose** was to place LSD in or on something such as a sugar cube or a bowl of punch; **dosed** punch was known at least in the San Francisco Bay Area as **fucko punch**. A sugar cube dosed with LSD was a **cube** or **sugar,** while an LSD-dosed cookie was a **wafer**.

Types of LSD had slangy names such as **blue cheer, Owsley blue dot, California sunshine,**

---

the Flapper used "greens" when she spoke of money. "Green" resurfaced again in the 1960s counterculture, where it played second fiddle to "bread" as the synonym of choice for "money."

grok
To possess total awareness of a concept or fact. *This term was invented by Robert Heinlein in* Stranger in a Strange Land. *It was generally used by those who had read*

the book, but also by some who had not.

groove
1. To enjoy a situation
2. Something or someone who is very enjoyable

groove, in the
In tune with what's going on

grungy
Shabby, dirty. *A surfer word that jumped to hippies and then lay dormant for several decades, only to emerge big-time as the sobriquet of a*

youth movement in Seattle in the 1980s.

hairy
Unexpected, difficult to deal with, frightening

hang loose
To relax. *A surfing term, adopted into hippie speech.*

hang tough
To persevere or endure

hang-up
An inhibition, mental block, or psychological problem. *Salaets defined a hang-up as "Inside your head, not outside your noggin, but hasslin' and bouncin' around . . . the interior. They can be drip-dried and hung out until things are cool again."*

happening
A planned gathering where spontaneous or improvised activities take place. *The first recorded use of this*

Christmas trees, pink swirl, purple dome, purple haze, or **white lightning. Brown acid** was LSD which induced unpleasant side effects, gently mocking the announcement at Woodstock that there was some brown acid going around that was "not specifically good." LSD was measured in micrograms, or **mikes;** enough LSD for four users was known as a **four-way wedgie.** A regular user of LSD was a **head, acid head, acid freak, cube head,** or, simply, **experienced.**

To ingest LSD was to **eat acid** (Jefferson Airplane took the eating metaphor a step further in *White Rabbit,* attributing to the Dormouse in the Wonderland-set song the exhortation to "Feed your head..."), to **bust a cap,** to **drop acid,** to **drop a cap,** or to **turn on.**

Some took more care than others when planning to use LSD. To Timothy Leary and Richard Alpert, the **set and setting** were critically important; planning a serene physical setting for the drug use and making sure that one was spiritually prepared for the voyage were both significant considerations.

The LSD intoxication was known as an **experience** or, more pervasively as a **trip; innerspace** was the innermost self, reached through LSD. A bad LSD experience was a **bad trip, bum trip,** or simply a **bummer.** Continuing the travel metaphor, a **guide** or **groundman** was a person who sat with an LSD user during a session; the term **travel agent** applied either to the guide or to the person who provided the LSD for the **trip.** A person under the influence of LSD was said to be either **flying** or **behind** the drug; in her hippie guidebook, Ann Mathers included a chapter with "places to go behind lsd." **Flashback,** a word borrowed from the movies, came to refer to feelings or sensations reminiscent of LSD experienced while not under the influence of the drug.

Given the extreme outlaw nature of LSD use, it is remarkable that several LSD-inspired words migrated from argot into mainstream colloquial speech with meanings far broader than the LSD-specific meanings with which they began their slang journey. *Trip, bad trip,* and *bummer* are all used 30 years after the appearance of LSD without any taboo connotations.

---

word was in 1959 by Allan Krapow in conjunction with a performance work at the Reuben Gallery in New York, advertised as *"something to take place—a happening."*

harp
A harmonica

hassle
1. To bother someone
2. An annoyance or inconvenience

head
1. A hippie
2. A devotee of a particular drug, as in

ACID HEAD or POT HEAD
3. A chronic drug user. *Although the word has a strong*

hype
1. A hypodermic needle used to inject drugs
2. To create a bogus situation or hoax

association with hippies and the 1960s, it was used as early as 1937 to mean a habitual drug user.

head shop
A store catering to drug-using hippies, selling legal drug paraphernalia and

The Other Drugs

While LSD and marijuana were the clear favorites, drugs in other shapes and sizes were not unknown in the hippie culture. With some exceptions, hippies accepted established drug argot when talking about drugs other than grass or acid. With some tragic, notable, high-profile exceptions, hippies in large part eschewed "hard drugs" and needles, but they were not unheard-of commodities.

Heroin was known as **h, horse, junk, scag,** or **smack**. To inject a dose (**fix**) of heroin was to **mainline, shoot,** or **spike**. An addiction was a **jones** or **monkey** (on one's back); to be addicted was to be **strung out**. To withdraw from an addiction was to **kick,** while to do so without the aid of medication was to go **cold turkey**. To take an overdose of heroin was to **o.d.** These were all well-established members of the drug argot community before hippies discovered the joys of heroin.

Amphetamines or stimulants were known as **beans** (usually referring to Benzedrine specifically), **forwards, leapers, thrusters, ups, uppers, whites,** or, most commonly, as **speed,** with a frequent user known somewhat derisively as a **speed freak**. Specific drugs were known as **benny** or **big Ben** (Benzedrine), **crank** (methamphetamine), **crystals** (methedrine) or **dexie** (Dexedrine). On the natural front was cocaine, known as **coke, blow, nose,** or **snow;** cocaine was chopped into fine lines and snorted, or **tooted. Wired** was a word generally reserved for describing someone under the influence of a stimulant.

Tranquilizers or central nervous system depressants were called **backwards, downers, rainbows, R-do's** or **reds** (usually Secanol); a **speed ball** was a mixture of depressant and stimulant, usually injected, often fatally (as in the case of actor John Belushi). **Hash** was hashish; **ludes** or **sopors** (named for the soporific effect of the drug) were **methaquaaludes; 'shrooms** or **silly-cybon** were hallucinatory mushrooms; and an **amy, snapper,** or **popper** was an amyl nitrite ampoule. **Heavenly blues** were morning glory seeds, reputed to produce mild hallucinations; **mellow yellow** was a major hoax of the 1960s, where dried banana skins were reputed to have an intoxicating effect when smoked.

experience-enhancing accoutrements such as incense or strobe lights

heat
The police. *The rock group Buffalo Springfield in "For What It's Worth" sang of a demonstration, "What a field day for the heat. A thousand people in the street."*

heavy
Serious, worthy of serious consideration. *John Lennon knew of what he sang on "Abbey Road" when he said, "She's so heavy..."*

hep
Hepatitis. *"Hep" was rarely used by hippies to mean "aware."*

high
1. Drug-intoxicated *Salaets described this sense of high as "somewhere in the direction of up and parallel to but running in the opposite direction of down."*
2. Exhilarated, euphoric

hitch
To hitchhike

hustle
1. To take advantage of
2. To beg

if if
The International Federation for Internal Freedom, created in 1962 by the original Harvard Research Group for "work" not affiliated with the University

in
In tune, accepted

into
Interested in, engaged in

jam
1. To leave
2. To play music without rehearsing

jive
1. Talk that makes no sense
2. Untrustworthy

juice
Influence

Keep the faith, baby!
A parting remark, borrowed from Adam Clayton Powell

kicks
Fun, thrills. *Robert Gold traces "kicks" back to 1928 in his Jazz Lexicon and identifies 1950 as the year in which it really took off. Bobby Troup gave "kicks" a big lift in 1946 when he wrote "(Get Your Kicks On) Route 66," with the wonderful exhortation to "get hip to this timely trip." This word's hip pedigree was called into question when Paul Revere and the Raiders, a musical group catering to the preteen set, recorded a song called "Kicks."*

killer
Extremely good, sensational

laid-back
Relaxed

law, the
Police

lay on
To give, as in "Let me lay some of this great dope on you."

liberate
1. Free from tradition, convention and authority
2. Steal. *In a richly ironic twist, "liberate"*

was widely used during World War II by members of the armed forces as a sardonic euphemism for stealing. That which the hippies thought they had coined had in fact been coined twenty years earlier by those whose authority they now challenged so openly.

lick
A short musical phrase. *Robert Gold identified "lick" as a popular word used by jazz musicians from 1930 until 1945 when it fell into the black hole of "obsolete except when used historically." Like many other jazz and jive terms, it found its way back into the hippie lexicon of the late 1960s.*

like
That is... *A filler, hesitation word, or intensifier. As Salaets wrote, "an adjective, unless used otherwise."*

lose your cool
To lose one's temper or to become flustered

make
1. To identify someone

2. To buy drugs
3. To have sexual intercourse

make it
To leave

make the scene
To be part of the hippie counterculture

man
A generic filler or expletive

Man, the
Police, or other authorities. *Another holdover from the 1950s.*

maxi-
Large

mega-
Extremely large

mellow
1. Mildly drug-intoxicated
2. Calm, LAID BACK

mind-bending
Having the effects of a hallucinogen

mind-blowing
Being a sudden shock or uncommon experience

mind-expanding
Creating a vague state of increased awareness

mini-
Small

mojo
A charm or amulet.

Probably of African origin and related to the Fulani word "moco'o" (medicine man), "mojo" had been used to mean amulet by African-Americans for several centuries before being discovered by the hippies in the 1960s.

monster
A tremendous success

most, the
The best

natural
A natural hair style favored by black nationalists and black hippies, long and frizzy, also known as an AFRO

nitty-gritty
The crux of a situation

now trip
The philosophy of living in the present, not the past or the future. *The principal life outlook taught by Fritz Perls at the Esalen Institute, Big Sur, California.*

nowhere
Something that is dull and boring. *Seemingly a quintessential sixties word?*

Not exactly. It was first recorded in this slangy sense in 1935, and was part of a slang rhyme—"Like Jack the Bear/ Just ain't nowhere..."

old lady
Girlfriend

old man
Boyfriend

out of it
Oblivious

out-of-sight
So good as to defy categorization or description, most often used as an exclamation

outrageous
Very good

pad
An apartment, room, or house. *A term coined in the 1930s that passed through generations of Bohemians to the hippies.*

panhandle
To beg. *In his 1931 Tramp and*

Underworld Slang, *Godfrey Irwin characterized "panhandle" as an old word for begging. Both begging and the term "panhandling" were fashionable in the hippie counterculture.*

pick up on
To become attentive to something

pill, the
The birth control pill

plant your seed
To spread the hippie philosophy by example

plastic
Less than genuine

plastic hippie
Someone who occasionally donned what they thought was hippie garb and tried to pass as a hippie without making a commitment to the lifestyle. *In about 1968, I went to see Arlo Guthrie perform at the Main Point coffee house in suburban Philadelphia. As I waited in line with friends, a hippie-looking young man with a long scarf moved to the front of the line and into the club. I explicitly dismissed him to my prep school friends as a plastic hippie. He was Arlo Guthrie. I was wrong.*

pig
A policeman

primo
Excellent

Psych!
An exclamation used
when one has fooled
someone else

psych out
1. To figure out
2. To manipulate and
fool someone

put down
1. To criticize
2. To stop doing
something, as in "I'm
trying to put down
smoking dope."

put on
1. To deceive
2. A deception. *In*

*this sense, a put-on is
a deception or hoax.*

R

ralph
Vomit

rap
To talk, to
discuss thoroughly.
*A major word in its
own right in the late
1960s, "rap" became
a monster word in
the late 1980s and
early 1990s with the
proliferation of hip-
hop culture. A closer
look at "rap" can
be found in Chapter
10.*

real, it's been
An expression mean-
ing little more than
"it's been good talk-
ing with you"

Really!
An exclamation of
agreement

relate to
To feel sympathetic
towards. *A little bit of
pyschobabble usually
used in an annoying
fashion, although at
times with humor,
such as "I could sure
relate to a piece of
that pie."*

...right...
An expression used
as a rhetorical device,
either for emphasis
or to ascertain

whether the listener is
following.

Right on!
A term of agreement.
*The term had definite
political overtones,
and was a rallying
cry of the Black
Panther Party for Self
Defense. It migrated
from the radical youth
movement to counter-
culture and became a
common figure of
speech, usually as an
adjective, among hip-
pies, as in "He's a
right-on guy."*

righteous
Very good. *Not exactly
a new word in the
1960s, it was used as
early as 1938 in this
slangy sense.*

rip-off
Something which is a poor value

rip, rip off
1. To steal (something) or cheat (someone)
2. To copy

rush
1. The initial barrage of a drug's effect
2. A sudden sense of euphoria or excitement, drug-induced or not

S

scene
1. A place where something
is happening
2. An interest
3. A style of living. *A big, very vague hippie word.*

score
To buy. *Although the word is straight from drug addict argot (circa 1936), it was playfully used in other contexts, such as "I'm going down to the A&P to score some orange juice."*

screw
1. To have sexual intercourse
2. To cheat or treat poorly

sell out
1. To return to a conventional lifestyle
2. To compromise or
abandon a principle for the sake of expediency or money. *In the mid-1960s, the Who released an album entitled* The Who Sell Out, *punning on ticket sales at a concert and the commercialization of rock and roll.*

send
To excite or move

set
A group of songs in a performance

shades
Sunglasses

shine on
To ignore something or someone

short
A car

shuck
1. Deception
2. To deceive. *Most often this was used as part of the expression "shuck and* JIVE." *Although hippies used "shuck and jive" as a*

square
Out of touch with current trends and styles. *In the us-and-them world of slang-speaking youth, "square" was popular in the 1940s and 1950s. Chapter 5 contains an up close and personal look at "square."*

single cohesive state-ment, the words had distinct meanings in black vernacular English. "Shuck" implied insincere flat-tery, while "jive" sug-gested deception.

skin
A handshake or some form, as in "Give me some skin..."

solid
Very good. *As modern as "solid" may have sounded in the 1960s, it was a major adjec-tive of praise in the slang of the 1940s.*

spaced *or* **spaced out**
Completely inatten-tive, perhaps because of drug intoxication

spade
An African-American. *As was the case among the Beats of the 1950s, there were hippies who felt that "spade" could be used without giving offense. This may have been true in some circles; however, it is also true that "spade" has a long history of being used in a clearly derogato-ry way and this sense of "spade" has always carried the warning note "usually taken to be offensive" in Merriam-Webster dictionaries.*

split
To leave

static
Criticism

straight
1. ESTABLISHMENT-oriented, less than HIP
2. Heterosexual

super
Outstanding

surreal
Dreamlike, irrational

swing
To act in an unfet-tered manner. *Used more commonly out-side hippie circles in the late 1960s, but not unheard of among hippies.*

teenybopper
A young teenager or preteen who identified with the hippie culture and affected the fashions but not the ethos of the times. *The earliest use I have found of this expression is in a Ralph J. Gleason column in the* San Francisco Chronicle *of April 21, 1965, where he refers to "super grubby teenie boppers." In late 1966 and early 1967,*

the expression was used to refer very specifically to groups of Berkeley High School students who congregated on the 24000 Block of Telegraph Avenue in Berkeley. In defense of the teenybopper, the Toronto Star opined on October 30, 1966, that teenyboppers were trendsetters because they were "The only people brave enough to try outrageous new fads."

they
Everyone outside the counterculture, as in "They think they know."

thing
A way of life, a calling, or an interest. *In* Electric Kool-Aid Acid Test, *Tom Wolfe wrote: "Thing was the major abstract word in Haight-Ashbury. It could mean any-thing, isms, life styles, habits, leanings, causes, sexual organs."*

threads
Clothes. *Very much a beat word, used in early hippie days.*

thumb
To hitchhike. *Maurice Weseen included "thumb" as a synonym for hitch-hiking in his 1934*

Dictionary of American Slang. *As was the case with begging/panhandling, when hippies rediscov-ered the joys of hitch-hiking, they also rediscovered a venera-ble piece of slang in "thumb."*

tight
Close, intimate. *This word had limited application in hippie speech with a definite meaning. Thirty years later it became a major player in collo-quial speech among young people.*

together
Aware of who one is and what one wants to do

Too much!
Overwhelming, very good

tribe
1. A small commune or community
2. The hippie coun-terculture taken as a whole

trip
1. A drug experi-ence, usually involving hallucino-genic drugs
2. Something out of the ordinary
3. To ingest a hallucinogenic drug
4. To think or fantasize about something. *An indis-pensable hippie word.*

trip out
1. To take a hallucinatory drug
2. To experience hallucinations while under the influence of drugs
3. To get lost in a fantasy

truckin'
Moving along or persevering. *Truckin' was a dance in the 1930s, a fact which R. Crumb probably knew when he used the expression in his comics. Also, the name of a well-known song by the Grateful Dead.*

tune in
To focus on something, most often the inner self and/or cosmic truth

turn-on
A sexually arousing action

turn on
1. To use drugs
2. To introduce another to something
3. To alter awareness, with or without drugs
4. To become intently aware
5. To provoke a sexual reaction

turn-off
Something that disgusts or repels

turn off
To disgust or otherwise repel

ultimate
The best

uncool
Tactless, naive, dangerous. *A potent word with overtones of ostracism.*

underground
1. The entire hippie counterculture
2. Politically radical
3. A group of fugitives from the law, as in "the Weather Underground," which referred to the clandestine wing of the radical student organization The Weathermen.

up
1. Amphetamines or stimulants
2. Happy, elated

up front
Open, straightforward, upright

uptight
Bound by convention and unable to enjoy life. *Salaets' definition was "Tikked off, unhappy, zilched, mad over or at or about, and furthermore....The opposite of down loose."*

vibes *or* **vibrations**
A sense of what is happening derived almost purely from intuition

way out
Beyond explanation. *This expression could*

zilch
Nothing. *Perhaps an echo of Joe Zilsch of the 1920s, "zilch" was also a feature of mainstream 1960s slang. See Chapter 7 for a further note on "zilch."*

Such a Deal...

In the pro-drug counterculture of the 1960s, he (or sometimes she) who sold drugs was held in some esteem. The seller of drugs was known as one's **connection,** a **dealer,** a **pusher,** or **my man** (a term used by Cab Calloway in his 1932 composition *The Man from Harlem,* and by Warren Zevon in the mid 1970s in "Carmelita," where the buyer "goes to meet my man, he hangs out down on Alvarado Street, by the Pioneer Chicken stand"). **Pusher** was not that popular a term, a rare instance were hippies did not embrace a clichéd term with negative connotations. To sell drugs was to **deal** or **push,** while to buy was simply to **make a buy** or to **score.** If one was **holding,** he had drugs in his possession; if he had no drugs, he was **clean.**

The argot of drug dealers dealt in quantities, such as **baggie** (a plastic sandwich bag full of marijuana) or **matchbox** (a matchbox full of marijuana), **dime bag** (an old expression for ten dollars' worth of drugs) or **nickel bag** (five dollars' worth), a **lid** (an ounce of marijuana), or **mikes** (micrograms of LSD). It was a common practice to dilute drugs with a foreign substance before sale, both to maximize profit and to reserve some purer drugs for the dealer's personal consumption; this practice was known as **cutting** or **stepping** on the drug. Mindful of this practice, someone making a buy might ask for a **taste,** a sample or very small amount of the drug before buying.

The drug dealer's nemesis was the **narc** or **nark,** an undercover narcotics agent. Steve Salaets' definition of "narc" aptly illustrates the low regard in which a narc was held: "Sneaky mutha who belongs to Mickey Mouse Club Established Thinking Society, and one who comes down on and does away with stashes and dopers."

be used to describe either something good or something bad.

where it's at
The core of what is important or what is happening

where your head is
What is happening inside your deepest thought processes

white light *or* **the great white light**
A phase in a LSD TRIP, encompassing a discovery of the true inner self as seen through an all-encompassing white light

wicked
Extraordinarily good. *Never that popular a*

hippie word, it resurfaced with New England teenagers in the 1980s as a well-liked intensifier, as in "wicked good" or "wicked cold."

wig
The mind. *"Wig" was used in the mid-1950s and was an important word in the slang lexicon of both the Beats and the hippies.*

wig out
To lose control, often during a drug experience

wiped out
Exhausted and drained, usually after a drug experience. *A classic surfer expres-*

sion that migrated to hippie speech and then into mainstream colloquial speech.

withal
Money. *The hippie culture was not money-oriented, and there were few slang words for money. This is one of only several modest examples.*

Wo! Wow!
All-purpose exclamations, usually indicating some level of surprise

zap
To overcome, overwhelm, or destroy

Word History: Freak

Freak, a major player in the youth slang of the hippie movement and rap/hip-hop culture, has lived a distinguished life of slang. *Freak* has been used for decades to mean a person with a physical oddity, a true eccentric, a sexual deviate, and an ardent enthusiast.[2] In the 1940s, *freak* took on a special meaning among jazzmen and, to a limited degree, among young jazz enthusiasts. The May 1943 issue of *Down Beat* explains *freak* as follows:

"Freak" or "hokum" music, to New Orleans musicians, meant a way of playing which was in sharp contrast to the "legitimate" style of the downtown (Creole) players. The "freak" musicians produced the hottest, most exciting music; their playing was spontaneous and unorthodox, broadly vocalized—and, at times, embellished with "novelty" effects. . . . And "freak stuff" could be carried as far as the Livery Stable Blues which Keppard and Big Eye Louis used to play—as Carey tells it—with laughing cornet and wailing clarinet parts which were not, perhaps, in what we might like to call the best tradition. Broad as our definition must be, however, it is clear that "freak" has a special and significant meaning, which should not be confused with the ordinary, derogatory sense of the word.

Freak lay low during the 1950s, although the August 10, 1954, issue of *Look* magazine reported in a "Reference Guide to Teen-Age Conversation" that *freak* was a term of endearment.

Rested from its lack of work in the 1950s, *freak* leapt into the hippie lexicon almost effortlessly to play its first major part in the drama of youth slang. Having been called freaks by straight society, hippies quickly assumed the label with glee, calling themselves freaks at least by 1967. When journalist Hunter S. Thompson ran for sheriff of Pitkin County, Colorado, he ran under the banner of "Freak Power." Jerry Rubin, who advocated a militant blend of anarchistic politics and hippie values, embraced *freak*, spelling it "freek" as a further act of insolence.

Freak took on several drug-related meanings during the hippie years, with *speed freak* being commonly used to refer to someone who habitu-ally misused amphetamines, and *freak out* used to describe bad experiences with hallucinogenic drugs. As was the case with *trip*, *freak out* soon took on a broader meaning, referring to any dramatic loss of control. A third meaning for *freak out*, a gathering of hippies, is often forgotten. (See *New Yorker*, February 25, 1967; *Springfield* (Mass.) *Union*, March 27, 1967; *National Observer*, April 3, 1967; *Time*, June 30, 1967.)

All the while, *freak* retained its meaning as an ardent enthusiast, with examples such as *hope freak* (*Look*, April 18, 1967), *watch freak* (*The Village Voice*, February 22-28, 1968), *film freak* (*Newsweek*, September 21, 1970), *ecology freak* (*Newsweek*, July 3, 1972), *media freak* (*New York Review of Books*, March 9, 1972), or *fungus freak* (*Newsweek*, January 15, 1973).

Showing its resilience and versatility, in the idiom of rap and the hip-hop culture, *freak* has taken on several meanings, including someone who is sexually promiscuous (close to the historical use of *freak* to denote a sexual deviate), an appealing girl (compare to the definition for *freak*—"girl, usually pretty"—given in *American Speech*, December 1955, as having been in use at Wayne State University), and to have sex, to perform, or as the name of a dance.

Word Histories: Far Out and Out-of-Sight

Far out! Outta sight! Both of these vintage exclamations of the 1960s have roots that go back far beyond the 1960s, to the turn of the century.

Far out was used by Frank Norris in *McTeague* (1899) to mean extreme and imaginative. Despite this early use, it was not picked up again for several decades. Robert S. Gold writes in *A Jazz Lexicon* that in the 1940s *far out* "became integral to bop and cool," but the first written use that I have found is from 1954, when *Time* magazine used the expression to describe Dave Brubeck in the November 8 issue and again to describe Stefan Wolpe in the November 22 issue; in both examples, *far out* was used to mean experimental and out-of-the-mainstream. Through the end of the decade, *far out* as applied to jazz or other artistic expression enjoyed considerable popularity.

At the same time, *far out* underwent a generalization process, easing out of its jazz-specific meaning and into a more general superlative meaning. It was used by the hipsters and Beats and by those who were trying to exploit the Beatnik image, to mean astonishing or excellent. The hippie use, then, simply followed on the now-familiar jazz-to-Beat-to-hippie slang trail.

Like *far out*, *out-of-sight* can point to serious literary roots. As Richard H. Peck of the University of Virginia noted in *American Speech* (1966, pages 78-79), *out-of-sight* was Bowery slang for astonishingly excellent in the 1890s, and was used by Stephen Crane at least four times in *Maggie: A Girl of the Streets* (New York: 1893). Visiting a museum, our heroine utters, "Dis is outa sight." She could have been speaking 70 years later.

Lester V. Berrey and Melvin Van Den Bark identified *out-of-sight* as a slang synonym for five categories—beyond comparison, very supe-

rior, excessive, completely, and expensive—in the *American Thesaurus of Slang* (New York, 1942), but I found little other evidence of the term's use until the early 1960s.

Although *out of the world* (or *out of this world*) was from 1925 on the accepted jazz idiomatic phrase for something that was good beyond mortal experience or belief, *out-of-sight* was not entirely unknown in jazz circles. For example, in the January 5, 1961, issue of *Down Beat*, there is a pointed reference to the phrase *out-of-sight*. The June 20, 1963, issue of *Down Beat* similarly stated "This record is out of sight."

In the mid-1960s, both James Brown and Little Stevie Wonder popularized the term in song lyrics, and it became an ultimate accolade in youth slang. It is an expression that was appropriated by hippies, marginalized, and then forgotten, living on in the works of Stephen Crane.

The Whole World Was Watching

The 1960s were a tumultuous decade politically, and a sizable radical youth movement grew out of the Civil Rights movement and organized opposition to the war in Vietnam. The language of the Movement (the broad unorganized coalition of individuals and groups working for social, political, and economic change) was generally long on humorless, sloganeering jargon and short on slang.

That said, the Movement was not completely devoid of either humor or slang. The vernacular of the Movement drew upon the language of hippies, the language of the Black Panthers (drawn in turn from prison slang and street slang), and Marxist-Leninist rhetoric. Marxist rhetoric was potentially stultifying, but it was possible to use heroic proletarian lingo to debate what Chinese restaurant to call for dinner. Staid political jargon could be and was mocked by those radicals who didn't check their sense of humor at the door; while not slang, it provided a certain levity to Movement speech.[3]

Political slang was richest when it came to talking about the enemy. Police were known as the **heat, the Man,** or, most commonly, as **pigs**. *Pig* was a Black Panther term; the Panthers defined *pig* as "A low natured beast that has no regard for law, justice, or the rights of people; a creature that bites the hand that feeds it; a foul, depraved traducer, usually found masquerading as the victim of an unprovoked attack." Surely unbeknownst to the Panthers, *pig* had been defined in precisely this sense (police) in George Matsell's *Vocabulum: The Rogue's Lexicon* (New York: George Matsell & Company, 1859).

The porcine metaphor quickly spread into the white radical youth movement with variations such as **bacon, pork** ("Fork the pork!" and "Today's pig, tomorrow's bacon" were popular chants), and the hog call of **Sooo-eee**. The term *pig* was used both as a noun and as an adjective, as in "pig judge" or "pig lawyer." It caught on so strongly (thanks in no small part to the performance

Word History: Hippie

In the late 1960s, Americans could not help but have some appreciation of what a hippie was. A hippie, though, was not always a hippie.

Before the 1950s, *hippy* went through several short-lived lives as slang. It was used to mean smart or fashionable in a play copyrighted in 1924 and first performed in 1925, *The Fall Guy* by George Abbott and James Gleason, in a reference to "a hippy little automobile." In the 1940s and 1950s, *hippy* briefly emerged as meaning ample-hipped. In this sense *hippy* can be found "Among the New Words," *American Speech,* April, 1941, and in an advertisement for a diet food concentrate in powder form in 1958 ("Too hippy? Be happy! The Trim-Eze Way!").

In the 1950s, *hippy* or *hippie* took on a somewhat derisive tone when applied to those who posed as hipsters but were not in fact the genuine article. In his remarkable *A Jazz Lexicon,* Robert

S. Gold identifies this use as "current since c. 1945"; his first citation is to *Night Light* by Douglas Wallop (New York: W.W. Norton, 1953). Slightly later examples include:

Headline: "Indubitably Perturbable, Those Harpin' Hippies" (Ralph J. Gleason's "The Lively Arts," *San Francisco Chronicle,* July 11, 1957)

State Senator Bob McCarthy checked into the Beverly Hilton the other day and registered resolutely: "Sen. Robert I. McCarthy, 2041 Broadway, CITY." The desk clerk, a hippie, dug it... (*San Francisco Examiner,* August 14, 1957)

Headline: "A Big Night in North Beach: The Poets Cry Out 'Zen Nuts, Hippies, Squares'" (*San Francisco Examiner,* August 31, 1959)

Bobby Darin, a hippie from New York City, Tonsil No. 1 in the "new Noise" sweeping

of the Chicago Police during the Democratic Convention in 1968) that police organizations throughout the United States countered with billboards proclaiming "Pride, Integrity, and Guts") or showing a policeman rescuing a child with the banner headline: "Some call him Pig." White radicals seized upon another Panther term, **Right on!,** and shifted its use from a simple exclamation of affirmation to an adjective meaning good ("a right-on guy").

In Berkeley, Alameda County sheriffs came to be known as the **Blue Meanies** (the forces of evil in the Beatles' cartoon movie *Yellow Submarine*) because of their blue helmets and jump suits. Agents of the FBI were known as **feds, feebies,** or **suits. The Man** and **the Establishment** were used interchangeably to refer to any and all authority.

Internal differences invoked similar scorn, particularly when it came to **trots,** Trotsky-inspired sectarians such as the Progressive Labor Party and the Spartacist League (the **Sparts**). **Crazies** were anybody more outrageous than you, and there was always a candidate out there. The **Fuck Heads** were a splinter group in the Berkeley Free Speech Movement (which they called the "Filthy Speech Movement"), who insisted on testing the concepts of free speech with profanity, not political content.

Talking about doing something was more popular than doing it, especially when it was talk like **"off** the pig," a vague cry to kill police. If something was actually done, it was more likely an action, a minor act of vandalism. To **trash** something was to vandalize it, while to trash someone was to criticize them. **Sniping** consisted of posting leaflets and posters, usually with homemade wheat paste. For a demonstration possibly involving a confrontation with the police, one laced up one's heavy work boots, or **shit-kickers**. To reshape mass consciousness through actions was, in the lingo of the usually humorless radical Weathermen, to **massify**. Within the movement, **heavy** took on new meaning as an adjective, either meaning somebody with some degree of power or influence within the Left or denoting an element of physical danger, as in "a heavy action is gonna go down next Thursday."

America, completely conquered all the New York hippies. (San Francisco Examiner, June 9, 1960)

Two of the sturdiest souls in jazz sound off on Bean Bags (Atlantic)—a title, as hippies know, that announces the commanding presence of Coleman (Bean) Hawkins and Milt (Bags Jackson). (Playboy, July 1960).

Then the hippies, they come on cool—they will let me make it if I dig to! Ha!!! ("Silverstein in Greenwich Village," Playboy, September 1960)

And these are not musicians, for the most part. They are hippies who hang out with musicians. Like once upon a time there used to be a crowd of guys who used to hang out in front of Birdland. (Playboy, November 1960)

Like so many talents, Bill [Henderson] has made it slowly. One day, people in the trade

turned around, and there he was, singing in a big voice and with a style that was hip without being hippie. (Down Beat, November 10, 1960)

In baseball, Durocher is regarded as a hippy. Alston runs with the squares. ("Durocher Miscast in L.A. Yes Man Role," San Francisco News-Call, January 11, 1961)

Hugh O'Brian sizzled in one midtown spot when a William Morris agent told a table of hippies how much he disliked O'Brian while the cowboy star was standing just a couple of feet away. ("Memo from John J. Miller," San Francisco Chronicle, February 12, 1961)

Melina Mercouri, the Greek film star who's become a big thing with hippies over here, has been shopping for a Paris apartment. ("Voice of Broadway: Dorothy Kilgallen," San Francisco News Call-Bulletin, March 24, 1961)

The married Alec Guinness and a stunning starlet have been trying to act nonchalant but the hippies have them pegged as a twosome in spite of their casual air. ("Memo from John J. Miller," *San Francisco Chronicle*, May 14, 1961)

Vince Edwards' temperament on the "Ben Casey" set has the Hollywood hippies asking: "Is he kidding?" ("Memo from John J. Miller," *San Francisco Chronicle*, February 10, 1963)

Dick Haymes has the hippies at the Racquet Club in Miami amazed at the way he's boozing as if there is no tomorrow. ("Memo from John J. Miller," *San Francisco Chronicle*, September 29, 1963)

"I'm still a jazz musician," he [Buddy Greco] *says, listing several side efforts of late, "but years ago I was REALLY a hippie."* (*San Francisco Chronicle*, March 8, 1964)

...[Jonathan] Winters has been known in the business as a comedian's comedian, cherished wherever the hippies have gathered. (*New York Times Magazine*, March 28, 1965)

To the casual observer, *hippy* was perhaps first used in its new sense in 1963, when the Orlons took the song "South Street" to Number Three on the Billboard charts with the catchy question, "Where do all the hippies meet?" and the emphatic answer "South Street. South Street." However, the hippies of which the Orlons sang were most definitely not hippies in the post-Beatnik sense of the word but rather the pre-Beatnik hipster sense of the word.

The first use of *hippie* in the new 1960s sense of the word appears to have been in a series of articles on San Francisco's Haight-Ashbury neighborhood by Michael Fallon which began running in the *San Francisco Examiner* on September 5, 1965. Still using *beatnik* in the headline ("A New Paradise for Beatniks"), Fallon used *hippies, heads,* and *beatniks* interchangeably.[4] To what extent Fallon was using *hippie* in its quasi-pejorative 1950s sense as opposed to bringing a slightly new twist to the word is not clear, but it is clear that in late 1966, national attention was drawn to the *hippie* phenomenon in San Francisco, and the word took

off. *Beatnik* was still used to describe hippies at times through the 1960s, but once *hippie* got going, there was no looking back.

Word History: Mellow

At first glance, *mellow* is a quintessential 1960s word, perfectly describing the laid-back, bemused, pleasantly stoned hippie lifestyle. As slang, though, *mellow*'s lineage is impressive, an old-money word if ever there was one.

Since at least 1690, *mellow* has been used as slang to mean slightly and pleasantly intoxicated. It is defined in this sense by Gent (1690), Grose (1785), and Farmer and Henley (1890). Ben Franklin listed *mellow* in his 18th century contribution to the study of slang, *The Drinker's Dictionary* (1737); a century later, Lord Byron used *mellow* in the slang sense, lyricizing about speeches made by men who were "half mellow." Despite the other trails taken by *mellow* over the years, this meaning survives today.

In the 1930s, jazzmen appropriated *mellow*, which jumped comfortably into jive use. The definitions given in the jazz dictionaries don't really do *mellow* credit; Calloway was satisfied with "all right, fine," while Mezzrow said "Feeling good, especially after smoking marihuana." Song titles with *mellow* in them provided catch phrases; "Fine and Mellow" (Billie Holiday, 1939) and "Mello as a Cello" (Joe Venuti and His Blue Four, 1935) are two examples.

Mellow was a prominent word for Slim Gaillard in the late 1940s. The house organ of Capitol Records described Gaillard's use of *mellow* as follows:

For example, when he uses the word "mellow" (and he does constantly), Slim adds the sound "reeny" to the "mellow." (*The Capitol*, March 1946)

In fact, when Gaillard published his *Voutionary* in May 1946, he identified the publisher as "Mellowreeni Pub. Co."

As was the case with many jive words, *mellow* entered the idiom of mainstream teenagers in the 1940s. The *Ladies Home Journal* of December 1944, told us in an article entitled "Is Your Sub-Deb Slang Up-To-Date?" that a mellow man was an attractive boy, a use mirrored in the *Freckles*

and His Friends comic strips of July 19, 1945 ("Ever since June's map appeared in the magazine, she's been getting mushy mail from mellow men!"), September 8, 1945 ("I need your help mellow man"), and April 18, 1946 ("Relax, mellow man, leave it to me!").

Unlike most of its jazz/jive compatriots, though, *mellow* seems to have skipped the 1950s and the hipster/Beat generation, although Lord Buckley did use *mellow* in one of his classic routines in *Hiparama of the Classics*—"ZOOM, Up go Nero, he feel mellow in-deed...."

Next came the 1960s and a new sense of *mellow*, albeit a logical extension of the historical slang—drug intoxicated. Two definitions offered during the hippie years demonstrate the dangers of defining slang. In 1971, Dr. Eugene Landy, who later achieved some level of fame as the psychiatrist to the Beach Boys' Brian Wilson, defined *mellow* as "Just good, pleasant, not very high or very low"; this definition illustrates the dangers of defining slang in a conventional context. At about the same time, Steve Salaet's *Ye Olde Hiptionary* came out, defining *mellow* as "colored either bright fuschia or (curiously) yellow," and as "a sort of softness, not readily seen, but easily felt when feeling mellow." Mr. Salaets' definitions illustrate the danger of defining slang while in an unconventional state of mind.

Several songs nearly did *mellow* in, such as Donovan Leitch's 1966 "Mellow Yellow"[5] and Olivia Newton-John's 1974 "Have You Never Been Mellow"; however, the Grateful Dead went a ways towards rehabilitating the word in "Truckin'" ("Sometimes, you've got to mellow slow..."). In the early 1990s, the very trendy musical group the Red Hot Chili Peppers turned to *mellow* in "Mellowship Slinky in B Major."

Meanwhile, despite the atrocities committed on *mellow* by hippies, it thrived in other subcultures. Within the surfer subculture, *mellow* was well-established to describe a laid-back, relaxed lifestyle and as a general purpose superlative, and black vernacular was spinning *mellow* into much more interesting variations, meaning a friend (term of address), a lover (noun), and intimate (adjective). Within the idiom of rap, *mellow out* means to relax and calm down, a meaning strongly evocative of "Mellow Down Easy" (W. Dixon, 1955: "You mellow down easy when you really want to blow your top...").

Despite preconceptions, then, *mellow* is not just a trite hippie word which began with Donovan and ended with Honda commercials aimed at Northern California. From Lord Byron to Lord Buckley, from Ben Franklin to Cab Calloway, and from the Grateful Dead to the Street, *mellow* has been around.

Word History: Trip

Trip, seemingly an entirely innocent noun and at times an innocent-sounding verb ("Trip the light fantastic/on the sidewalks of New York..."), found itself stigmatized with an unshakable association with LSD and other psychedelic drugs in the 1960s.

Trip was not all innocence, though. It had been used in underworld slang since the 1930s to refer to an arrest, conviction, and sentence that led to incarceration. It was not without drug uses before the 1960s, either, for Peter Tamony tracked down *trip* used in the context of heroin use from *The Connection* (1957), a play by Jack Gelber staged in New York in 1959 and set in San Francisco's Broadway ("Tripping Out from San Francisco," *American Speech*, Summer 1981). Tamony further hypothesized that *trip* had made the leap from prison slang (meaning, according to a glossary issued by the California Bureau of Corrections in 1962, "fantasy, day dream fable, factual or fictional") to street drug use.[6]

In any event, *trip* was almost immediately ensconced as both a noun and verb in connection with the use of LSD. During his 1967 trial for marijuana possession, author Ken Kesey explained to Judge Joseph Karesh that a trip was "A happening out of the ordinary when induced by a psychedelic drug" (*San Francisco Chronicle*, April 12, 1967).

When was *trip* linked to LSD? In January 1966, Stewart Brand and others produced the Trips Festival at Longshoreman's Hall in San Francisco. This is the earliest written use of the word in conjunction with LSD that I have found, although a September 25, 1965, article in the *San Francisco Chronicle* about the closing of the Blue Unicorn, a Beat-oriented coffee shop, uses the adjective *trippy* as meaning "great." Where there is *trippy* must there have first been *trip?* In any event, in the first major book about LSD, aptly entitled *LSD* by Richard Alpert and Sidney

–in

The 1960s loved -in's. Until the 1960s, verbal phrases formed with *in* as the second part of a compound, such as *drive-in* or *break-in*, only suggested inward motion: the car is driven into the drive-in; a burglar breaks into a building during a break-in. New in the 1960s was the use of the combining form *-in* to imply that the activity was an organized political demonstration of some sort.

Although **sit-in** can be traced back to 1947, it did not catch on until after February 1, 1960, with a sit-in taking place at a segregated Woolworth's lunch counter in Greensboro, North Carolina. Four black civil rights workers sat-in at the lunch counter, demanding service and refusing to leave until they were arrested. The sit-in as a tactic in the war for civil rights was a logical extension of the sit-down, a tactic used by the more radical wing of American labor, the Congress of Industrial Organizations, in the 1930s; instead of simply striking, workers occupied their places of work, refusing to leave until their demands were met.

Teach-in (a loosely structured symposium on a single issue) was the next major -in, starting with a teach-in about the war in Vietnam at the University of Michigan in March 1965. Not far behind it was **be-in,** first widely used in conjunction with a gathering in Golden Gate Park, San Francisco, on October 7, 1966, observing the effective date of legislation making LSD illegal in California.

In an exhaustive article which appeared in the February 1968 edition of *American Speech*, Kelsie B. Harder reported recorded uses of the following staggering list of *-in* variations: **arrest-in, bat-and-ball-in, bitch-in, bleed-in, buy-in, camp-in, chew-in, cook-in, couch-in, debate-in, deer-in, design-in, drop-in, eat-in, fat-in, feed-in, fish-in, flower-in, fly-in, freeze-in, grade-in, graze-in, hang-in, hitch-in, jail-in, kiss-in, learn-in, leg-in, lie-in, loot-in, love-in, march-in, meal-in, moon-in, pray-in, preach-in, read-in, recite-in, rent-in, rest-in, roost-in, sail-in, scrub-in, shit-in, shoe-in, shop-in, shrink-in, sin-in, sing-in, sleep-in, slop-in, smoke-in, snarl-in, squat-in, stall-in, stand-in, stomp-in, study-in, summer-in, sweep-in, swim-in, think-in, wade-in, walk-in, wed-in, weep-in,** and **wheel-in.** Additional contestants found in the Tamony archives include **clean-in** (*San Francisco Chronicle*, January 23, 1967) and **mill-in** (*San Francisco Chronicle*, March 28, 1967).

On a personal note, while incarcerated in Washington, D.C., in May 1971, during the May Day demonstrations against the war in Vietnam, I was horrified when my cellmates announced to our jailers that we would conduct a **piss-in** at a given hour. The hour came and went and, thankfully, there was no piss-in.

The ultimate commercialization of poor *-in* came with Rowan and Martin's *Laugh-In,* a variety show which appeared on NBC first as a special and then as a weekly series from 1967 until 1973. At the time it was seen as an intrepid wrecker of taboos worthy of its association with *-in,* although by latter-day standards its verbal wit and sexual puns are quite tame.

The vernacular's infatuation with *-in* faded in the late 1960s, with the suffix *-gate* taking its place after the 1972 break-in at the Democratic National Committee's offices in the Watergate complex in Washington.

Cohen (New York: New American Library, 1966), *trip* appears on the dust jacket, defined as "a psychedelic experience."

Although firmly grounded in the language of LSD, *trip* soon ventured out to a more general use in hippie slang. It could mean an absorption in or obsession with an interest, attitude, or state of mind (as in an *ego trip, nostalgia trip, death trip, power trip, guilt trip*), a scene or lifestyle (as in knowing "damn well what the trip was when they entered the gates" of a motorcycle club), an experience not necessarily induced by drugs (as in the Grateful Dead's singing "What a long, strange trip it's been"), or to focus intently on

The Walls Come Tumblin Down

One lasting linguistic outgrowth of the 1960s was a radical loosening of verbal taboos. Language which had been studiously avoided for several centuries burst into mainstream speech; formerly forbidden words such as *fuck* and *shit* became mainstays of youth speech.

Americans had never been shy about oaths and curses. Blasphemy, though, was the challenge-to-taboo of choice until about 1870. With the adjustments to American society produced by the Civil War came a shift from blasphemy to obscenity and scatology. Even so, *fuck, shit,* and their ilk were off-limits for most Americans, and certainly most young people.

On the battlefields of World War I and to a far greater degree World War II, verbal taboos were the first casualties. *Fuck* and its variants were ubiquitous, used as standalone expletives, as curses directed at a person or situation, or as intensifying adjectives or adverbs. In *I Hear America Talking,* Stuart Flexner reflected on *fuck, screw,* and *shit* in World War II and wrote that "it almost seemed no serviceman could complete a sentence without using one of them."

Veterans brought their disregard for language taboos home with them, and slowly their use of profanity spread throughout American society. To a slight degree, *fuck* found its way into the speech of 1950s youth, largely in the guise of the exclamation **Fucking A!** ("I agree with you!"), an interjection which was used by the j.d. (juvenile delinquent) or greaser wing of the not-quite-mainstream youth. Similarly, several variants were used by Beat youth, probably most notably **fuck up** (a huge error). Curiously, **B.F.D.** (big fucking deal) slipped into informal speech of the 1960s mainstream youth in an innocent manner which seemed not to challenge taboos, much like *snafu* had 20 years earlier.

Even so, it was not until the hippie movement of the 1960s that American youth embraced pro-

something (as in "tripping out on the Rose Garden"). Despite its LSD-specific birthright, *trip* became an all-purpose, vague hippie word—"That's his trip" being an ambiguous and non-judgmental way of explaining away somebody's behavior.

Trip faded from the scene in the 1970s and early 1980s, emerging later as a big word in hip-hop/rap. In *A 2 Z: The book of Rap & Hip-Hop Slang* (New York: Boulevard Books, 1995), Lois Stavsky, I. E. Mozeson, and Dani Reyes Mozeson identify seven different uses of *trip*, several of which (an unforgettable experience, to enjoy, to experience the unexpected) mirror the non-LSD uses of the 1960s. The major rap meanings, though, are new for *trip*. *Tripping* as meaning either overreacting or having fun and *tripping on* as meaning insulting are brand-new and unexpected meanings for the venerable *trip*.

* * *

[1]The most prevalent words from Asian cultures used by hippies were **avatar** (a messiah), **dharma** (the right thing to do, the proper way of life; Jack Kerouac's study of Buddhism and his use of the word in the title *Dharma Bums* did much to popularize this word), **god's eye** (brightly colored, concentric squares woven by Indians for use in their religious rites), **guru** (a person who acts as a teacher in matters of fundamental spiritual concern), **hare krishna** (a phrase invoking the name of the great prophet, intoned in a chant), **Kama Sutra** (a sex manual from India, discovered and studied by hippies), **karma** (fate), **mandala** (a Hindu or Buddhist mystic symbol of the universe that is typically in the form of a circle enclosing a square), **mantra** (a Vedic hymn, prayer, or mystic formula used devotionally), **maya** (the powerful force that creates the cosmic illusion that the phenomenal world is real), **nirvana** (a state of inner unity and peace after the disappearance of all worldly desires), **sansara** (the indefinitely repeated cycle of birth, misery, and death caused by karma), **satori** (a sudden and stunning enlightenment attained by intuitive illumination, the spiritual goal of Zen Buddhism; Jack Kerouac popularized this word with his late novel, *Satori*

---

fanity as a fixture in their speech. Although hippies could complete a sentence without using profanity, they often chose not to. While **balling** was probably the slang synonym of choice for engaging in sexual intercourse, **fuck** was freely used in its pure sexual sense. **Fuck over** was used to mean to cheat or otherwise treat poorly; to **fuck up** was to err in a colossal fashion (a very popular concept and expression from World War II); and to be **fucked up** was to be drug-intoxicated or recovering from having been drug-intoxicated. Youth were not blind to the shock value of *fuck*, and nobody who was present for the May Day demonstrations in Washington, D.C., in the spring of 1971 will forget the thrill of Country Joe McDonald leading tens of thousands in the modified F-I-S-H sheer, spelling out F-U-C-K.

Motherfucker was a special word in the hippie and radical youth movements. While it could be used as an insult, it could also be used as a friendly form of address. Moreover, it could be used to refer to an authority figure. In the song "We Can Be Together," the Jefferson Airplane sang with great anti-authoritarian zeal, "Up against the wall motherfucker, tear down the walls...."

Pissed off (now universally understood to mean angry) is so far from taboo today that it is difficult to appreciate just how rude it once was, or that **piss** was one of the FCC's seven deadly sinful words. Similarly, **shit** came out of its taboo closet and became an all-purpose hippie word which, in quintessential vague hippie fashion, could describe (1) something good, (2) something bad, (3) marijuana, or (4) things—"stuff" as George Carlin would put it.

The best efforts of hippies notwithstanding, several verbal taboos stood for another decade, and in fact still stand. One recent victim has been **suck**; as will be seen in Chapter 11, *suck* moved off of the taboo list into mainstream speech in the late 1980s and early 1990s, with racial epithets assuming the most-forbidden status once enjoyed by *fuck, shit,* and company.

in Paris), **third eye** (a small diffractor worn on the body to catch light), **yin-yang** (a Zen Buddhist symbol, loosely representing the unity of opposites), and **zen** (truth seeking through introspection, intuition, and rejection of rational thought).

[2]In a 1981 column, William Safire reported a 1906 use of *freak* in this sense, quoting from a stenographic record of a trial in which a witness referred to someone as a "Kodak freak." The next earliest written record of *freak* used in this sense is in Robert Gold's *A Jazz Lexicon;* Gold quotes Duke Ellington as saying in 1946, "I'm a train freak."

There may be an even earlier hit than Safire's 1906 citation. In "College Words and Phrases," *Dialect Notes,* Volume II, Part 1 (1900), Eugene H. Babbit defined freak as "someone who is exceptionally proficient in a given area." This is not at all far-removed from the ardent-enthusiast meaning of the word.

[3]The ideological *liberate* could be used in a gently mocking tone to mean "steal," *affinity group* could stop meaning "study group" or "cell" and simply mean the group of friends that was sneaking out to see Mick Jagger and the Rolling Stones despite the sexist lyrics of "Under My Thumb," or *correct line* could be lifted from its Marxist-Leninist roots and used to ask, "What's the correct line on going up to Tilden Park and turning on this afternoon?" Similarly, *mass line* (the for-public-consumption explanation of an action or theory) could be used to describe any less-than-truth, *united front* (short-term coalition-building with non-communist groups) could be applied to any situation where unity was needed, and *revisionist* could be and was used well beyond its historical application to Stalin. *Bourgeois baggage*, a dogmatic phrase, was often shortened to *baggage* and used in a broad sense that gained a foothold in the language of therapists.

[4]In a June 24, 1971, letter to the editor of the *San Francisco Chronicle*, one George E. Poggi of San Francisco suggested that "recent etymological research at the University of Oklahoma has pretty well established that hippie derives from the great Mexican god Xipe, the X of course being pronounced as H. Xipe was the god of corn." A ruse? A forgotten theory? A prank?

[5]*Mellow yellow* briefly enjoyed a slang mean-

ing of scraped, dried banana peels, which were rumored to have a psychedelic effect when smoked. A team of UCLA psychiatrists determined in 1967 that "there are no known hallucinogens in bananadine" and that the entire mellow yellow craze had been a ruse from the start.

[6]In *Skeleton Key: A Dictionary for Deadheads* (New York: Main Stream Books, 1994), David Shenk and Steve Silberman write that "Soldiers at Edgewood Arsenal stole the drug for their own purposes, and the word 'trip' was coined." This is a fascinating lead, but unfortunately it lacks, for the time being, documentation.

Sources and References

Aside from underground comics, the lyrics of rock songs, and underground newspapers, the most amusing, most frustrating, and ultimately the most useful sources of information for hippie slang are some of the hippie-inspired glossaries and word lists that resulted from indigenous efforts at hippie lexicography. A few of these home-cooked efforts that I consulted include: *The Hip Pocket Book* by Ann C. Mathers (New York: Aphromode Press, 1967), which captures the naïveté and innocence of the era; *The Hip Glossary of Hippie Language* by May Lay and Nancy Orban (San Francisco: self-published, 1967), a copy of which was kindly provided by the Western Historical Manuscript Collection at the University of Missouri, Columbia and which falls into the from-the-heart but not-that-instructive category; and, my favorite, *Ye Olde Hiptionary* by Steve Salaets (Las Vegas: self-published, 1970), a witty, clever, whimsical, and loving glossary.

Another effort by participants, *LSD* by Richard Alpert and Sidney Cohen (New York: New American Library, 1966), is valuable for dating LSD terms. Also on the drug front, Ernest L. Abel's *A Marihuana Dictionary: Words, Terms, Events and Persons Relating to Cannabis* (Westport, Connecticut: Greenwood Press, 1982) and *The Slang and Jargon of Drugs and Drink* by Richard A. Spears (Metuchen, New Jersey: Scarecrow Press, 1986) are helpful for the historical context of hippie drug argot.

Useful works written by outsiders looking in include *It's Happening: A Portrait of the Youth*

Scene Today by J. L. Simmons and Barry Winograd (Santa Barbara, California: McNally and Loftin Publishers, 1966); *The Hippies* by the correspondents of *Time* magazine, edited by Joe David Brown (New York: Time Incorporated, 1967); *The Hippies* by Burton H. Wolfe (New York: Signet Books, 1968); and Kenneth Hudson's *Dictionary of the Teenage Revolution and its Aftermath* (London: Macmillan Press, 1983). While Hudson's work spans several decades and is focused on the United Kingdom, his etymological work on several words was and is particularly helpful.

A map of "Haight Ashbury San Francisco Hippieville" published by "W.T. Samhill" (as in "What the Samhill...?") in Sausalito, California, in 1967, contains a slight treatment on the language of hippies ("Parlez-vous Hippi?"), while the April 1966 issue of *Mr.* magazine contains "The Hippie's Lexicon" by Allen Geller.

For the language of rock and roll, Tom Hibbert's *Rockspeak! The Dictionary of Rock Terms* (London: Omnibus Press, 1983) is a good source of information. Although amusing, I have found *The Language of Rock and Roll* by Bob Young and Micky Moody (London: Sidgwick & Jackson, 1985) to be only peripherally valuable.

Useful sources for the language of the Movement include *The Underground Press in America* (Bloomington, Indiana: Indiana University Press, 1970); Jerry Rubin's *Do It! Scenarios of the Revolution* (New York: Simon and Schuster, 1970); Abbie Hoffman's *Revolution for the Hell of It* (New York: Dial Press, 1968) and *Woodstock Nation* (New York: Vintage Books, 1969); and *The Sixties Papers: Documents of a Rebellious Decade* by Judith Clavir Albert and Stewart Edward Albert (New York: Praeger Publishers, 1984). In this area, I have also benefited from conversations with Stew Albert, Bill Monning, and Laurie Zoloth-Dorfmann.

CHAPTER 9
The 1970s and 1980s
▼

"Gag me with a spoon!"

A fter the sound and fury of the 1960s, the nation let out a collective gasp and began to try to digest the tumult that had seemingly visited every corner of the society. The war in Vietnam had bitterly divided the country; the images of the war which endured were not pretty—National Guard troops killing students at Kent State University and Jackson State College in May 1970, the victims of the My Lai massacre, a South Vietnamese officer coldly shooting a suspected Viet Cong in the head from point-blank range, a young girl scorched by napalm running naked from the horror, and the panic associated with the fall of Saigon in 1975. The results of three consecutive presidential elections were profoundly affected, if not decided, by assassins, and the early 1970s saw first a vice president resign after it was learned that he had accepted envelopes of cash bribes in his office at the Executive Office Building and then a president and his attorney general resign hip-deep in political scandal. The

Illustrations by Matthew Martin

civil rights movement, which had begun with such noble aspirations and hope, had been devastated by assassination, racist terror, and then internal bickering. Our national ace in the hole, economic prosperity, was besieged by the dual threats of the oil crisis and inflation.

The excesses of the 1960s youth in revolt produced a popular cultural reaction—bland was briefly in. Insipid, clichéd, and prosaic music performed by such "artists" as Tony Orlando and Dawn, Barry Manilow, Debby Boone, and Morris Albert (who among those who lived the 1970s can forget "Feelings"?) enjoyed some degree of popularity, and the utterly vapid *Love Story* passed for literature.

Out of the ashes of this monotony a youth culture arose, as it always has. As the country lurched to the right in the 1980s, led by older religious and cultural conservatives, young people found their voice. Unlike the hippie counterculture of the 1960s, though, there was no single movement that captured the hearts and minds of the young. Disco was a brief fad, but hardly a movement. The punk scene was a fringe movement whose very radical nature dispelled popular support, while the grunge movement was regional. Skateboarders and Deadheads all had their place, but they were essentially parochial cultural movements. The movement which probably exerted the greatest countercultural impact was the hip-hop and rap movement (see Chapter 10), and it defined music, fashions, and speech without defining a lifestyle.

If there was a single unifying cultural force, it became MTV with its pastiche of music videos and hip-talking, ultra-trendy video jockeys. MTV first appeared in 1981, and by mid-decade it was in full stride, defining the cutting edge of popular culture. To the extent that there was a unifying generational theme, it was the slick and daring, commercialized hip message of MTV.

The Language of the 1970s and 1980s

In the winter of 1971, Stephen Dills of the University of South Dakota suspended publication of the journal *Current Slang* which he had issued on a quarterly basis for five years. He did so because, he believed, slang was on the wane:

Apparently the burst of invention typical of the last five years is over. The rate of additions seems to be slowing down. Terms as old as three and four years now make up the bulk of the items submitted.

While the gloomy state-of-slang forecast issued by Professor Dills may have been true for several years, it did not hold true for long.[1] Despite the notable absence of a single, unifying countercultural movement which could be expected to spawn a slang lexicon, the 1970s and 1980s were a golden age of youth slang.

Just as popular culture backed away from the intemperance of the 1960s, the slang of young people too moved away from the slang of the 1960s. Where both mainstream 1960s slang and the speech of hippies drew in large part on the jive speech of Harlem in the 1920s (via jazz musicians to hipsters to the Beat 1950s to the 1960s), the slang of the 1970s and 1980s was, until the emphatic influence of rap and hip-hop in the late 1980s, for the most part free of the influence of black street vernacular.

Instead, youth slang of the 1970s and 1980s relied in large part on the clever, sardonic use of standard English. *Arbitrary, attitude,*

bank, beige, bitter, brick, budget, cashed, cold, costing, cozy, fold, generic, guns, hungry, junks, load, moldy, perpetrate, precious, quaint, rank, rat, roller, rush, savage, serious, shine, shred, team, thrash, toxic, work, wrap, wreck, and *wretched* all took on slangy meanings that deviated from standard usage in clever ways.

A final feature of the slang of the 1970s and 1980s is the degree to which slang-speaking youth trampled on grammar and syntax. In *Slang U* (Harmony Books, 1989), Pamela Munro of the University of California at Los Angeles took a novel approach to slang, analyzing the grammatical aspects of college slang.

Two pronounced facets of the grammatical mayhem visited upon the language by slang in the 1970s and 1980s are worthy of note.

First, in telling a story, the phrase "he said" or "she said" or, for that matter, anybody saying anything, all but disappeared. Instead of the standard English "He said, 'I don't want to go,'"

one of several variations would be heard, any and all of which were more than a little annoying to the older generation:

(1) *He's, "I don't want to go..."*
(2) *He's like, "I don't want to go..."*
(3) *He's all like, "I don't want to go..."*
(4) *He's all, "I don't want to go..."*
(5) *He goes, "I don't want to go..."*

Secondly, intensifiers knew no borders when it came to part of speech. For example, **big time** was used in the middle of a sentence as an adverbial intensifier—"I was big time interested in going to the concert." In the same vein, **total** moved from simply an adjective and became an adverbial intensifier, playing in place of the adverb formerly known as "totally," as in "She is total shameless, running off to Las Vegas like that." Many other intensifiers used by young people underwent a similar transformation.

A Word List of the 1970s and 1980s

ace
To do very well

acid
Steroids. *A curious transfiguration reflecting a cultural shift, from LSD in the late 1960s to steroids in the 1980s.*

aggro
Angry. *A clipped, hipped "aggressive," from Australian slang via surfers.*

animal
A wild and crazy guy. *This term came into the slang idiom in the 1940s, went into hiding, and then emerged with a vengeance in the 1970s with the movie* Animal House.

arbitrary
Irrelevant

ass out
In trouble

attitude
Arrogance

B.A.
To expose one's bare ass

bad news
An unpleasant or demanding person or situation, as in "That girl Terry's going out with is strictly bad news."

bag some rays
To sunbathe. *An echo of the 1960s "catch some rays" and "soak up some rays"*

bank
Money

bank on
To beat up

beam out
To daydream. *This*

expression was derived from the oft-uttered command on Star Trek *of "Beam me up, Scotty."*

beemer
A BMW car

beige
Dull

bent
Deranged

bite
1. To duplicate without consent
2. To be very unpleasant

bitter
Annoyed

blow away
To be astonished

blow off
To reject or ignore

bogue
1. Totally disgusting. *"Bogue" and its parent "bogus" had been used in black vernacular for several decades to mean false. In the drug argot of the*

1950s and early 1960s, "bogue" meant craving for drugs. The word was taken up by a new generation in the 1970s and given a broader negative meaning. Hackers loved the word, spinning off several variants as part of their rich idiom, described further in this chapter.
2. To smoke a cigarette

bones
Money

bonzai
Enormous

boom
A radio, tape player, or CD player. *A shortened form of "boom box."*

boppers
Shoes

box
A radio, tape player, or CD player. *A shortened form of "boom box."*

Not specifically good...

In the 1970s and 1980s, *bad* came to mean for young people what *good* means in standard English, leaving a linguistic vacuum for the negative side of life. Nature abhors a vacuum, and a bevy of slang *"bads"* leapt into the breech: **bald, beat, budget, buggy, bunk, burnt, bush, crappy, d, dank** (also very good), **deadly** (also very good), **from hell, gnarly** (also very good), **greasy, harsh, heinous, killer** (also very good), **lame, painful, sucky** (making its passage of conversion from taboo of the 1970s to unblushing youth slang of the 1990s), and **weak**.

dragon
A person with bad breath

AHEM

boxie
A girl with dyed blonde hair. *Contrast with* LOXIE—*a boxie gets it from a bottle.*

brain-dead
Extremely tired

break out
To do something unexpected or new

brick
To be afraid. *Probably derived from the quaint "to shit a brick" when frightened.*

budget
Insufficient, unqualified

bummed out
Bored

burly
A difficult task

bust
1. A rude insult
2. A good shot in basketball

butt-lick
A sycophant

buzz crusher
A killjoy

C

cashed
Completed, drained

checking
To pull down someone's boxer shorts as a surprise

cheese
Something that is outdated

chew on
To bother

chickenshit
A coward

chief
A term of address that can be used with almost anyone safely

chill *or* **chill out**
To calm down and regain one's poise

choke
To fail under pressure, to do poorly

clock
1. To acquire
2. To hit somebody

clue
A sense of what is going on. *If someone does something that brings into question his or her awareness of what is going on, you might suggest, "Catch a clue!"*

clueless
Hopelessly incompetent and out of touch with current trends

cold
Unpleasant

costing
Expensive

cozy
Dull

crank
To do very well

crash and burn
To do poorly

creep
To flirt

creepers
Thick-soled black shoes

crew
A group of friends

Cujo
A dangerous, risk-taking person. *Derived from the book by Stephen King and subsequent movie.*

cut up
To act bizarre

D

dicked
Assured of achievement

dingy
Mindless

dip
To eavesdrop

dismiss
To break off a dating relationship

do
A hairstyle. *In the African-American community, "do" was*

Hid, Hein, or Honey?

Slang words to describe physical beauty or the lack thereof were abundant. A pretty girl was a **Betty** (from the surfer idiom, derived from a cartoon character in the *Flintstones*), a **filet** (love those meat images!), a **freak, nectar** (again, a surfer word that made it mainstream), or a **treat**. A good-looking boy was a **biscuit, honey,** or **stud muffin**. In search of an adjective instead of "attractive," the young resorted to **buff, crushin'** (usually describing clothes), **fresh** (usually applied to a female), **fine, hot, mint, saucy, smokin', stylin', tender,** and **tough**. **Babe** worked both sides of the street, meaning an attractive person regardless of gender.

Something or someone that was very appealing was simply **death**. "You kill me" and "you slay me" are earlier examples of slang use of death to express attraction.

Instead of the simple old "ugly," the youth of the 1970s and 1980s might use **hein** (a clipped "heinous"), **hid** (a clipped "hideous"), **nasty, scary,** or **skanky**. To describe an ugly person, one could exploit **bushpig, skag** (usually applied to girls), **skank, troll** (usually applied to girls), or **Wilma** (an ugly girl; another allusion to the *Flintstones*).

---

used to refer specifically to an artificially straightened or "processed" hairdo, with the derivatives "do-cap" and "do-rag" used to refer to caps and scarves worn while the chemical process was taking place. In the late 1980s, it was embraced by mainstream youth to refer to any haircut or style.

do righteous
To perform well

dog
To spurn in a brutal fashion, to treat somebody badly

drag
To feel sick or listless

drill on
To beat up

drop some iron
To spend money

duckets
Money. *In the 1920s, a Flapper used the term "ducat" to refer to subway tokens or money. Not much is new.*

duff
To do poorly

duker
A massive bowel movement

dump
To break off a dating relationship. *As Elise Hancock observed in her 1988 article on student slang, when a young person said "We're still going out but we decided we should see other people" it was a good indication that the speaker*

had been dumped.

dust
In big trouble, as in "If you're late, you're dust."

easy
Adaptable, affable

express
Presently disposed to party

fashion risk
Unattractive clothing

file
Dangerous

fire on
1. To hit
2. To rebuke

five-finger discount
Shoplifting. *"Five-finger" and "five-fingers" were used in underworld slang to refer to a thief at least as early as the 1930s, and Five Fingers was a popular movie in the early 1950s about a master thief. "Discount" was added to the historical "five-fingers" and captured the imagination of the young.*

flake
To fail to follow through on your commitments

flaming
Very angry

flex
To show off

flip *or* **flip out**
To be shocked

flip off
To give the finger

fold
To become exhausted

front
1. To put up a front, to pose
2. To embarass someone

fry
An unpleasant experience, as in "What a fry!" *An unusual outgrowth of the well-known "fried" (drunk), recorded among high school students in Michigan in the early 1980s.*

funky
1. Smelly
2. Good in a soulful way, usually applied to music
3. Eccentric but not unacceptable

G

gagger
A disgusting person

gank
To flirt

generic
Dull

gig
A dance. *For decades, "gig" meant a job, originally for a musician.*

give a melvin
To hoist someone off their feet by their underwear

globes
Breasts

glued
Emotionally stable

gooey
Girlfriend

granola
A person who is a throwback to hippie days

grease
1. To kiss passionately
2. A meal

grind
To eat

gothic
A style involving black clothes, black lipstick, pale face

Chilly Most and Cherry-Good and Cool

The young person of the 1970s and 1980s had a wide choice of slang to fall back upon when trying to convey that something was cool or good. There were a number of words that meant what *cool* had meant to past generations. **Boomin', caj, cas, cazh, chilly, chilly most, coo', cosmo, crit, critical, fresh, godly, happening, hot, hype, icy, justice, rad, radical, raw, rude, ruff, studly, stupid fresh, trick, wicked** (an important word), and **wild** were all *cool*-clones in the seventies and eighties.

When it came to quality, why say "good" or "excellent" when you could say **ace-high, all that, awes** (a clipped form of *awesome,* which had passed into obsolescence), **badass, beauteous, bonus, cherry, choice, chronic, classic, cooking, crankin', crucial, dank, deadly** (also could mean very bad), **decent** (also could mean very bad), **def, deffest, dope, dual, electric, fierce, fly, fully, fully-on, golden, hardcore, hellified, hot, hype, intense, jamming, killer, mean, outrageous, primo, psychotic, raw, rockin', savage, sick, slammin', smoking, smooth, solid, stompin', sweet, swift, tasty, the kind** (da kine), or **vicious**?

Chicano Slang

Mexicans and Mexican-Americans have always played a vital role in the border states of California, Arizona, New Mexico, and Texas. In the 1970s, the efforts of Cesar Chavez to organize migrant farm workers in California brought national attention to Mexican immigrants, who had been nearly invisible on the national scene since the zoot suit riots of the 1940s.

Chicano (Mexican-American) youth in America have their own, quite rich language. Although most of the Chicano dialect is a form of Mexican Spanish known as *calo* or *pocho,* a few English expressions were used with regularity. **Low and slow** referred to the **lowrider** style of driving and could serve as a metaphor for other activities; to **khaki down** was to dress in khakis, a pressed white tee shirt, and perhaps a flannel shirt. **Ay te guacho** (pronounced eye tay watcho) is a perfect example of Spanglish—based on English words and Spanish sounds, it meant "I'll see you."

Aside from the term *Chicano,* only a few words have worked their way into English-speaking slang; **barrio** (the Mexican part of town) and **macho** (virile) are two that made the journey. Few outside California would know that **Califas** was California, or that **Aztlan** was the ancient and future kingdom of Mexico, including the southwestern United States.

Greetings included **Que honda?** (what's up) and **que pasa?** (what's going on?). Disbelief akin to "no way!" could be expressed by **Chale!** Other commonly used words were **chisme** (gossip), **fuchi** (ugly, disgusting), **placa** (one's nickname, spray-painted in a personalized style), **ranfla** (car), and **trucha** (aware, hip). When spray-painting one's placa or painting a mural, the initials **c.s.** (**con safo**) were sprayed, almost as a talisman against rival gangs painting over the mural or name.

---

grip
Control, some glimmer of what is going on, as in "Get a grip!"

grub
To eat in abundance

guns
Muscles

gutter wear
Very hip clothing

hack
To escape undesirable people

hank
A licentious girl

happy camper
Someone who is having fun.
The term is probably more popular in the negative—"She was not a happy camper."

hardcore
Extreme

heads
People, as in "I'm bringing six heads to the party."

heifer
A fat girl. *In the early 1800s, a "heifer" was an attractive young girl.*

high-siding
Cruising

hippy witch
A girl dressed in hippie-style clothing

history
Out of the the picture, as in "She's history— we broke up two weeks ago."

hit on
To try to pick someone up

hittin'
Good tasting

holler at
To talk to

Holmes or **homes**
A term of address for a male friend

homey
A close and reliable friend

honking
Enormous

hook
To catch on

hook or **hook up**
To connect with someone

horsebag
A loose girl

hoser
A jerk

hoss
A muscular man

hungry
Horny

Chicano slang words that were applied to people included **chuco** (a clipped "pachuco"), **bato** (guy), **bato loco** (completely wild guy), **cabron** (literally one who has been cuckolded, used as a slightly disrespectful equivalent of "dude"), **buey** (literally an ox, used to mean a dumb person, usually intensified by **pinche,** about the equivalent of "fucking"), **carnal** (blood brother), **chiflada** (a wild child who is always running around), **chingon** (big shot, roughly the counterpart of "big fucker"), **culero** (asshole), **ese** (guy, the linguistic equivalent of "hey man"), **gabacho** (an Anglo, or white person), **huevon** (lazy person, derived from the image of a man whose testicles [huevos] are huge because he is so lazy), **metiche** (a meddler), **mojado** (an illegal immigrant, literally a "wet one," similar to the English "wetback"), **pendejo** (literally a pubic hair, used to describe a very stupid person), and **ruca** or **ruco** (one's girlfriend or boyfriend).

A party was a **pachanga**, where there might be **mota** (marijuana) or **carga** or **chiva** (heroin). If there was trouble (**pedo**) or fights (**chingasos**) at the party, it might devolve into a total disaster (**desmadre**) and the police (the **chota**) might be called.

Leaving, one often said, **"Ya estufas"**—enough already.

Sources: I spent 12 years of my youth working for Cesar Chavez, and I heard most of this slang on a daily basis. Written sources were *Barrio Language Dictionary: First Dictionary of Calo* by Dagoberto Fuentes and Jose A. Lopez (La Puente, California: Sunburst Enterprises, 1974) and *Regional Dictionary of Chicano Slang* by Dr. Librado Keno Vasquez and Maria Enriqueta Vasquez (Austin: Jenkins Publishing Company, 1975).

I

illin'
Not feeling good about life

in one's crack
Excessively inquisitive about someone else's business, as in "Virginia's driving me crazy—she's totally in my crack about what's going on with Darrell and me."

industrial
Very worthy, reliable

Izod
A preppy

J

jack
Excited

jacked
Happy

jack up
To kick in the rear end

jake
To stand somebody up

jam
To go smoothly

jeek
Stylish

jingus
Bogus

jockin'
Hanging on to your boyfriend

Judy
An overweight girl

juiced
Very excited

juicer
A user of steroids

juke
1. To avoid
2. To hit
3. To dance, to enjoy a party

jungle fever
An attraction between people of different races

junks
Expensive basketball shoes

K

kickers
Shoes

kipe
To steal

L

lardo
A fat person

Trek Talk

A small but vociferous group of young people spent the 1970s lost in *Star Trek*, a futuristic television show which enjoyed far more popularity in syndication in the 1970s than it had during its initial three-year run ending in 1969.

To the general population of young people, *Star Trek* was good for several catch phrases. **Beam me up, Scotty** (uttered by various characters during the show when they wanted to be transported back to the spaceship) could be used anytime that one found oneself in a strange or bizarre situation, while Spock's **"Live long and prosper"** had some currency as a sardonic goodbye. The expressions **beam** and **talk to Scotty** used by crack cocaine users and dealers were derived from *Star Trek*.

True devotees of *Star Trek* developed a broad vernacular of their own.[2] First and foremost, a devotee was not, repeat—not—known as a **Trekkie**. While that term was used extensively by the public at large to describe *Star Trek* fans, it was shunned by serious fans, who preferred and used **Trekker**.

In large part, the language of Trekkers took on the sound and character of clipped military jargon. A Star Trek (ST) convention, an integral part of Trekker life, was known as a **con;** variations spun off that, including **fancon** (a convention organized by fans), **minicon** (a small convention), or **procon** (a convention professionally organized). Similarly, "magazine" was shortened to **zine** (perhaps the earliest use of this clipped slang which surged to the surface of the 1990s underground publication world), which evolved to produce **crudzine** (a shoddy magazine), a **letterzine** (a magazine containing only correspondence), a **newszine** (a magazine containing information but no fiction), or a **prozine** (a slick magazine published by professionals). **Zine** could also serve as a clipped prefix, as in **zined,** a magazine editor.

A Trekker whose focus was on collecting tapes of *Star Trek* episodes was known as a **clipper**. Trekkers as a collective being were known as **fandom;** a brand new fan was a **neofan,** a relatively new fan was a **fifth generation fan,** a famous fan was a **BNF** (big name fan), and the plural of fan was **fen**.

Like all exiles, Trekkers hoped for a return of their show, or revival. They got it.

---

leech
Somebody who won't leave you alone

legal
Twenty-one years old

load
A car

loaf
A fat person

lose it
To lose control or one's poise

loving life *or* **loving it**
In good shape

loxie
A natural blonde. *As in Goldilocks. Contrast with* BOXIE.

lunchin'
Daydreaming, temporarily or permanently. *Derived from "out to lunch."*

machine
A motorcycle

mack
To flirt

melba
Peculiar

mellow out
To calm down. *Despite the indignities heaped upon "mellow" in the 1960s and the scorn which would greet most uses of "mellow" in the 1970s and 1980s, "mellow out" still enjoyed a fairly broad following and was used without*

hint of irony or mocking.

mental
Crazy, weird, strange, peculiar

molded *or* **moldy**
Embarrassed, humiliated

nuke
To destroy

Mickey D's
McDonald's

posse
A group of friends

precious
Dull

psyched
Worked up, elated,
prepared

punt
To give up on. *A foot-
ball expression that
made its way into the
general population's
slang idiom via young
people.*

O

on a mission
Looking for some-
thing

P

party down
To have a good time

perpetrate
To put up a false
front, to pretend

piece
Junk. *Just as World
War II's "sad sack of
shit" became simply
"Sad Sack" in the
comics, so has "piece
of shit" become
"piece."*

pimp *or* **pimp out**
To be cheated

player
Someone who
succeeds in romance

poser
Someone who imitates
the style without
understanding the
substance

Q

quaint
Dull

Drugs

Although the sexual mores of the 1960s spilled over into the 1970s, the drug culture of the hippie movement abated quite dramatically in the 1970s, if not drug use. Marijuana continued to hold its attraction to young America and picked up several new slang names—**alfalfa, bammer, blunt, bone, boom, bud, chronic** (from rap), **doobage** ("doobie" from the 1960s + "-age" as an all-purpose intensifier of the 1970s), **dube, geeba, hooch** (an obvious throwback to the 1920s when the Flapper used *hooch* to refer to prohibited alcohol), **hooter, ned, oz, sens, spleef, tree,** and **tweed.** *Bud* was custom-made for humor based on the Budweiser beer slogan "This Bud's for you." To smoke marijuana was to **bake, blow jaw,** or **smoke a bowl.** To be under the influence of marijuana was to be **baked.**

New to the drug scene in the 1970s was MDMA, known most popularly as **ecstasy.** An amphetamine similar in molecular structure to mescaline, it was made illegal in 1987 under the emergency scheduling powers of the Drug Enforcement Agency. To its devotees, it was also known as **X, E, M** or **Double M.**

Surfing in the Seventies

Fads come and go, and even though mainstream youth somewhat lost sight of the surfing culture in the 1970s and 1980s, the surf culture did not lose sight of itself. To those who surf, surfing is not a fad, but a way of life, and the subculture of surfing continued to flourish despite the Beach Boys' fall from grace and the lack of mainstream focus on surfing. As the subculture flourished, it continued to generate slang. Just as old surfer slang had worked its way into the mainstream, so did some of the newer surfer slang. However, where the surfer slang of the 1960s migrated to popular youth culture largely by the lyrics of songs, the surfer slang of the 1970s was transported into popular youth idiom largely via the San Fernando Valley. **Aggro** (aggressive, an Australian slang word picked up by California surfers), **amped** (overexcited), **dweeb** (a loser or social outcast), **epic** (very good), **full-on** (completely), **gnarly** (good, a term possibly coined at a beach with Monterey cyprus trees and their gnarled roots), and **rad** or **radical** (very good) all worked their way through the Valley into popular slang.

Within the surf subculture itself, **grommet** replaced **gremmie** as the nonderogatory term for a beginning surfer, while **Val** or **Valley** cropped up as a derogatory term for people who live inland. A **shoulder hopper** was someone who cut in front of you on a wave, suggesting that conditions were too crowded, or **zooed out**.

New words were developed to describe ocean conditions. **Barrel** replaced **tube** to describe the hollow part of a curling wave. A **double-overhead** wave was one that was twice as tall as you; huge waves that were as powerful as a Mack truck were said to be **macking,** waves blown over by winds coming into shore were **blown out** or **mushy,** and waves consistently breaking large were **going off**. If the surfing conditions should include any hammerhead sharks, they were called **formula ones**.

Surf boards themselves picked up several new slang words. A **big gun** was a board designed especially for big waves, while a **thruster** was a board with three fins. Although **aqua boot** sounds like a piece of equipment, it in fact meant to vomit in the ocean. New slang words for technique included the **caveman campfire squat** (squatting on the front of a long board with one's hands stretched out in front like warming over a fire), **off the lip** was a maneuver in which the rider surfs to the top of the lip of a wave and then back down again, while **reentry** was to do the same thing, but to leave the wave into the air before returning back down the wave.

Sources: Once again, I relied on Trevor Cralle, author of *Surfin-ary,* in compiling this look at surfing language from the 1970s.

A Dissertation on Regurgitation

Anthropologists of the future who study the slang of the 1970s and 1980s might conclude from the many expressions and terms that describe the act of vomiting that American youth had little time for any activity other than vomiting.

The verbs **blow, lose,** and **toss,** the last two of which were standalone terms for vomiting, spawned a slew of vomit synonyms, including **blow chunks, blow cookies, blow grist, blow lunch, lose it, lose lunch, lose one's groceries, toss cookies, toss groceries,** and **toss tacos.** Similarly, **Ralph** and **Earl** meant to vomit, as did their cousins **call Earl, talk to Earl, talk to Ralph on the big white phone,** and **go to Europe with Ralph and Earl in a Buick. Fred** and **Hughie (call Hughie)** also lent their names to the act. Borrowing terms that had been prominent in earlier generations and coining new terms of their own, they certainly had a rich and varied vocabulary when it came to regurgitation.

The toilet as the receptacle of vomit figured largely in the language of regurgitation. **Bow to the porcelain god, drive the porcelain bus, hug the porcelain god, make love to the porcelain goddess, marry your porcelain mistress, pray to the porcelain god, pray to the enamel god, talk into the porcelain telephone, worship the throne,** and **worship the porcelain god** all meant the same thing, and it was not pretty.

There were a number of miscellaneous expressions (**be to the curb, chew the cheese, chum the fish, decorate your shoes, laugh at the carpet, reverse gears, ride the Buick, sell Buicks, shoot your cookies, spill the blue groceries, spit beef, technicolor yawn, throw donuts, water buffalo,** and **waste groceries**) and then an impressive, graphic-sounding string of single-word synonyms, including **barf, bison, boag, boot, burl, chummy, chunk, hack, spew, spule, wheeze, woof, yak, yank,** and **zuke.**

rack *or* **rack out**
To sleep

rage
To party

raggin'
Well-dressed

raging
A good, fun time

rank
Nauseating

rank out
To back out of a

situation, as in "Joey was going to go with us to the shore, but at the last minute he ranked out."

rat
A devotee, as in "mall rat" or "gym rat"

'rents
Parents. *Originally a 1960s term, still in use in the late 1980s.*

ride
A car

rider
A copycat

rip
A bad deal or cheat. *A clipped form of the 1960s expression "rip off."*

road dog
Your best friend

road trip
A spontaneous drive or walk

rock your world
To beat you up

rocker
Anybody into heavy metal

roll
A fat person

roller
A policeman

rush
To challenge someone aggressively

sagging
A style of wearing one's pants low at the waist, breaking over the shoes

Exclamations!

The clever, pithy, and witty interjection played a major role in the speech of young people in the 1970s and 1980s. Most often, a one-word or two-word rejoinder was quickly thrown back into the conversation, not unlike a game of the dozens toned down for aggression and animosity. So broad-ranging was the lexicon of exclamation that it was nearly possible to carry on an entire conversation constructed of nothing but intensifying interjections. Examples include:

Abuse!
You certainly scored on that last disparaging remark!

Agony!
How vexing!

Basic!
How right you are!

Be real! *or* **Get real!**
You've got to be kidding! Be realistic about this!

Bite me!
Shut up!

Bonus!
Great!

Burn!
I just insulted you in a clever and stinging fashion!

Clamp it!
Be quiet!

Come in Berlin!
Pay attention to what I am saying!

Cool beans!
I'm doing great! *This expression was always used as a response to the question, "How are you?" regardless of the form in which the question was asked.*

Cram it!
I don't care for what you are saying! *An abbreviated "cram it up your ass!"*

Eat chain!
Drop dead! *From "eat a chain saw."*

Eat me!
Shut up!

Face!
That was quite an insult!

False!
I don't believe that what you just said is possible!

Fear!
That's a frightening thought!

For real, even?
Are you serious?

Fuck me hard!
Damn!

Get a grip!
Come to your senses!

Get a life!
Stop pursuing the trivial line of questioning or thinking or speaking in which you are engaged and focus on something

more important! *In 1905, the mocking cry of "Get a horse!" was a popular catch phrase, directed at the newfangled invention of the automobile. In 1958, the Silhouettes had a smash hit "Get a Job," again evocative of the sentiment of this expression.*

Get a room!
Your open sexual activity has crossed the line of acceptable public display of affection!

Get off my jock!
Stop harassing me!

Get up!
Well done!

Get yours!
I hope that you find what you want!

Go for it!
I encourage you in what you are doing!

Good answer!
Cool! *A catch phrase borrowed from* Family Feud, *a television quiz show.*

Good call!
Good thinking! Good

move! *The phrase has an obvious sports origin.*

Happens!
I am sorry to hear that bad news! *Usually uttered with some degree of sarcasm.*

Hard way to go!
Boy, that is bad luck!

Ho!
Great!

I heard that!
I agree with you! I dig!

I'm down!
I agree with you!

It ain't all that!
You are surely exaggerating!

It rules!
It is wondrous!

Mess 'em up!
Good luck!

My bad!
My mistake—sorry! *A playground basketball term that made it off the playground.*

No doubt!
I am in total and ardent agreement with you!

No, duh!
That's obvious!

Not!
What I just said is obviously not true! *Actor/comedian Mike Meyers made "Not!" the interjection of the 1980s and 1990s, but he did not invent the denial-after-the-fact usage. The late Charles Poe, a serious student of vernacular English, found the precise usage made famous in "Wayne's World" in a 1936 novel,* Wind Over the Range.

Pick up your face!
You just did something quite stupid and should consider how you will recover from the gaffe!

Rat on!
I agree with you! *A play on "right on!"*

Roller!
A policeman is coming and you would be advised to stop whatever it is you are doing!

Rude!
What you just said or described is rude! *In the 1992 movie* Buffy the Vampire Slayer, *a chorus of Valley Girl types improve on this with a disdainful "Rude? Much??"*

See ya!
What you just said makes me want to leave!

Shot who?
What did you just say?

Skin it!
Slap my hand! *A variation on "Give me five!"*

Take a picture!
Stop staring at me!

Take it down a thousand!
Calm down!

Wake it!
Pay attention! Wake up!

Whatever.
While I may not agree with what you just said, I do not choose to waste my time arguing with you about it just now.

Wit!
That was a really stupid joke you just told!

Word
An interjection used when you have nothing of substance to say, or—Yes!

Naked!
I agree with you!

The Lively Language of the Deadhead

As the 1960s blurred into the 1970s and eventually the 1980s, at least one relic of the 1960s gathered momentum each year, the Grateful Dead. The Grateful Dead burst onto the psychedelic scene of San Francisco in the mid 1960s, epitomizing the carefree and bemused spirit of the times. Unlike most of the other rock bands of the era, the Grateful Dead did not stop playing. They recorded and toured nearly incessantly until the summer of 1995 when their lead guitarist and spiritual center, Jerry Garcia, died.

Around the Grateful Dead there grew a tribe of devoted followers, known both disparagingly and proudly as **Deadheads**. This group of young people developed a distinct culture and a distinct idiom, which is the subject of a careful and caring book, *Skeleton Key: A Dictionary for Deadheads* by David Shenk and Steve Silberman (New York: Mainstream Books, 1994). Like the Grateful Dead, the vernacular of Deadheads is humorous, clever, and at times self-mocking.

Deadheads drew upon the travels of Ken Kesey and the Merry Pranksters in the 1960s for the metaphor to describe being part of the tribe—you were **on the bus**. A common Deadhead greeting drew upon the lyrics of an oft-played song, **"Hey now!"** Among the several concepts with no direct nomenclature in standard English was the practice of Deadheads of giving something to someone without expectation of an explicit return favor. Deadheads knew this as **to sesh**.

In the parking lot before and after a Grateful Dead concert, Deadheads would gather in **drum circles**. Deadheads, who perhaps had **maxed out** by packing ten people into a single motel room, now dressed in their show clothes, or **dead threads**, would gather around, and different instruments of percussion, swirling dancing, and howls from the crowd blended together. Deadheads in need of a ticket for the concert would ask others for an **extra** or a **miracle** (derived from the song, "I Need a Miracle"). Among their number might be a **wook** or two—extremely hairy hippies who appear to live in the woods and are reminiscent of the hairy wookie character in the *Star Wars* trilogy. There would definitely be a Deadhead or two who had ingested LSD and who was walking around with a **useless smile**.

Each group of friends would designate somebody for **line duty**—waiting in line at general admission concerts for the concert to open. When the doors opened, the **runner** would sprint for the concert floor to stake out good areas for the friends. At reserved seating concerts, you could always **stub down** to better seats by having friends in better seats pass their ticket stubs up to

---

savage
Harshly. *Used as an adverb, as "He was dumped savage."*

scab
An undesirable, unappealing person

scam
1. To lie
2. To flirt

scoff
To obtain, steal, or "borrow." *A benign term, almost a euphemism for "steal."*

scoop
To kiss

scoop on
To flirt with, try to pick up

scope
To look for or at someone or something

scope out
To survey and evaluate something

scrub
A younger person, perhaps a freshman

scum *or* **scumbag**
An undesirable, unappealing person

serious
Intense, powerful

shag
To lift someone off their feet by their underpants

you for your use in getting down to the better seats.

There was a rich vocabulary used to describe a Grateful Dead concert itself. A **breakout** was the first time that the band played a particular song in concert. The transition between songs was known as either a **doorway** (an effortless, subtle passage) or a **splice** (an abrupt leap to the next song). During a song, the band might give a false suggestion that they were about to make a transition to a song; this was a **tease**. When the band played intensely and well, they were, simply put, **hot**.

Deadheads appreciated the different talents of the different band members, and had a vocabulary for each band member. Guitarist Jerry Garcia's guitar-playing techniques included **fanning, scrubbing, the tuck, the machine gun,** and **the butterfly**. When rhythm guitarist Bob Weir dramatically leaned into the crowd at the height of an intense improvisation, it was known as **the lunge**. A particularly loud and powerful bass note or chord played by electric bassist Phil Lesh (whose side of the stage was known as **the Phil Zone**) was a **biscuit** or a **Phil bomb**; Lesh's thunderous bass introduction to the song "The Other One" was known simply as **The Roll**. Percussionists Mickey Hart and Bill Kreutzmann traditionally opened the second set with a percussion session known as **Drums,** in which they explored **The Zone**.

During the concert, some Deadheads (**railrats**) liked to stand as close to the band as possible. Others found a little more room and engaged in **space dancing,** a free form, liquid dance. Still others moved around the concert hall, taking in the show from different perspectives; this practice was known as **swimming**.

A subset of Deadheads obsessively sought to acquire tapes of as many Grateful Dead concerts as possible, be they tapes made from the band's sound board or recorded by fans in the crowd. Tapes are rated by the number of times they have been duplicated since the source tape; each duplication is known as a **gen** (clipped "generation"), and exceedingly clear tapes are **crisp** or **the kills**. The section of the crowd where tapers gathered was known as **the pit**. To tape-record over a previously recorded tape was known as **retreading;** when taping (**spinning**), the moment when one had to change the tape was known as **the flip,** which one tried to time to take place between songs. When somebody said **list,** it was understood that the reference was either to a list of the songs played at a particular concert, including transitions, or a list of concert tapes in one's collection.

After following the Grateful Dead around on tour for several weeks or months, even a tough Deadhead might end up with a case of **road burn**. At the end of the tour, the Deadhead was faced with the task of adapting to the real world again, a process simply known as **reentry**.

shine	**shred**	**skate**	**slime**
To ignore or disregard	To do well.	To avoid one's obligations	A lowlife
	Surf slang that made it mainstream.		
shit list			**smoke**
An imagined list of unpopular things or people	**skanless**	**slaps**	To defeat
	Acting as if better than others, as in	Sandals	
			snake
	"Ever since Adam started going out with	**sleeze**	To steal
shoot hoop	Evie, he's all skanless	An undesirable, unappealing person	
To play basketball	and won't hang out with us anymore."		**snap**
		slim	To break a promise, as in "She said she would stay around,
		Girlfriend	

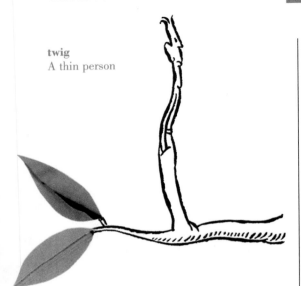

twig
A thin person

squeeze
1. Inadvertent, fluky
2. Romantic partner, as in "main squeeze" and "side squeeze"

stoner
Someone who looks like he or she uses drugs too much

stressing
Losing poise while under a strain

stud
A successful male

suck
To be utterly inadequate, objectionable, or undesirable. *In the 1980s this word still retained some of its sexual taboo, which all but disappeared by the 1990s.*

suck up
To try to curry favor

sucky
Awful

sweat
To give somebody a hard time

swift
Imaginative, intelligent, usually said sarcastically.

swoop on
To make a pass at

take a chill pill
To calm down

talk shit
To emphasize the negative aspects of a situation

tard
Someone who is slow on the uptake. *A clipped "retard."*

team
Dressing in a manner that easily identifies

but at the last minute, she snapped and went off with that rich squid she met at the pool."

so fast
Enthusiastically, as in "I'd go out with her so fast!"

spacing
Not paying attention

spank
To defeat soundly

spazz *or* **spazz out**
To become overexcited and lose one's cool

special
Dull

spent
Money

spikes
Shoes

sprung
Deeply infatuated

Intensified

The 1970s and 1980s were intense decades, and the language of young people reflected this proclivity to intensify. A recurrent theme throughout the language of these decades is the bent to emphasize.

Instead of "very," one could say **butt, fully, full-on, furiously, hella, in a big way, largely, major, tons, too, totally,** or **way.** Disc jockey M. Dung, the morning man on KFOG in San Francisco for much of the 1980s, popularized *way* in several different manners, including "Not that way!" and "A-way!"

Other words and phrases whose purpose in life was to lend severity and fervor to the sentence were **...and a half, factor** (as in "There was a high sleaze factor in the bar so we jammed"), **mode** (a noun that added on to another noun serves as an intensifier, as in "I was in a major heartbreak mode when she dumped me"), **mondo-** (an intensifying prefix), **-fest** (a suffix denoting an abundance of the noun), and **up the ying yang.**

Valley Girl

The distinctive patois of the Valley Girl was a hallmark of the early 1980s. Firmly grounded in the speech patterns of teenage girls from the San Fernando Valley in suburban Los Angeles, Val Speak became a highly visible, oft-mimicked caricature that inspired a handful of fad books.[3]

National exposure to the Valley Girl as cultural icon was due in large part to the uncanny ear of Moon Zappa and her father, the late Frank Zappa, an avant-garde composer. In 1982, Ms. and Mr. Zappa recorded "Valley Girl," a precious pastiche of the language that Ms. Zappa heard when in the malls of the San Fernando Valley. Heavily laced with humor and irony, the song spotlighted a typical Valley Girl waxing eloquently about the shopping joys of the Galleria in Encino, the horrors of a gay English teacher (a **bu-fu,** clipped for *butt-fucker*), a bad experience at a nail salon, and the tribulations of orthodontics.

The vocabulary of the Valley Girl was derived in large part from the slang of surfers; her language consisted of one part vocabulary and one big part attitude—materialistic, jaded, intentionally dim, melodramatic, and heavily sarcastic. She was nothing if not ironic. Completely conscious of her distinctive speech, the Valley Girl in Moon Zappa's song asked, "Whatsa matter with the way I talk?" Her signature phrase was **fer sure,** always spoken with a high level of sarcasm. The same incongruity could be achieved with **I'm sure, I am SO sure,** or **Oh right!** In 1995, she came back to life in a vibrant little movie, *Clueless,* adding **as if** (I don't believe you!) and **Tscha** (Surely you jest!) to her public vocabulary.

Something that pleased the Valley Girl was **awesome, bitchin, cazh** (a clipped "casual"), **gnarly, raspy,** or **tubular**—most surfing slang that Valley surfers took home with them. As was the case with much of the slang of young people in the 1970s and the 1980s, the speech of the Valley Girl was replete with dramatic intensifiers, such as **super-super, totally, to the max,** or **way.** Anything that was not good was **beastie, crill, grisly, grody, grody to the max,** or **ill;** something very disgusting would prompt the exclamation—**Bag it!** Vomit metaphors were prevalent, such as **barf me out** or **gag me with a spoon.**

The Valley Girl and her speech were a fascinating case of life imitating art imitating life. The model of the Valley Girl was firmly based in reality, then subjected to exaggeration and parody; teenage girls who were predisposed to the Valley Girl ethic embraced and built upon the caricature.

As a fad, the Valley Girl faded, not before a forgettable 1983 *Valley Girl* movie starring Nicholas Cage and Deborah Foreman. Because she had sprung from reality, she herself did not fade. Years after she burst onto the scene, she is with us still in the hearts, minds, and speech of young girls.

---

one with a particular group, as in "Simon's just too team with all his Seventy-Sixers gear and his Doctor J. this and Doctor J. that."

teamer
Someone who does not use drugs

thrash
1. To excel at

something
2. To dance

throw down
To foment or inflame an argument

tight
Intimate, close

tight-assed
Uptight in the sixties sense of the word

toast
In big trouble

to the curb
Unbecoming, as in "Linda's all excited about the new dress she bought, but if you ask me, it's strictly to the curb."

tool
1. A fool

2. To do very well

toxic
Surprising

trip
To act like a fool

trippy
Far out

tube *or* **tube out**
To watch television

Disparaged in the 70s and 80s

Youth slang of the later 1970s and the 1980s is brimming with words and expressions roughly meaning to disparage, tease, or criticize harshly. While the hip-hop/rap/black **dis** (clipped "disrespect") was by far the most prominent, other synonyms were to **bag on, burn, bust one's ass, cap, clown, cut, cut down on, cut on, dust, face** (derived from the Asian concept of saving or losing face), **gaff, gouge, haze, jerk, munch on, peg, rag on, slam, slap down,** or **slice up**. An insult was a **bust** or **face**, while to be on the receiving end of things was to **catch flak** or **catch shit**.

tunes
Music of any sort

tweak
To hurt or injure

tweaked *or* **tweaked out**
Inattentive, day-dreaming

tweaker
Someone behaving in an irrational manner

unglued
Angry, out of control

wail
To beat somebody up

waldo
Out of it, as in "That new kid in Biology class is totally waldo—clueless to the max." *Derived from the popular Where's Waldo picture books of the 1980s, where the object is to find Waldo, a nerd, in a busy and complicated picture.*

wanked out
Fatigued

wanna-be
Someone who strives to be something else or act like someone else

waver
A new-wave teen who is into the post-punk club scene

wench
Girlfriend

whack
A jerk

whacked
Crazy, messed up

winks
Sleep

wonk
Someone who is devoted to one discipline to the detriment of living a real life

woof
To boast

work
To defeat

wrap
A girlfriend

wreck
To fight

wuss
A coward, a weakling

yen
Money

yoked
Very athletic

zels
Pretzels

zone
To daydream to an extreme

zoo
Any crowded or confused situation

You Say Good-bye and I Say Hello

Salutations and farewells are often fertile ground for slang, probably because the first and last words exchanged are important areas for establishing and affirming coolness. The 1970s and 1980s were no exception.

Greetings fell into two categories. First was the simple exclamation. "Hi" was too simple; instead there was **Hey!** or **Yo!**, a traditional greeting among Italian-Americans in South Philadelphia that was made famous by Sylvester Stallone in the movie *Rocky* and then embraced by the language of the hip-hop culture. Hip-hop inspired variations used outside the small inner circle of hip-hop included **Yo, homes!** and **Yo, G!**

The second type of greeting was the question, the functional equivalent of "how are you?" and "what is new?" Variations on the ever-popular **What's happening?** included what sounded like **Sappnin'?** or **Zappenin'?**, while **what's up** sounded like **Buzza?, S'up?, Wassup?,** or **Zup?**. Other greetings were **How do?, What it is?,** and the less dramatic but ubiquitous **What's shaking?**

When it came time to say **Sko** (let's go), young people of the 1970s and 1980s had a broad range of words to use instead of simply "leave." Verb synonyms included **bail, beat feet,**

blaze, blow, blow this joint, blow this popsicle stand, blow this taco stand, bolt, boogie, book, book it, break camp, disco (one would have to assume that this term was an updated "boogie"), **haul buggy, haul ass, honk on, jet, matriculate, motivate, motorvate, roll out, slide, split, step off, truck,** and **vamp**.

Good-byes included **Awright den, Catch you later, Check you, Chill with you later, Hasta** (from the Spanish "hasta luego" or "hasta la vista," popularized in the movie *The Terminator*), **I'm history, Later dude!, Peace!,** or simply **See ya!**

The Gay Vernacular

The early 1970s saw a great leap out of the closet for homosexual America, led by young homosexual America. As young gays built communities in cities throughout the country, they quickly fashioned and acquired a considerable gay vocabulary. Until the early 1970s, the gay world and gay language were dominated by adults. It was not until the urban gay surge of the 1970s that young gays found a community, their voice, and a language. Without a community, there can be no slang. With the community came a bountiful slang; both were glorified by Lou Reed in "Walk on the Wild Side," with the emergence of the **sugar plum fairy** as icon.

Gay speech relied in part on the slangy and dramatic use of adjectives borrowed from standard English; **brilliant, clever, divine, elegant, flawless, gallant, ravishing, royal, smart, sweet, tacky,** and **tasty** all took on a sarcastic slang edge to their meaning. Exclamations, such as **Baby discovers!** (said when somebody figures something out or finds something they like) or **God help us all and Oscar Wilde!** played an important role in the gay vernacular. Gossip too was an important part of the gay social fabric, either in person or by the **sewer line** (the telephone, used for gossip).

Another homosexual was known as an **auntie** (usually an older homosexual), **belle, boy** (usually used in the plural), **broad, femme, nelly, fluff, flamingo** (an elegant dresser), **freak, girl, himmer, honest girl** (an open homosexual), **kid** (usually used in the plural), **man's man, miss,** or **natural**. A new, young arrival to the gay scene, perhaps staying at the **French embassy** (the YMCA, fertile grounds for gay youth), was a **candy kid, canned goods, fresh fruit, new**

Word History: Bodacious

Bodacious enjoyed two huge bursts of favor in youth slang in the 1980s thanks to the movies, first in 1982-1983 after release of *An Officer and a Gentlemen* with its catchy if lurid expression "bodacious ta-ta's" (impressive, large breasts) and then again in 1989 with *Bill and Ted's Excellent Adventure* in which Keanu Reeves and Alex Winter perfect dude-speak, relying in a very catchy way on *bodacious*.

Bodacious (an intensifying combination of *boldly* + au*dacious*) got its start in life as the adverb *bodaciously* with an earliest recorded usage of 1832. It has a definite homespun ring to it, and in fact in the preface of the *Sketches of David Crockett* in 1833 one finds this passage: "I cannot regale you with the delicate repast of a constant repetition of the terms bodyaciously, teetotaciously, obfisticated, etc."

Eleven years later, in 1843, it first appeared as an adjective, signifying "complete and thorough." *Bodaciously* (at times spelled *bardaciously, bidaciously, bodyaciously, boldacious,* or

boudaciously) enjoyed great popularity for about ten years, capturing the public's imagination as a word worthy of the migration west.

By the 1870s, use dropped off considerably. In the 1930s, *bodacious* crept into Harlem jive as *bardacious* (*Literary Digest*, Volume 124, No. 21, page 30, December 4, 1937) and, probably more importantly, into the speech of Snuffy Smith in the *Barney Google* comic strip by Billy DeBeck. It remained, though, a quaint Southern expression, charming and amusing in a provincial way, the type of word that caption writers would use with a picture and headline—"Hill Billy Aims To Keep Bride, 12—[a couple] who think her fibbin' about her age being 16 so they could get married is just bodacious" (*San Francisco Examiner*, July 5, 1938).

In the late 1950s, the copy writers for Phantasy Records dug up *bodacious* in an advertisement for Lenny Bruce, whom they described as Bodacious, Loquacious, Audacious, Sagacious, and Tenacious (BLAST).

In 1973, *bodacious* made a bid at a comeback when Martin Balin, formerly of the Jefferson

ground, or **untried.** One's **Adam** was his first male sexual partner, while to **change your luck** was to take a black lover for the first time.

Before the days of AIDS and safe sex, it was not uncommon to search graffiti on bathroom walls (the **menu**) for names and telephone numbers of potential encounters, perhaps to take back to one's **cage** (a dismal apartment). To **advertise** was to wear seductive clothing, while to **cancel the act** was to break a date. A **ballad** or **commercial** was a flimsy, tired excuse, and **wet lashes** were the morose details of a melancholy story. In the early 1970s, the police were very much a problem, and were known by a rich variety of slang names, including **Lilly** and **Alice.**

In response to a simple greeting of "hi," the clever retort was **Higher.** There were many good-byes, none more eloquent than **Toodles.**

Sources: C.J. Scheiner of Brooklyn furnished me with a copy of *Gay Girl's Guide to the U.S. & the Western World* (third edition, privately printed in the 1950s), which contains a bright little glossary. Madeline Kripke of the East Village found me a copy of *The Queen's Vernacular: A Gay Lexicon* by Bruce Rodgers (San Francisco: Straight Arrow Books, 1972). As I reread Rodgers, I am always struck by just how fine a compilation it is, one of the best slang dictionaries of the 20th century. Other valuable sources for gay slang include G. Legman's "The Language of Homosexuality: An American Glossary" in *Sex Variants: A Study of Homosexual Patterns* (New York: Paul B. Hoeber, 1941); *The Guild Dictionary of Homosexual Terms,* with an introduction by Dr. Albert Ellis (Washington: Guild Press, Ltd., 1965); and *Gay (S)language* by H. Max (Austin: Banned Books, 1988).

Airplane, launched a short-lived new band known as Bodacious. The band never caught on, and use of the term withered. After a strong but parochial appearance in CB trucker lingo between 1975 and 1977 meaning a clear radio signal, *bodacious* finally made the big time again thanks to the silver screen. Today, it survives as either a cultural reference to "bodacious ta-ta's" in *An Officer and a Gentlemen* or as a parody of dude speech.

Word History: Dude

Dude has raged within youth slang since the early 1980s, egged on by the Teenage Mutant Ninja Turtles, Jeff Spicoli (of *Fast Times at Ridgemont High*), Bill and Ted (of *Bill and Ted's Excellent Adventure*), Wayne and Garth (of the "Wayne's World" sketch on *Saturday Night Live*), and comedian/actor Pauly Shore. *Dude* has an astonishing range, acting both as a synonym for "guy" or "fellow" and as a verbal filler in the same class as "like," "he's all," or "you know?" From the school playground to twentysome-

thingers, where would youth slang of the 1980s and 1990s be without *dude*?

Dude is, of course, no neophyte, newcomer, or novice. As a piece of American slang, it has seen a startling number of births and deaths, rising from the ashes with new meaning. *Dude*'s first incarnation came in the late 1870s and early 1880s when it came to mean a man extremely fastidious in dress and manner, a dandy, fop, or swell. The etymology for this incarnation is less murky than many, with the apparent source being *dud,* an English cant word for an article of clothing (and the apparent source of duds for clothes). In the August 2, 1941, issue of *The Saturday Evening Post,* Booth Tarkington described the original dude as "marked particularly by the extreme height of his round white cylinder of a collar, by the spoon-shaped crown of his hard hat, by his razor-pointed hoses, by the flare of the skirts of his Chesterfield black frock coat, by the shortness of his fawn overcoat, and, above all, by such tightness of his trousers that no one could explain how he got his feet through them."

Heavy Metal

In the 1960s, many streams converged into the river of rock and roll. In the 1970s, the river of rock and roll split into many streams. One such stream was **heavy metal;** in the late 1970s, the expression, which was coined by William Burroughs in *Naked Lunch* and then popularized in the 1968 song "Born to Be Wild" by Steppenwolf ("heavy metal thunder"), was applied to a form of rock and roll which theretofore had been known simply as **metal**. The music in question is loud, ponderous, and dense. In *Rockspeak!* (London: Omnibus Press, 1983), Tom Hibbert describes the prototypical heavy metal lead singer as "clad usually in tight trousers of velvet or leather material," growling lyrics that can be characterized as either "macho-sexual" or "mytho-militaristic."

Within heavy metal were several sub-species, including **speed metal** (very fast music, such as Anthrax and early Metallica), **thrash metal** (very fast music with angrier lyrics and a meaner sound than speed metal), **death metal** (not as fast as speed or thrash, but more angst-ridden, often dealing with Satan or sodomy), and **doom metal** (slower music, very gloomy, dealing with the darker side of life).

The young attracted by heavy metal were nearly all white, nearly uniformly suburban, and predominantly male. They were known as **headbangers, heshers,** or **metalheads;** a **Motorheadbanger** was a devoted Motorhead fan. **Up the Irons!** was a common greeting or simple exclamation between devoted Iron Maiden fans. Superlatives favored by headbangers include **hostile** (used in a shout of approval, as "Yeah, fuckin' HOSTILE!"), **rude,** and **brutal**.

A heavy metal concert was definitely an audience-participation event. The performers would often **stage-dive,** leap off the stage into the crowd, while concertgoers could **crowd-surf** (lie on your back and be passed overhead through the crowd). Most concertgoers would **headbang** or **bang** (smash your head up and down to add to the enjoyment of fast music), often resulting in **whiplash** after the concert—"Dude, the show was killer but I really got whiplash."

At a concert, **moshing** is a big-time activity—running around, often **rotted** (intoxicated), and crashing into other people doing the same thing within a circular area, the **mosh pit**. At times this was also referred to as **thrashing** or **slam dancing,** but these terms were found more at punk shows. After a concert you were likely to have a ringing in your ears known as **concert-ring;** no complaints though, for there was a ready-made reply to complaints about loud music—If it's too loud, you're too old.

To the **headbanger** in search of love, **grids** were breasts, often modified by **excellent** in a slangy sense. A **hagmeyer** was, as the word suggests, an unattractive girl. A complete jerk was a **ted,** while someone who ran out of partying energy too early was simply a **sniveler**. A **skid** was an out-of-date, out-of-fashion fan, wearing outdated tee-shirts and out-of-style pants.

Sources: Many of these terms were provided by Berkeley metalhead Seamus O'Reilly; others were gathered from the pages of *Rolling Stone*

In the late 19th century, *dude* was born again, this time as a city dweller unfamiliar with life on the range, especially an Easterner in the West. The dude became a predictable character in the western tales of Mark Twain, Bret Harte, Artemus Ward, Owen Wister, and Zane Grey, as well as the epics of Hopalong Cassidy and other celluloid cowhands. While newer uses have come, the tenderfoot meaning of *dude* remains strongly implanted in American vernacular.

In the late 1930s, *dude* began another metamorphosis, evolving into a synonym for "guy." In the *They'll Do It Every Time* comic strip of February 23, 1939, the brother calls out to his exhausted sister, "Hey, Sis! Some dude here on the phone wants to talk to you." According to Richard A. Hill of Taylor University, author of "You've Come a Long Way, Dude" in *American Speech*, Volume 69, Number 3 (Fall 1994), railway workers began to use *dude* to refer to conductors, soldiers began to use *dude* to refer to fresh recruits, and pachuco youth in Mexican-American barrios began to refer to each other as *dude*.

Dude's next big move was in the slang idiom of the surfer community. It was a basic component of surfer slang, used as a term of address or as a descriptive noun applied to a fellow surfer. It was one of the major surfer contributions to hippie dialect in the late 1960s and 1970s, serving as a slangy, inside synonym for "guy," usually prefaced by "some" or "this" or "hey."

Never quite dying out in the 1970s, *dude* resurfaced with a vengeance in the 1980s, both meaning "guy" and serving as an all-purpose intensifier. It is a word with an attitude, a word that could mock itself and avoid marginalization.

Word History: Humongous

Humongous was a big, if not humongous word for the young of the 1970s, graphically and vividly and intensely conveying implications of immense size, of unexpected Swiftian proportions. It is clearly a synthetic word, perhaps forged through a blend of *huge + monstrous*, but what of its synthesis?

It was first recorded by three senior linguistics majors at Brown University who during the 1967-1968 school year conducted a large-scale study of slang in use at 18 universities. In 1968 they published the results of their study, which was designed by Professor W. Nelson Francis, as *College Undergraduate Slang Study*. Included within the 227-page glossary of words collected

Booty-Coot— You know, Sex!

The sexually "liberating" ethos of the late 1960s defined the 1970s and the early 1980s, when lax attitudes towards sex were confronted with the AIDS epidemic and a reaction of mores. The youth slang vocabulary involving sex (**booty** or **coot**) was prolific.

Desperate for sex? You were **wretched**—a clever application of standard English. An erection, known to past generations as a *hard-on* or *boner*, was a **woody**, again conveying a graphic physical image. Sexually suggestive clothes or boots were **C.F.M.**—come fuck me.

Cutting to the chase, to engage in sexual intercourse was often described in verbally aggressive slang. Synonyms for the most taboo of verbs were to **boff, boink, bone** (male usage), **boost, bump, do the do, do the wild thing, do the nasty, do the deed, dog, G, gash, get busy, get together, grind, hose** (male usage), **hound, jab** (male usage), **jump her/his bones, lay pipe** (male usage), **plug** (male usage), **pole** (male usage), **prod** (male usage), **rout, scrap, square the circle, stick** (male usage), **thump, womp on,** or **work**. Oral sex performed on a boy was **giving cone**, while a girl who engaged in serial sex with different boys in a single session was taking part in a **bunch punch**. On the "safe" side, a condom was a **party hat**.

Doing Nothing

The young of the 1970s and 1980s had a number of ways to describe the act of doing nothing with friends. To **cold chill, hang, hang out, jell** (a modern-sounding term first recorded in the early 1930s at the University of Missouri), **jell out, kick it, lamp** (the word suggests that it derived from the very urban visual image of young people congregating around a lamp post), **veg**, and **veg out** all meant to loaf with friends. And to think of all those years with nothing more than "hang out" to describe what we were doing!

one finds *humongous,* defined simply as "a great deal (of something)."

Humongous lay low for several years, next appearing in the May 23, 1973 issue of the *Denver Clarion,* the student newspaper at the University of Denver. As the 1970s moved towards the 1980s, *humongous* gained a little momentum. It was used in an advertisement in the *Miami Herald* on February 15, 1975; it was noticed by L. M. Boyd in his syndicated Answer Man column on June 16, 1978, as the "newest word in the English language"; it was discussed in the *Baltimore Sun* on August 9, 1978; and it worked its way into *Time* on December 4, 1978.

While humongous never achieved Slang God status, it was a catchy and appealing word, from the Davey Crockett "more syllables is more better" school of wordsmithing. It is still heard today, especially among younger slang speakers who cannot resist the way the syllables just roll off the tongue.

Word History: Like, Part Two

When last spotted in the 1950s, *like* had undergone two separate assaults, first on its status as a preposition ("Winston tastes good, like [not as?] a cigarette should") and then as meaningless verbal filler in the speech of hipsters and Beats. In the 1970s and 1980s, full-scale warfare was on, with *like* plunged into three more battles.

One onslaught on *like* was to make it an adjective meaning "approximately," as in "He was, like 50 years old."

A second converted it into what linguists call a discourse marker. In this sense, *like* serves no grammatical function, but instead affects the meaning of what is said in an intrusive, ungrammatical fashion. As a discourse marker, *like* focuses attention; it can intensify ("He's, like, pissed off"), soften ("I'm, like, sorry that I'm late"), distance the speaker and avoid forthrightness through hedging ("Would you, like, go to the movies with me on Saturday?"), and add irony ("I'm like totally surprised!").

A further transmutation produced what is known as the quotative *like.* Used only in the present tense, it provides a perfect barrier of blurred vagueness. When a girl says, "So then Darren's all like—I don't want to see her anymore," she may have used *like* to preface a direct quote, a paraphrase, or a projection of what the person was thinking. Because the quotative *like* does not always precede a direct quote, it is not a substitute for the verb "say"; instead, it provides a stream-of-consciousness toggle switch between direct and indirect quotation, between thought and speech, between objective and subjective, and between real and perceived—the ultimate 20th century speech mechanism.

Sources: I, like, relied on "Like is, Like Focus" by Robert Underhill, *American Speech* (1988); "For Teenspeak, Like Another Meaning for the Multipurposeful Like" by Richard Bernstein in the *New York Times* of August 25, 1988; "It's, Like, Totally Unnecessary, But It's, Like, So Totally Versatile" by Malcolm Gladwell in the *Washington Post* of May 18, 1992; and "The word that is, like, everywhere" by Kate Kelly in *USA Today* of May 27, 1992. I also live among many who, like, like *like*.

Slang of the Aloha State

Young people in Hawaii have their own slang, which came of age in the 1970s and 1980s. In Hawaii, the cultures and languages of China, Japan, the Philippine Islands, Portugal, and Samoa converge with native Hawaiian and American English of the mainland. The result is a spirited, vivid, and slang-driven Pidgin.

Leaving aside the loan words from other languages, the localized pronunciations (**An' den?** [and then?], **any kine** [anything], **ass why** [that's what], **da** [the], **dat** [that], or **dem** [them]), and the Pidgin constructions (**across** for across from, **already** for yet, **anybody** for everybody, **before-time** for earlier, **below of** for below, **but** used at the end of sentence in place of though, **like** for want, **good** for very, etc.), Hawaiian youth enjoyed a rich body of English-based slang.

Common greetings were variations on mainland greetings of the time—**Howzit?**, **Wha's da haps?**, or **Woddascoops?** Likewise, when it is time to **bag,** the parting of **Easy!** is a cool cousin of "take it easy."

Beyond greetings, the most indispensable words of Pidgin slang were **brah** (brother, good friend, roughly akin to the African-American *bro'*), **da kine** (an all-purpose, all-meaning expression), and **shaka** (right on!). **Shaka, brah!** migrated from Hawaii into mainland surfer slang, but no further.

Several commonly used adjectives show just how expressive good slang can be—**had-it** (tired), **lack** (without refinement or without money, or without both), **nails** (not good), **pumpin'** (going strong), and **safe** (not cool). A very cool guy was a **jammer,** while just any guy was a **buggah**. To do anything risky or naughty was to **catch thrills,** to do anything fast was to **run speed limit,** to fight was to **scrap,** while to relax was to **coast.** To date without going steady was **tripping,** while to have sex was **poking squid,** a vivid and explicitly vulgar expression used by boys away from the hearing of girls, or at least girls whose squid they entertained any hope of poking.

To talk about somebody or something in a disparaging fashion was to **talk stink,** while the **stink eye** was an entirely disapproving look. A customary argument-ending rebuke was simply **You know da rules.**

Sources: *Da Kine Talk: From Pidgin to Standard English in Hawaii* by Elizabeth Ball Carr (University Press of Hawaii, 1972) is a scholarly but caring work that focuses on the Pidgin aspects of colloquial speech in Hawaii. *Peppo's Pidgin to da Max* (Honolulu: Peppovision, 1981) and *Peppo's Pidgin to da Max Hana Hou!* (Honolulu: Peppovision, 1982) are love songs to the multicultural, multilingual slang of Hawaiian youth. While perhaps lacking in scholastic rigor, they are fine, affectionate, and spirited indigenous efforts.

Word History: Punk

When punk rock came onto the scene in 1976 and with it the punk scene, a venerable old slang word was given new life.

Historically, *punk* has been one of the more versatile slang words in the language. In *Words: A Connoisseur's Collection of Old and New, Weird and Wonderful, Useful and Outlandish Words* (New York: Delacorte Press, 1982), Paul Dickson devotes an entire chapter to *punk*, coming up with no less than 43 different slang definitions of *punk*, not counting *punk* derivations. Major slang meanings attached to *punk* in the past include bread, a homosexual (especially a young boy attached to an older homosexual), a young animal, and a beginner at a task or job.

In the late 1940s and early 1950s, *punk* took on a special meaning when applied to a teenager—it meant trouble. With the rise in juvenile delinquency all across the United States after World War II, the country needed a word to describe the hoodlums; *punk* answered the call, and served admirably in headlines:

"55 Peninsula Teeners Open Anti-Punk Drive: Burlingame High School Boys Vote to Look Like Gentlemen, Not Hoodlums" (San Francisco News, February 22, 1950)

"Punk Forays Must be Promptly Reported" (San Francisco News, March 16, 1950)

"Punks Caught Robbing Safe: Hoodlums Renewing Attacks on Teeners" (San Francisco News, April 14, 1950)

Tank Time!

It was always **tank time** (time to drink) somewhere, time for **the doctor** (alcohol) or a **frosty** (a beer). Young Americans returned to alcohol with a passion in the 1970s and 1980s. To describe their bouts with alcohol, they had a slang vocabulary both old and new.

To drink was to **catch a buzz, catch a load, catch one, chug** (to drink without pause), **crack some suds, do shots** (to drink hard liquor by the shot glass), **hammer, pop tops, pound beer** (to CHUG beer), **shotgun** (to drink a can of beer through a hole in the bottom), **sip suds, slam, swill,** or to **tip back.** In a case of reverse migration, a drug word from the 1960s, *bong*, was resurrected in the context of alcohol; a **beer bong** was a device consisting of a funnel attached to a tube for rapid (a) consumption of beer and (b) intoxication. A **hairball** was an obnoxious drunk.

The slang idiom for drunk was wide and deep, often playing on a theme of destruction. **Basted, blasted, blind, blitzed, blitz-krieged, blotto, blown, blown out, brewed, crazy, crushed, faced, fried, fucked, gone, hammered, heated, hurting, juiced, keyed, laid out, lit, locked, looped, messed up, obliterated, outta hand, pickled, pissed, planted, plastered, plowed, polluted, ripped, shit-faced, shredded, slammed, sloshed, smashed, snockered, tanked, thrashed, toasted, totaled, trashed, tweaked, twisted, under the table, wasted, whipped, wiped out, woofy, wrecked,** and **zooed** all meant more or less intoxicated. Many of these words were used by earlier generations of young people when they spoke of being intoxicated—**fried, juiced, plastered, polluted,** and **tanked** were all used by the Flapper when she indulged in too much bootleg liquor—and many of the other adjectives still in use in the 1970s and 1980s were regularly used in the 1950s and 1960s.

The late 1970s and 1980s were a time of drinking games, including **Caps** (players throw bottle caps into glasses), **Categories** (players must take turns naming items in a chosen classification), **Hi Bob!** (played while watching the *Bob Newhart Show* on television, everyone takes a drink every time that an actor says, "Hi Bob!"), **Quarters** (varying rules, generally involving players bouncing quarters off the table into a shot glass), and **Thumper** (each player has a different made-up name to which he or she must respond when called).

Skateboarding: Early Years

After a first incarnation as a brief but intense fad in 1964 and 1965, skateboarding ebbed. The introduction of the polyurethane wheel by Frank Nasworthy in 1973 breathed new life into skateboarding, which boomed in 1974 and which has not looked back since. In the two-plus decades since skateboarding's resurgence, a robust culture has built around the skateboard, largely consisting of white, middle-class boys. To them, the skateboard is not just mobility, it is a way of life, a tribe with its own dress code, tastes in music, and slang.

Many skateboarding (also known as **plank riding**) terms were borrowed directly from surfing—**coffin** (riding lying on one's back), **geek** (an awkward skateboarder), **goofy-footing** (right foot forward), **gremmie** (a young, inexperienced skateboarder), **hodad** (a novice), **hotdogging** (high-profile, trick-oriented riding), **kamikaze** (a risky position for riding), **nose** (the front of the skateboard), **pearling** (falling off the board), **radical** (demanding, intense terrain), **stoked** (excited), and **wipe out** (a bad spill).

A number of slang terms were developed for skateboarding technique. **Body cranking** or **body tacking** refers to twisting the body to increase one's speed. **Doing a run** is to ride a long distance without falling or stopping, while **gliding** is to ride in a straight direction, with few or no turns. **Pool riding**—skateboarding in an empty swimming pool—was always fun; if a pool was not available, skateboarders looked for **moguls** (a ski term), small rounded bumps to skate up and down. To ride **daffy** was to straddle between two boards, to **catamaran** was to ride with a friend on two boards, facing each other and linked with legs and hands connected, and a **bunny hop** or **frog jump** was a small leap of board and rider off the ground, achieving an **ollie** (completely aerial situation). Using the **kick** (a raised tail) on the board, a rider might try a **wheelie** (lifting the front wheels off the ground); more experienced riders might try a **heelie**, lifting the rear wheels off the ground. To stop the board, a rider uses a **toe tap**, repeatedly touching the toes of one foot to the ground. A rider who knows exactly how to negotiate a given course is said to **have it wired**.

What if things go wrong, perhaps as a result of the **wobblies** or **wobs** (intense vibrations while going fast)? To **chew it** is to fall off the board, as a result of which one can expect a **bongo** (bruise or injury) or at least **road rash** (scraped skin).

Sources: I relied on Trevor Cralle's skateboarding files, the Tamony archives, and the glossaries in *The Skateboarder's Bible* by Albert Cassorla (Philadelphia: Running Press, 1976) and *The Complete Book of Skateboarding* by Laura Torbet (New York: Funk and Wagnalls, 1976).

"Collier's Article Discusses S.F.'s Punk Problems" (*San Francisco News*, April 21, 1950)

"Pro-Red Adults Blamed for Punk Gang Violence" (*San Francisco News*, May 9, 1950)

"East Bay Punk: Hall of Justice Escaper Identified" (*San Francisco News*, September 16, 1954)

After this brush with the wrong side of the law, *punk* eased back into its historical role, used by the young as a playground taunt and waiting in the wings for the Sex Pistols et al. Oddly enough, though, the term *punkrock* or *punk* as applied to a style of rock and roll was in place and ready well before Sid Vicious and Johnny Rotten shocked the world in 1976, as evidenced by the following:

...especially those with an ear for the nice-wrought mainstream punk raunch and snidely clever lyrics. (*Rolling Stone*, April 15, 1971)

The Punk Scene

The Punk Movement took hold in London in the summer of 1976 and by 1978 had worked its way to the United States. Highly visible and heavy on outrage, it ultimately had a minimal effect on popular youth culture at large. While the fashion (spiked hair known as **liberty spikes,** often dyed bright colors, body piercing, thug clothing and boots, and highly noticeable tattoos or **tats**), lifestyle (living in warehouses or squatting in abandoned buildings, often resorting to **dumpster diving** for food), and music (loud, harsh, clashing, often atonal or off-tune) were big on anger and shock value, most young people never got closer to the punk scene than the postcard of flagrant and flamboyant punks that someone sent home from London or New York.

The language of the punk community (the **scene**) was not without its vivid moments; it simply does not appear to have had much luck in influencing the vernacular of mainstream youth.

Within the punk movement, **hardcore** was almost synonymous with *punk*. The hardcore punk was the American 1980s version of the punk, trend-conscious and correctly dressed (as punk dressing went). **Skins** (clipped "skinheads," a term used in the *San Francisco Chronicle* as early as 1965) were an integral part of the punk scene; while most of the racist, anti-Semitic element of the punk scene were skins, by no means were most skins anti-Semitic racists. A **lounge lizard** was a young person whose life revolved around the alternative, punk night club scene. This seemingly modern word was commonly used by Flappers in the 1920s to mean a well-dressed ladies' man. After 60 years, the word was dusted off, given a new meaning, and revived. **Bag lords** were at the other end of the punk scene—punks who scrounged food from dumpsters. A **chickie broad** was a woman who was not part of the scene; **lolla-lucka** was a term used in place of "motherfucker."

Music was a large part of the punk scene. A concert was a **show,** always a show and never a concert. The quasi-ceremonial, violent-looking, fervent male-dominated style of dancing at a punk show was known as **thrashing** and **slam dancing**. Further thrills were possible with **stage diving,** the practice of running across the stage at a show and flinging oneself into the audience. Poor musicianship was known as **scats**.

Probably the most popular drug within the punk scene was methedrine; those who advocated staying away from methedrine were known as the **straight edge** movement. To say that someone was **amped** meant that they were acting in a bizarre fashion, either due to a personality quirk or amphetamines. If you had enough **billys** (money), you could rent a **drum** (an apartment). If you were feeling melancholy, you were feeling **bumly**.

Sources: Primary sources for the language of the punk scene are *Modern English: A Trendy Slang Dictionary* by Jennifer Blowdryer [Waters] (Last Gasp, 1985); *The Philosophy of Punk: More Than Noise* by Craig O'Hara (AK Press, 1995); and *Street Style* by Ted Phlemus (Thames and Hudson, 1994).

...and in that respect *Grand Funk* may have performed quite a symbolic act, seeing as the spirit of American punk rock certainly lives on in GFRR (if in erratic amounts).... (*Rolling Stone,* January 6, 1972)

...they take the spirit rather than the sound of fifties rock as their inspiration—particularly the Dionysiac illiteracy of Jerry Lee Lewis and Little Richard. "Punk-rock" has become the favored term of endearment. (*New Yorker,* December 9, 1972)

Punk-rock is a fascinating genre: Getting into it requires endless hours at flea markets and junk stores, but when the reward is some apex of vinyl mania like "Voices Green and Purple" by the Bees you don't complain. Punk-rock at its best is the *closest we came in the Sixties to the original rock-abilly spirit of rock & roll. (Rolling Stone, January 4, 1973)*

...[of] the Tubes plays very good guitar and synthesizer-dominated rock that varies from punk to heavy metal to avant-spacey. (Rolling Stone, November 20, 1975)

When the punk scene caught fire in London in the summer of 1976, punk was in the wings, ready, willing, and able. By the fall of 1976, punk was seeing duty describing the new scene— "Punks are greasers with art" (New York, September 20, 1976).

Today the punk survives to some limited degree, providing an identity for a small number of young people, enough though that the term *punk* has retained its 1976 meaning 20 years later.

* * *

[1]In the quite amusing *Stuck in the Seventies* (Chicago: Bonus Books, 1991), Scott Matthews and his fellow authors reflect on the slang of the 1970s: "We apologize for the constantly overused words 'wicked' and 'cool.' We tried to add variety to our adjectives, we really did. But we failed."

[2]The language of *Star Trek* was the sole focus of M. J. Fisher's *The Strekfan's Glossary of Abbreviations and Slanguage* (Toledo, Ohio: Kzinti Press, 1976) and "Star Trek Lives:

The Winners and...

The social outcast, he who was hopelessly out of step with current fashions and trends, the misfit— the Loser—could be described in any number of ways, as an **assface, asswipe, Barney** (an allusion to Barney Rubble, a lovable but dimwitted character on the *Flintstones*), **boofa, bub, cadet, cheesehead, dexter, dickweed, dickwad, dildo, dink, dipstick, dirtball, doofus, dork, duck, dweeb, fetus, full hank, geek, gimp, goob, goober, goose, lop, McFly** (from a character in the movie *Back to the Future*), **narc, spud, squid,** or **twink**.

Adjectives for the person who was out of date, out of fashion, or just plain out of it included **bunk, cheesy, cob, diseased, gay** (curiously divorced of any reference to sexual orientation), **lame, punk, sick, tacky, uncool,** and **weak**.

Over in the stupid department were the **airhead, arbuckle** (probably from the not-too-bright character in the *Garfield* comic strip), **ditz, doughhead, gourd, gumby** (after the animated clay figure in the children's television show of the 1950s, reintroduced to a new generation through Eddy Murphy's comedy skits on *Saturday Night Live*), **hubba,** and **twit**. They weren't stupid, they were just **ditzy** (absent-minded) or **queer** (like "gay," often used in contexts having nothing to do with sexual orientation).

The Slang Yack of the Computer Hack

In the later 1970s and the 1980s, a vibrant subculture grew up around computers. As dehumanizing as computers may seem or be, the culture of **hackers** (an amorphous, not easily defined word—a clever computer person) was one of the most animated and dynamic, if idiosyncratic and odd, of the era. Largely male, entirely brilliant and most often obsessive, hackers developed an entire society and a considerable idiom. Their language was dominated by jargon, but there was a strong element of clever, sardonic, and allusive slang and slangy jargon to it.

Slang played an important role when it came to describe failure and success. An assortment of words were applied in a negative sense, including **blechterous** (disgusting), **disgustitude** (the state of being disgusted; a playful construction similar to **barfulation** or **barfulous,** both of which refer to disgusting situations), **vanilla** (standard and boring), **bogus** (nonfunctional because of a poor design feature; this word evolved into the noun **bogosity**), **bad** (broken because of design), **casters-up mode** (broken), **crufty** (poorly built), **demented** (poorly designed), **fried** (not functioning because of a hardware failure), **gedanken** (not thought out well, from the German *gedanken*—thought), **gnarly** (enigmatic and intricate), **hosed** (not functioning), **interesting** (bothersome, arduous, or both), **obscure** (not easily understood), **pessimal** (as bad as things get, the worst case scenario), **tanked** (not functioning), **trivial** (easily worked out), **uninteresting** (subject to being solved simply by dedication of resources or, if solved, not helpful), and **wonky** (broken). When a computer froze up in its operations, it was said to be **catatonic, hung,** or **wedged.** A program or computer that ran slowly was said to **chug, grind,** or **grovel.**

On the good side of the page was **cuspy** (exciting), **clean** or **elegant** (simple yet profoundly clever), **fine** (not quite as exciting as *cuspy*), **funky** (works in a quirky way, best left untouched), **infinitely fine** (very good), **flavorful** (pleasing), **insanely great** (so good that only the best minds could appreciate how great), **moby** (large, complicated, and awe-inspiring, derived from *Moby-Dick*), **tense** (imaginative and practical), and **well-behaved** (said of a program that does its job without problems).

Mythical and magical imagery was an integral part of hacker slang. A person who was very adept at solving difficult problems was known as a **guru,** a **kahuna,** a **lord high fixer,** or wiz-

Trekker Slang" by Patricia Byrd, which appeared in the Spring 1978 issue of *American Speech*. Additionally, "Star Trek" linguists have cultivated and published several "dictionaries" of foreign languages encountered in space.

[3]*The Totally Awesome Val Guide* by Jodie Ann Posserello, as told to Sue Black (Los Angeles: Price-Stern/Sloan, 1982); *The Valley Girl's Guide to Life* by Mimi Pond (New York: Dell, 1982); and *How to be a Valley Girl* by Mary Corey and Victoria Westermark (New York: Bantam Books, 1982) all contain glossaries of ValSpeak. Pond's is the most extensive, followed by Corey and Westermark.

Sources and References

Written sources for slang of this period which I have found particularly helpful include the chapter on "Teen and High School Slang" in Paul Dickson's *Slang!* (New York: Pocket Books, 1990); *College Slang 101* by Connie Eble (Georgetown, Connecticut: Spectacle Lane Press, 1989); and Pamela Munro's *Slang U: The Official Dictionary of College Slang* (New York: Harmony Books, 1989). Other useful sources include "Razorback Slang" by Gary N. Underwood of the University of Texas, Austin, which appeared in the Summer 1975 issue of *American Speech;* "Zoos, Tunes and Gweeps: A

ard; their problem-solving was known as **black art, casting the runes, examining the entrails, incantation, magic** (or **black magic** or **deep magic** or **heavy magic**), performing a **rain dance,** or **waving a dead chicken**. A dormant program was known as a **daemon,** a **dragon** was a program that only performed secondary tasks, and **voodoo programming** was the use of a system that one does not truly understand (derived from George Bush's attack in the 1980 Republican primary on Ronald Reagan's economic theories as "voodoo economics").

Jargon was far more common than slang when it came to describing the actual operations of a computer, but there were some strong slang entries in the field, especially when it came to making mistakes or solving problems. Examples include **adger** (to make a reckless mistake that could have been avoided), **banana** (a problem that never seems to stop, derived from a joke about spelling *banana* in which the punch line is "I know how to spell it, I just don't know when to stop"), **blivet** (an unyielding problem), **big win** (serendipity), **chrome** (a showy feature that adds little to a program, emphasizing style over substance; also known as **content-free**), **cokebottle** (a character that is not on one's keyboard), **crawling horror** (an old computer or program that a hacker keeps functioning), **feep** (the beep made by a computer), **kludge** (a crude solution to a problem), and **happily** (said of a program that is blissfully unaware of an important fact in its environment). The perforated edges of printer paper torn off after printing were known as **chad, perf,** and **selvage.**

An entire slang vocabulary existed to describe life outside the computer screen. To **fuel up** was to eat; other food-related slang included **great wall** (a group trip to an Asian restaurant), **laser chicken** (microwaved chicken), and **stir-fried random** (home-cooked stir fry, made with assorted refrigerator findings). To **birble, flame,** or **rave** was to talk too much; **flame** later took on a different meaning—to post an inflammatory or insulting message on the Internet.

The small group of computer wizards who hacked into computer systems where they were not specifically welcomed (**crackers**) had their own idiom. To **phreak** was to crack into a computer system, while a successful or difficult-to-break computer security system was **fascist.**

Sources: Richard Perlman has interpreted the language and culture of hackers for me over the years. Useful written sources include *The Internet Dictionary* by Christian Crumlish (San Francisco: Sybex, 1995); *The Devouring Fungus: Tales of the Computer Age* by Karla Jennings (New York: W.W. Norton and Company, 1990); and *The New Hackers Dictionary* edited by Eric Raymond (Cambridge, Massachusetts: MIT Press, 1991).

Dictionary of Campus Slang" by Elise Hancock in the *Journal of Higher Education,* Volume 61, Number 1 (January/February 1990) [the article was orginally printed in the *WPI* (Worcester Polytechnic Institute) *Journal* in 1988]; *Piled Higher and Deeper: The Folklore of Campus Life* by Simon Bronner (Little Rock: August House Publishers, Inc., 1990); and the "Dictionary of BHS" in the 1990 Berkeley (California) High School yearbook. I also gathered material from a presentation by James C. Stalker (Department of English, Michigan State University, East Lansing) to the American Dialect Society and National Council of Teachers of English in November 1992, on "Taboo Language in the Classroom."

In addition, Paul Dickson has made available to me more than a hundred slang surveys which he conducted among high school students in the late 1980s. During the decades in question I was a close reader of *Rolling Stone,* a periodical with its ear to the ground of youth slang.

CHAPTER 10
Hip-Hop & Rap
▼

"To the hip-hop the hippy hippy hippy hippy hop and you don't stop."

Without doubt, the most vigorous youth culture to arise since the demise of the hippie movement in the early 1970s has been the hip-hop movement. Created as an alternative to the culture of gang violence in the mid-1970s in the Bronx and Harlem with the midwifery of Clive "Kool Herc" Campbell, Afrika Bambaataa, Grandmaster Flash, and DJ Hollywood, hip-hop culture as originally envisioned had three major components: rap music, breakdancing, and graffiti art.

By the mid-1980s, rap music as an expression of hip-hop culture had become the Next Wave of wider popular culture. Breakdancing was left behind as a fad, and graffiti art never moved beyond its stigma of vandalism, although it had an immense effect on commercial graphic art related to hip-hop culture. Rap music, though, with its heavy emphasis on beat and rhythm, scratching and sampling, rhythmic rhymes, and lyrics that were often based on powerfully realistic images of violent inner-city life, not only survived, it prevailed. Like the first gen-

Illustrations by Matthew Martin

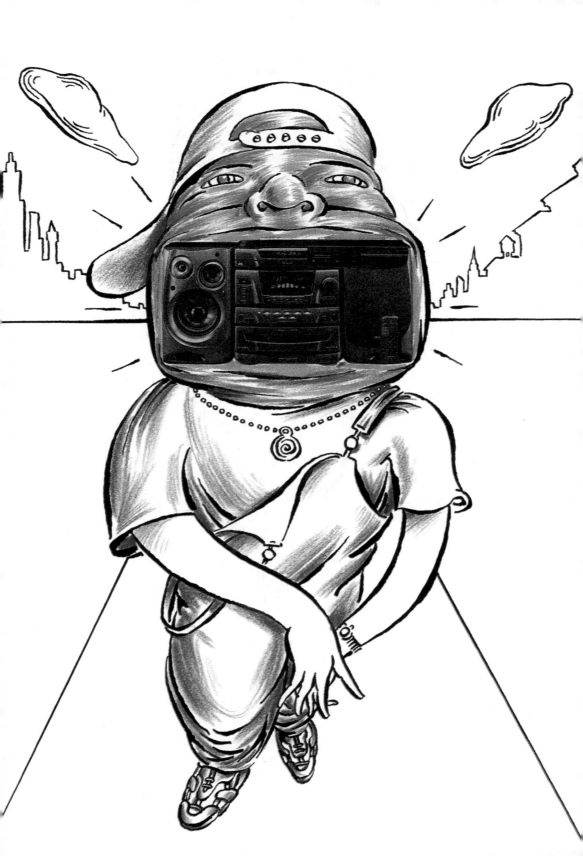

eration of rock and roll in the 1950s, rap had an unmistakably seditious and menacing edge, both in its celebration of ghetto life and its defiant youth stance. And, like the first generation of rock and roll, it seized the attention and interest of young people.

In the late 1980s rap gained enormous popularity. The early 1990s saw hip-hop culture defining popular youth culture to a startling degree. Fueled by movies, radio airplay, MTV exposure, and definite parental disapproval, rap soared.

Unlike the hippie movement where anyone could don a tie-dye shirt and become a weekend hippie, the hip-hop culture did not provide a lifestyle that most American young people could completely embrace. Simply put, white teenagers could not, as much as they might wish to, become black. They could and did, however, listen to the music, dress the dress (emphasis on high-cost sneakers, sagging pants, hooded baggy sweatshirts, and baseball caps), mirror the hair cuts, adopt the rap vocabulary suitable for their daily lives, mimic the cadence of street speech, and admire from a safe distance the lives of prominent black rappers and athletes. On a different level, rap provided a connection to the lives of those living in the chaos of inner cities, a connection that brought with it a degree of awareness of social injustice.

For the youth of the inner city, rap played a very different role. It was a true source of Afrocentric pride, bright and bold, street and chic, fly and fresh. It defined black culture with a cocky, macho braggadocio that was more than just a little appealing to teenage boys.

In the early 1990s, rap veered towards commercialization and trivialization as the mainstream forces of advertising and marketing began to appreciate its money-making potential. Hip-hop culture responded with a countertrend towards the gangsta ethic. In this context, early, more joyful rap sounds hopelessly dated and, well, dopey to young people first attracted to harsher rap of the early 1990s.

In mid-decade, rap shows no sign of abatement. The hue and cry of fundamentalist Christians, lyric-guardian Tipper Gore, and presidential candidate Bill Clinton all increased its stature with youth, and it remains a defiant, insolent, threatening counterculture.

The Language of Hip-Hop & Rap

The hip-hop movement and rap music provided the biggest infusion of black street vernacular into youth slang since introduction of Harlem jive in the 1930s. The lyrics of rap music formed the primer for rap vocabulary, reinforced by So Hip veejays on MTV, disc jockeys on rap-format radio stations, and urban life movies such as *Boyz 'N the Hood.*

The idiom of rap is not entirely new, and certainly not as new as most of its practitioners would believe. Apparent neologisms such as **fly, fat/phat,** and **rap** are venerable slang, while much of the rap vocabulary dealing with violence can be traced to Harlem jive, gangster slang of the 1930s, or the war in Vietnam.

Because of its frequent preoccupation with the bleaker and more somber realities of black inner-city life, much of the vocabulary of rap is of little use in youth culture at large, other than as an extension of America's perennial fascination with violence. The status-oriented vocabulary though—the greetings, labeling as good or bad, teasing and insulting, discussion of leaving, and farewells—took hold on the slang of popular youth culture.

Whatever its sociolinguistic merits, the slang of the hip-hop culture and rap music is as vibrant, creative, innovative, and inventive a body of youth slang as has come along in decades.

A Hip-Hop Word
List

A-ight!
An exclamation of
approval

accessory
One's boyfriend or
girlfriend

ace
One's best friend

around the way
The neighborhood or
community

ass-out
Very

assed-out
In trouble

B-boy, B-girl
Someone who is part
of hip-hop culture.
*The "B" stands for
"breakdancer." There*

*is clearly an echo here
of the 1930s B-girl
(bar girl), who worked
in a tavern for the pur-
pose of encouraging
male patrons to drink.
While the practice and
word were phased out
in the United States
by the late 1960s,
both were prevalent
in Vietnam during
the conflict
there.*

bag
A bottle of beer

bail
To strut, walk in an
assertive fashion

banji
Tough

beastie
A person who looks
uncouth and threaten-
ing

beep
To page someone

Bet!
Certainly!

big up
To compliment

bitch up
To back down

blimp
To overeat

blow up
To become famous

blush
To try to hide
something

bone
1. A cigarette
2. A song on a
record

bones
Dice or dominoes

booming
Loud and good

booty-ass
Shoddy

Booya!
I approve!

bop
To walk in an
arrogant manner

break
To appear for the
first time

break night
To stay up all
night

bricks
Housing projects

broke
Injured

bronco
Individualistic

buck
Very

bucket
An old beat-up car

bugged *or* **bugged
out**
Crazy

buggy man
A homeless man

bump
To play music very
loudly

bumpin'
Spirited

burn
A cigarette

bust on the scene
To arrive

busted
Homely

butt
1. Very
2. Weak

butter
Smooth

Not Good

The language of the hip-hop culture is versatile when it comes to describing status. Something that is bad might be called **bank, burnt, corroded, cramped** (ugly), **crasty, nasty, p.j.** (pure junk), **played** or **played out** (old-fashioned), **toe up, torn back, trife, wack,** or **weak.** Slang for "weak" includes **bitch, booty, bootsy, lame, moist, punk** or **punk ass, slum, soft,** or **tired;** a weak man is known as a **bitch** or **pussy.**

C

cabbage
The brain

cable
A bulky gold chain

calendar
A year

catch wreck
To gain respect

check
1. To criticize
2. To stop what you are doing

chill hard
To survive, get by

chop
An ugly person

badass
Powerful, exacting deference

chopper
A big razor

chump
To take advantage of

cipher
Knowledge

clock
To observe or watch

clock dollars
To earn money

clock z's
To sleep.
The term "z's" has

been around as slang since the 1920s and is a universally recognized convention for conveying sleep in cartoons and comics. Rappers simply dressed up the old "z's" with new clocking to come up with this new/old expression.

club
To visit different night clubs

cold
Completely

To Establish Station

Most street culture revolves around rank, station, and the never-ending process of establishing and maintaining one's standing within the group. Hip-hop culture is no exception, and its slang idiom is laden with terms and expressions pertaining to status.

The insult is a key component in establishing station, and hip-hop knows a variety of words that mean "insult." To **answer, bag on, break on, clown, dis, dog, fade, heat, loud, play, rank on, riff on, shoot on, signify, snap, sound on, step off, talk trash, toast, trip on,** or **woof** is to insult in some form, be it mocking, ridiculing, or humiliating.

Pretending, part of the status game, is known as **comin' off, cross, fakin' the funk, frontin', game, jive, perpin', playin' that, playing it off, playin' yourself, popping shit, posing, shammin', shuckin,** or **woofin',** while someone who does so is a **poser, studio gangsta, wanna-be,** or **wigger.** (The black oral tradition historically reserved special meanings to special words, such as **shuck** and **jive,** which referred to ritualistic insults in very special senses. With the rise of hip-hop culture came a blurring of lines between types of insult, leaving a stew of synonyms rather than a selection of finely differing variations on a theme.) Taking things a step further, showing off is to **flex, front, profile, strut, style, truck,** or **vogue.** Bragging is **popping shit, riffin', talkin',** or **woofin';** a braggart is sometimes called **bragadocious** (a play on bodacious), while bragging itself is, succinctly put, **shit.**

Playground Basketball

Although not officially a part of the hip-hop culture's trinity (breakdancing, graffiti, and rap music), playground basketball is a powerful expression of black urban culture. The playground took the language of organized basketball, filtered it through the screen of black street speech, and produced a slangy vernacular with some application away from the game.

It starts with the basic vocabulary of the sport—the game (**ball** or **hoops**), the ball (the **apple** or, most commonly, the **pill**), the basket rim (the **cup, rack,** or **hole**), the lane (the **office, box,** or **death valley**), to jump (to **sky** or **rise**), rebounds (**pull, snatch,** or **yank**), to pass (**deal, dish,** or **look**) to score (**flush**), and the score (**count**).

To make a strong move to the basket (a **bust**) is to **Bogart** or **boogie**. While driving, a **juke** is an unexpected move, usually a decoy. In the shooting department, there is the short and simple shot (a **chippie**, a golf term), the shot that scores without touching the rim (**all net** or **nothing but net**), the long shot (to **pump from downtown,** similar to the baseball term **go downtown** for a well-hit home run), and the terrible shot (a **brick**). The player who shoots a lot is a **chucker, gunner,** or **heaver**.

On the defense (**D**), a check is a **feel,** while an aggressive and rough defensive player is a **butcher** or **hacker**.

At stake in playground basketball is pride, or **face**; and in playground ball, there are only two things that you can do with face—save it or lose it. Two expressions from the playground which enjoyed more general use were **li'l help** (a plea for assistance) and **my bad** (sorry, my fault).

Written sources for this look at playground basketball include the glossaries "Asphalt Argot" in *The In-Your-Face Basketball Book* (New York: Everest House, 1980) and *The Back-In-Your-Face Guide to Pick-Up Basketball* (New York: Dodd, Mead & Company, 1986) by Chuck Wielgus and Alexander Wolff, as well as a number of glossaries from newspaper treatments of playground basketball.

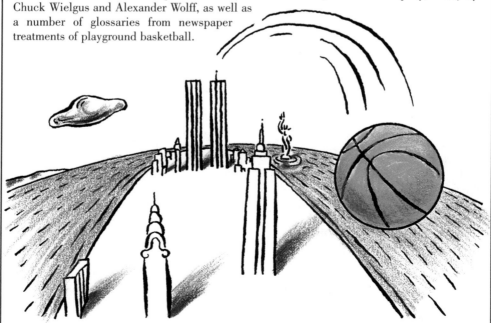

come correct
To excel

come up
To grow up

cram
To want very
badly

crank the beat
Increase the
volume of
music

crunchy
Embarrassed

D
Ready

dead up
Positively

deep
Serious

deese
Powerful.
A clipped form of
DIESEL.

dibs
One's house or
apartment

diesel
Someone with a large
and powerful body

dig
To understand, to like

digits
A telephone number

dizzy
Inattentive, impracti-
cal

dog *or* **dogg** *or* **dawg**
A friend

down
Attentive to styles and
fashions

down low
Quiet

down with
Zealous

drop science
To share knowledge

drop-top
A convertible. *Some*
will remember the

"drop-top Cadillac"
from Jim Croce's
1974 song "You Dont
Mess Around with
Jim."

fade
To ignore

fall off
To become less
popular

fave
Favorite

fiend
To act violently

flip
To betray

foul
Unsuitable

funk up
To increase the
energy level

funky
1. Original

2. Foul-smelling,
disgusting

game
Aware

gangsta
1. A gang member
2. A style of hard-
edged music originat-
ing in south-central
Los Angeles
3. One who is angry
or inclined to
violence

geek up
To teach

get over
To get by with
a minimum
effort

get served
To be defeated or
embarrassed

give it up
To express a greeting,
to applaud

Music

Music is a critical component of hip-hop culture, and it has its own fairly extensive idiom. To rap is to **break, bust, bust out, bust rhymes, chat, comp, cut, drop, flip, flow, freak, freak the beats, freestyle, give it up, hook, jam, kick, kick the ballistics, make noise, rhyme, rip, rock, scratch, shoot the gift, skip** or **throw out**. The beat is the **kick**; technical points include **sampling** (working popular songs into the mix) and the **hook** or **loop** (refrain). While rapping, one might acknowledge credit for creative input by giv-ing **big ups** or **shout outs**.

To **beatbox** is to make background mouth noises while someone else raps; to **cut** or **scratch** or **skip** is to manipulate a record on two turntables (**wheels of steel**) to create percussion. The sound system is known as the **boom box** or simply the **boom**, the **box**, or the **system**.

go out
To compromise one's beliefs

grease
To eat

grit
To eat

half-step
To start something which one does not finish

haps
The latest information

hard *or* **hardcore**
Violent, brutal, criminal

hawk
To ask for a favor

heavy
Serious

heffa
An ugly girl.
A deliberate misspelling of "heifer."

hi-sididy
Conceited

Hit me!
Call me on my pager

homeboy *or*
homie *or* **homes**
or **Holmes**
A close friend, especially from one's neighborhood

hood
A neighborhood

hood rat
Someone from the neighborhood

hurting
Lacking

ill
To perform very well

jack
A telephone

jack up
Beat up

jam
1. A song
2. To party

'jects
Housing projects

jerk
1. To take advantage of
2. To spend money freely

jib
Talk

jock
To follow, pursue

joint, the
The very best

Fashion

Along with music and language, the fashion of hip-hop has had a tremendous impact on American youth. The fashion of hip-hop itself is not without an idiom.

Words associated with clothes (**gear, jig,** or the older **threads**) include **daizy dukes** (short shorts), **doo-doo pants** (baggy pants), **hoodie** or **hoody** (a sweatshirt with a hood), **knot** (a necktie), **low riders** (sagging pants that ride low on the hips), **pum-pum shorts** (very short shorts), and **skully** (a wool stocking cap). Sneakers are known as **dogs, grips, jammies, kicks** (a jive word that Cab Calloway would have used in 1935, popping up in the middle of rap idiom), and **pumps,** while heavy boots are **B.B.'s, M.C. Boots, shit-kickers** (a holdover from the 1960s), or **timbos.** Wearing stylish clothes is **rockin, stylin',** or **voguein'.**

Hairstyles include the **caesar** (closely shaved with lines), **dreds** (short for dreadlocks, braided hair, characteristic of Jamaicans), **fade** or **cameo** (a sculpted haircut in which the sides are trimmed close to the head and the hair on top is cut flat), **'fro** (an Afro, or natural cut), **gumby** (a side-angled fade, named after a cartoon character repopularized by Eddie Murphy on *Saturday Night Live* in the 1980s), **high-top fade** (a sculpted cut), **J-C's** (short for "Jerry Curls"—wet, tight curls), and **mushroom** (a mushroom-shaped cut).

Greetings and Farewells

As with most slang vocabularies, the idiom of rap has a full range of greetings and farewells, ritualistic expressions that establish status.

"Hello" might be expressed as **Ayo, Eh G, Give it up, Hayo, S'up?, Wassup? Wassup, Money?** or **Yo**. Male terms of address include **ace, B, B-boy, blood, bro, brotha, brother, cat, cuz, dog, dude, G, homeboy, homepeep, home slice, homes, homey, hops, jack, loc, low, main man, money, money dog, money grip, mother, mutha, nigga, nigger, par, power, Slim,** and **soldier** or **souljah**. **B-girl, boo boo, girlfriend, homegirl, side kick, sista, squeeze,** and **tender** are all female terms of address. Often an expressive gesture accompanies the verbal greeting, such as **daps** (a slap or form of public greeting), **high five** (hands slapped shoulder-high or higher), **pound** (lightly pounding fists), and **props** (clipped for proper respects, or a closed fist, over and under tapped greeting).

To leave is to **Audi 5000, bill, blow, book, boogie, bounce, break, break north, buff, bux one, clock out, dip, flex, ghost, haul ass, jet, motor, outie, parlay, step off, swayze,** or **tear up**. A farewell could be expressed as **5000, Check ya, Good lookin' out, Gone, I'm outie, Later, Lay', Peace, Peace out, Sideways,** or **I'm swayze**.

jump off
To happen suddenly

keep it real
To be honest

kick that to the curb
To stop doing something

kill the noise
To become quiet

legit
Able, genuine

light
Attention

living large
Doing well

loc
Crazy.
Probably from Spanish "loco."

locin'
Going crazy

locs
Dark glasses

loud
To criticize

lucy
A cigarette

M

mack
A smooth operator

mad
Very

main squeeze
One's best girlfriend

make noise
To get attention

mark
Someone who acts stupid

milk
Smooth

moist
Weak

N

nasty
1. Sexually appealing
2. Sex, as in "doing the nasty"

ox
A razor blade

O

old school
Longtime friends

on the real
Truly

On the strength.
I agree.

open
Desperate

out box
The start

P

par
A friend, or partner

peep
To inquire into

peeps
1. Parents
2. Those who support you

perpetrate
To imitate or copy

petro
Worried

poppin'
1. Creative
2. Popular

power
Trusted friend

R

real, the
The truth

regulate
To exact retribution

riff
To start trouble, to complain

riff on
1. To inform on
2. To insult

rim
A hubcap

rip
To perform magnificently

rope chain
A large, braided gold chain

rump
Very good

S

scheme on
To watch closely

scrub
Someone with no talent

seeds
Children

set
A neighborhood

shank
A razor

shy
To avoid on purpose

six pack
Sculpted abdominal muscles

Whiling Time Away

As is the case with most youth, the hip-hop young spend a fair amount of time in an inert and languid state, relaxing. Whiling time away is to **chill** or **cold chill, cool out, ease, hang, kick back, kick it, lamp, limp, max** (**maxin'** and **relaxin'**), **mellow out, parlay, swing it,** or **will.**

The Vocabulary of Violence

The lyrics of rap music are undeniably permeated with graphic images of violence, and one of the leading criticisms of rap is that it glorifies violence. Given both the daily presence of violence in the inner-city neighborhoods which provide the cultural context of rap and the high level of violence depicted in mainstream television and movies, the singling out for criticism of the words of rap hardly seems fair.

In any event, there is a staggering vocabulary of violence which is found in the inner city, echoed in rap, and imitated in young white society.

To start with, what would once have been called a gang is called a **crew, posse, tribe,** or **troop,** and individual gang members or the criminally inclined are known as **gangbangers, gangstas, hardheads, headbangers,** or **roughnecks**. To participate in gang activities is to be **mobbin'** or **gangbanging**.

A word list just of terms for guns would run on for more than a page. The more generic terms are **bis, biscuit, burner, calico, chrome, chwop, click, clog, flamer, four pounder, gak, gat, gauge, glock, heat** or **heater, iron, jack, jammie, joint, niner, oowop, piece, pump, steel, strap, street sweeper, strill, tech, toast,** or **tootie**.

Ready to fight? Try **bang, beef, break on, bust up, crash, duke, flex, flip, funk up, gank, get busy, jap, jump, loc** or **loc on, muff, punk, rag up, reck, riff, roll, rush, set off, step to, style on, throw down,** or **wreck**.

To shoot someone is to **blast, buck, burn, bust a cap, cap, clip, dent, fade, fry, gat, ice, lead up, peel a cap, pop a cap, smoke, spray,** or **wet**. The terms **187, catch a body, check, do, drop, drop a body, dust, ice, off, pull the plug, put to rest, smoke, take out, waste,** and **wet** all mean to kill some-one.

The idiom of theft is just as impressive, with **bank, bite, boost, borrow, catch, chump, gaffle, gee, hawk, house, jack, pop, roll, stick, tax,** and **trim** all synonyms for "to steal." A **lick** is a robber.

The victim of all this mayhem? A **biscuit, bitch, buster, catch-wreck, chump, crab, herb, no-frill, punk, sucker** or simply **vic**.

Working the other side of the street are the police—**5-0** (from the television show *Hawaii 5-0*) or the derivative **fifty, b&w, blue bunnies, blue jeans, boop boop, the boyz, green pockets, jake, the law, little boy blue, the Man, Mr. Charlie, one-time, pigs, Willy Bo Bills,** and the **yank**. Many of these terms were in use before the rappers, with both **pig** and **the Man** having played major roles in the lexicon of the Black Panthers in the 1960s.

Arrested? No, **bagged, busted, canned, cuffed, gaffled, gagged, knocked, popped, served** or **tagged**. Destination jail? Try instead the **big house, bullpen, can, clink, grey goose, house of D.** ("D" being detention), **house of pain, joint, pen, slammer,** and **the wall**—many old-time words from criminal argot. A jail sentence is a **bid**, while **county blues** and **state greens** refer to jail uniforms.

sleep on
To ignore

slum
Weak

soft
Weak

solid
A favor

soup up
To compliment

stank
Ugly, disagreeable

static
Trouble

street
Authentic, hardcore, gritty

stress
To crave, to desire, as in "He's stressing Mary but she doesn't even know he exists."

stupid
Very

sweat
To admire

swollen
fat

take no shorts
To demand respect

tapped
Without money

The Talk of Tagging

Rap owes some debt, if only in spirit, to graffiti artists, subway defacers—**bombers, tag bangers** (signature artists only), or **writers,** who had a slangy jargon to describe their artistic expression. While graffiti art itself did not become the major fixture of popular culture that rap music did, the artistic style of its practitioners made a lasting impression on commercial graphic art associated with the hip-hop movement.

The personnel: A group of writers was a **crew** or **clique;** your buddy was your **writing partner;** and novices were known as **toys.** To be **down** with a crew was to be part of the group, while **up** referred to a prolific writer. In Philadelphia in the early 1970s, Cool Earl and Cornbread were definitely up.

The equipment: A **piece book** or **black book** contained a writer's rough sketches for a **piece** (clipped "masterpiece"); a **cap** was a nozzle that was fitted onto a can of spray paint, varying in width. Spray-paint cans were simply **cans.**

The canvas: A **flat** was a smooth-sided, older-style subway car which was conducive to the art, and a **ridgy** was a newer, corrugated subway car, far less conducive to the art. A **panel piece** was a piece below the windows or between the doors; a **top-to-bottom,** on the other hand, stretched from the top of the car to the bottom of the car; and a **window-down** was painted below window level.

Creating the art: To **burn, hit, kill, get over, get up,** or **terrorize** was to succeed in painting a train; an all-night tagging expedition was a **mission.** To **fade** was to blend colors; to **ice down** was to fill a wall or car with the painting; to **tag** was to include your signature in the piece; to **go over** was to paint over someone's tag; to **bite** was to copy another tagger's technique; and to **burn** was to reach a choice car before a competing crew in the ongoing **graf wars. Wildstyle** was the elaborate assembly of overlapping letters; a **bomb** or a **throw-up** was a profuse painting. The enemy was **buff,** which was any method used by the transit authorities to remove or erase pieces. **Motion tagging** was painting graffiti on a moving subway car; the safer route was to visit the **lay up,** or subway car train yard.

The result: Good was **king;** a good piece was a **burner;** and bad was **whack.**

Most rap glossaries contain at least a few words relating to graffiti. In addition, there is one graffiti-specific source that I have consulted: *Subway Art* by Martha Cooper and Henry Chalfant (New York: Holt, Rinehart and Winston, 1984).

The Bank of Hip-Hop

Hip-hop supplies an ample vocabulary dealing with money, including **aces** ($1 bills), **balls, bank, beans** ($1 bills), **bills** ($100 bills), **bingos** ($1 bills), **bones** ($1 bills), **booty, bore** ($5 bills), **bucks** ($100 bills), **clout, cream, dead presidents, dils** ($1 bills), **dividends, doe, ducats** or **ducs, ends** ($1000 bills), **Franklins** ($100 bills), **G's** ($1000 bills), **green** (a word used by the Flapper long before the Rapper), **grip, gusto, jacks** or **jax, Jacksons** ($20 bills), **jerkin', long dollars** (large denominations), **loochie, loot, papes, presidents, rollin' snaps, scrilla, trickin', yard,** or **year** (both $100 bills). Someone who is moneyed would be a **balla** or **baller**, a **fat rocker**, a **hard roller** or **high roller, large**, a **roller**, or **rollin'**.

---

tardy
Behind on news

throw down
To party

time
The latest situation

tip
A style

tipster
A groupie

tonk
A card game

trim
To pick a
lock

truck
To wear something
in a conspicuous
manner

twenty-four/seven
To be attentive 24
hours a day, seven
days a week

vibes
Instinctive sensations.
*Hippies were in tune
with "vibes" (see
Chapter 8), but the*

*vibes that hippies
picked up were of the
cosmic variety, where-
as the vibes referred to
here involve intuition
about a situation,
similar to street
smarts.*

Ville
Housing projects

wax
To defeat soundly in
competition

wheel
To ride in a car

Whoomp!
How exciting!

wild
To act crazy

wisdom
A girlfriend

with it
Part of the situation

Word! or **Word up!**
I agree!

Word History: Fly

Fresh and *fly*—both seem so new and modern and hip-hoppish, yet one is and one is not. Just as *fresh* can make the unusual claim of originality, so must *fly* stand up and be counted for what it is: a slang word with a long and noble heritage.

In the rap sense of the word, *fly* denotes good-looking, well-dressed, stylish, and cool, and it is usually applied to a woman. *Fly's* slang ancestry is varied, but its past points to its present.

The most well-established slang meaning of *fly* was in the argot of thieves, where *fly* meant sly, cunning, wide-awake, knowing, or smart. Joseph Wright in the *English Dialect Dictionary* (London: Henry Frowde, 1900), points to uses of *fly* in this sense as early as 1724 and in *Bleak House* by Dickens in 1853. It appears with this definition in *Vocabulum: The Rogue's Lexicon* by George Matsell (New York: George W. Matsell & Company, 1859), and *The Slang Dictionary* (London: John Camden Hotten, 1860). This use spilled into the 20th century, where, according to Robert L. Gold, it became "current especially among Negro jazzmen" beginning around 1900.

In the 1930s, *fly* began a transfiguration, moving towards a more general term of approval. In 1939, Peter Tamony made a notation of "Fly: All right, good," as used by Clarence Ison, a "young Negro prisoner" on his way to Terminal Island. That same year, the term was applied in a musical context in the April issue of *Metronome*, where one Bauduc is said to "really come on with some very fly and superb drumming."

In 1947, Walter Winchell, who had a close ear to the ground when it came to slang, wrote in the November 17 *San Francisco Call-Bulletin* about a "fly guy": "in hep lingo it means he's a manaboutown." In 1952, in *A History of Jazz in America* (New York: Viking, 1952), Barry Ulanov defined *fly* as "smooth; to describe looks or manner or performance, usually the first two." In his 1952 *The Jives of Dr. Hepcat*, Lavada Durst defined *fly* as "on the ball, smart, cute, handsome, good." Similarly, in 1972 in *Black Jargon in White America* (Grand Rapids, Mich.: William B. Eerdmans Publishing Company, 1972), David Claerbaut defined *fly* as either "stylish looking" or "attractive in manner, alluring in character." In his 1968 *Hy Lit Dictionary*, Hy Lit defined *fly* as well-dressed.

In the 1970s, a series of black exploitation *Super Fly* movies shone the spotlight on *fly*, which then retreated for another decade until it was revived by rappers, embracing both the 1724 sense of the word ("knowing") and the one that developed in the 20th century ("smooth looks," "stylish looking," and "attractive in manner, alluring in character." Like many of the first-generation rap slang words, *fly* fell into disuse by the early 1990s, but in mid-decade it is making a strong comeback, especially used by boys to describe girls who are attractive in manner and alluring in character.

Word History: Fresh

Fresh, used in the hip-hop culture since the 1980s as a term of high approval, is one of those rarest of slang words: an original addition to the idiom, totally lacking roots in Harlem jive or earlier relevant slang use.

It is generally agreed that *fresh* owes its life to the Fantastic Grand Wizard Theodore and the 5 MC's, a group in the late 1970s which would routinely rap:

We're fresh out of the pack,
you gotta stay back
We got one Puerto Rican and the
rest are black.

The phrase "fresh out of the pack" suggests nothing more than a claim of original artistry. The "out of the pack," though, was soon dropped from the phrase, leaving simply *fresh* as an ultimate accolade. While *fresh* had been used in a slang sense to mean slightly intoxicated, as recorded (Barrère and Leland's: *Dictionary of Slang, Jargon and Cant* [London: George Bell &

Breakdancing

One of the three original components of the hip-hop movement was breakdancing, which got its start in the South Bronx as an alternative to gang warfare. It consisted of highly rehearsed, highly acrobatic, highly stylized dancing, a form of street art or street theater that was most often performed either on sidewalks for tips or in organized competitions. In the end, breakdancing turned out to be a fad; while hip-hop moved on, breakdancing remained a craze that was fondly remembered but passed by.

In the language of breakdancers, though, one hears the early echoes of hip-hop language, the bridge from black street vernacular to the idiom of hip-hop. Leaving aside the many words used by breakdancers which are found in the lexicon of hip-hop, there were a handful of slang expressions and terms that were unique to breakdancing.

The term **break** itself is an old jazz term, meaning that the music and dancing continue within a song but the singer does not. By extension, in hip-hop culture a **breaker** was a dancer, and **breaking** was dancing. A group of breakdancers was a **crew**, a term which came to have a more generalized meaning. To **cut** someone was to expel them from the group of dancers.

A breaker's **dogs** are dancing sneakers, and **gear** is one's performance clothes. Also included in the breakdancer's essentials are a **box** (a large, portable tape player, short for **boom box**), used to play **jams** (tapes or songs).

There were three basic styles of breakdancing—**breaking, the electric boogie,** and **uprock**. Within each style there were a number of **pediments** (hand or head moves), all of which had catchy, slangy names. A breaker who was breaking very well was **in his power,** or really **rockin'**. To win a dance contest you had to **amaze 'em** and **take out** your competition. A word shared with graffiti writers was **bite,** which in the context of breaking meant to mimic another breaker's moves.

Useful glossaries and discussions of the language of breakdancing can be found in Mr. Fresh's *Breakdancing* (New York: Avon Books, 1984) and *Breakdancing* by William H. Watkins and Eric N. Franklin (Chicago: Contemporary Books, 1984).

Sons], 1897), it had never been used before as a general term of admiration or approbation.

Fresh enjoyed an intense burst of popularity as rap slang, as evidenced by the title of the first major treatment of rap slang, *fresh fly flavor* by Fab 5 Freddy in 1992. Although *fresh* faded and was soon stale within the strictly rap idiom, it established something of a toehold in the mainstream youth slang of the 1980s and 1990s, remaining a mid-level popular word to convey approval for someone or something.

Word History: Hip-Hop

As is the case with many slang words, the etymology of *hip-hop* is clouded, with at least two competing theories on the origin of the word, which describes an entire subculture, including music, dancing, art, dress, and speech. Although

Females

Rap is often criticized for the brutal treatment of women in the lyrics of its songs. While most rap lyrics are at worst candid and profane, there is a small but highly visible corpus of rap songs that treat women in a harsh fashion which warrants criticism.

The vocabulary for girl or woman includes **B-girl, bait** (short for jailbait, meaning under the age of consent), **bitch, bitty, G, group ho** (a group of girls), **honey, jill, niggette, shortie, squallie, stunt, tender, trick, wisdom,** and **yickenhead**. An attractive woman would be known as a **breed, honey dripper,** or **hottie,** while a licentious woman would be called a **freak, ho** or **hoe, hoochie, hood rat, juicer, salt shaker** (transmitting disease), **scab, scunt, skank, skeezer, stunt, stipster, trick,** or **yant**.

HO HO HO

the word is barely 20 years old, participants in its birth dispute its coining.[1]

In *fresh fly flavor,* Fab 5 Freddy (Fred Brathwaite) attributes the word to D.J. Hollywood, a rap pioneer at the Apollo Theater and Club 371 in New York:

The term originated in the mid-1970s during the beginning stages of what is also known as rap. It was first said by D.J. Hollywood, who, while playing records, would get on the mike and shout: "To the hip-hop the hippy hippy hippy hippy hop and you don't stop." This caught on and other pioneering D.J.'s and J.C.'s in Harlem and the Bronx picked up on it. It became the one expression used by everyone involved. Fans, when

explaining the previous night's party experiences, would use the word hip-hop to describe and identify what type of party it was.

Afrika Bambaataa, who founded the Zulu Nation, an Afrocentric group that worked to supplant gang violence with cultural competition (breakdancing and rapping) in the early 1970s in the Bronx, offers a different explanation:

Around 1974, a Bronx MC named Loveburg Starski used to always say, "Hip-hop, you don't stop." So I took the cliché from him, and I gave it as a name to the whole culture. Before that, people used to call us ditty boppers or b-boppers.

Rap on Sex

The hip-hop vocabulary dealing with sexual intercourse is rich in images of impact, but in that respect hip-hop is hardly alone. Rap expressions for having sex include to **bang, bob** (engage in oral sex), **bone, break off, bump and grind, bust a move** (make a sexual advance), **bust out, catch vapors, dick, dig out, do, do the grown-up, do the naughty, do the nasty, fake moves, get busy, get down, get the boots, give it up, go downtown** (engage in oral sex), **hit it, hit the kitten, hit the skins, jay, jock, kick it, knock the boots, nob** (engage in oral sex), **parlay, plex, rock, sex, slag, slam it, slide up in that, socialize, spank, stick,** or **trick off** (engage in oral sex). Among nouns referring to sex are **12 play, ass, freak, g, nasty,** and **wild thing**.

Good, Good Looking, Etc.

When it comes to adjectives to convey a favorable impression, hip-hop comes on strong. A simple "good" could be expressed as **all that, bad, badass, bitchin', bookoo funk, boomin', bumpin', butter** or **butterfingers, chill, cool** (yes!), **def, fat, firme, fly, foolish, fresh, funkified** or **funky, heavy, hittin', hot, hype, ill, in full effect, in the house, in there, kickin', the milk, move, natty, phat, poppin', propa** or **proper, retarded, righteous, rump, the shit, slam** or **slammin', smokin', smooth, straight, stupid fresh, sweet, tight, treach, vicious,** or **wicked.** "Good" with a fashionable twist might be **dap, dip, dope, flave, fly, funky, kick ass, rockin', thick,** or **tight-ass.** To enjoy success is to be a **baller, rocker,** or **roller** or to **blow up, get fat,** or **kick ass.** One who is successful is **high profilin', high rollin', hittin', in the house, in the mix, in the good,** or simply **large.**

One way or the other, sometime in the mid-1970s a D.J. in the Bronx said "Hip-hop, you don't stop," and the country was given the latest chapter in a century-long march of *hip*, even if this use appears to be based more on the scat phrasing of a Bronx deejay than the historical use of *hip*.

Word History: Phat

Phat at first glance is a virgin slang word, an inventive new superlative (meaning either sexy or cool) conceived of and delivered in the rap idiom of the hip-hop culture. In the Fall 1994 issue of *American Speech*, John and Adele Algeo postulate that *phat* may have been devised as an acronym for "Pretty Hips And Thighs"; others have speculated that it was drawn from "physically attractive." If you forget the cute spelling, though, and look at *fat*, the explanation is probably a lot simpler.

Early slang lexicographers B.E. Gent in the 17th century, Francis Grose in the 18th century, and John Camden Hotten in the 19th century all define *fat* as a slang term for "rich." That meaning survives in the 20th century in the slang of gamblers and African-Americans.

As sometimes seems to be the case with slang that begins its journey meaning "rich," *fat* at some point began to take on a more general meaning of good. For example, *American Speech* in 1955 defined *fat* (shortened from "fat and happy") as "in an excellent situation." In his 1968 *Hy Lit Dictionary*, the archetypal fast-talking Philadelphia AM disc jockey included *fat* as "great, cool, you dig it."

The "ph" spelling is a curious story, though, and it gets curiouser and curiouser the more you look. In two early rap dictionaries, *fat* was still *fat*. In *fresh fly flavor* (Stamford, Connecticut: Longmeadow Press, 1992), Fab 5 Freddy (Fred Brathwaite) defined *fat* as "Living well, doing well, being successful." The same is true in Deee-Lite's *The 376 Deee-Liteful Words* published by Elektra Entertainment in 1992 in which *fat* is defined as "great." By 1995, *phat* appears in *A 2 Z: The Book of Rap & Hip-Hop Slang* by Lois Stavsky, I.E. Mozeson, and Dani Reyes Mozeson (New York: Boulevard Books, 1995), defined as "superlative, cool."

This suggests that in the early 1990s, *fat* evolved to *phat*, but the trail is not that simple. For example, in an August 2, 1963, article on "Negro argot" in *Time*, one finds *phat* listed as one of several "adjectives of approval." Ace slang-tracker Connie Eble first recorded *phat* at the University of North Carolina in 1973; after that sighting, Eble did not see *phat* again until 1981, when it became a constantly reported slang word and spelling by Eble's UNC students. Curiously, Eble's students did not report *fat* until 1986, and by then *phat* had come to dominate the market. Given the relatively later change to *phat* in rap literature, one has to wonder at how this quirky spelling arose and how students knew this idiosyncratic spelling of a word that would have been often spoken but rarely written.

It seems fairly certain that *phat* is *fat*, and *fat* is by no means new slang; in the second half of the 1990s it seems to have passed its zenith of popularity and to have begun the slide towards disuse and—probably eventually—re-use. The playful if affected "ph" spelling (also seen, for example, in hip-hop spellings of *phunky* or *Phar*

Side) is nothing new. Young people in the 1920s spelled "rats" as "Rhatz!" and shortened "that's too bad" to "stoo bad." Similarly, the young in the 1960s read magazines that loved "tuff," intentionally called themselves "freeks" and considered the spelling of "Amerika" to be a political statement. Nor are the young the only slang-speakers to play with spelling. Earlier in this century typesetters referred to type that was easily set as being *phat*—and, neatly enough, type that was difficult to set was *lean*—just going to show that others have played here before. Indeed, in 1885, the Post Express Printing Company in Rochester, New York, published the "Phat Boy's Birds-Eye Map of the Saint Lawrence River" with a drawing of a corpulent boy. The temptation to play with the "ph" spelling has been with us for more than a century.

Word History: Rap

Rap's original meaning in standard English was a severe blow with a sword or cudgel. Although the meaning softened to mean a softer blow, by 1733 it had also come to mean to make a formal complaint or testify against someone. By the late 18th century, in America, it also came to mean a prison sentence or blame, as in "beating the rap" or "a ten-year rap." Portending meanings to come, in 1923 *put in a rap* took on a slangy meaning of criticizing.

Those who came of age in the 1960s or 1970s first think of *rap* as meaning to discuss something or hold a conversation, a meaning which was firmly attached to the word in the late 1960s. William Safire, who may have found an earlier use of *rap* in this sense by Damon Runyon in 1929 ("He never raps to me but only bows and takes my hat...."), has reported a piece written by Winston Churchill on August 5, 1933, in which Churchill wrote of a dinner party in Washington in which "...the pervading atmosphere of good sense and fellow feeling enabled us to rap all the most delicate topics without the slightest offense given or received" ("On Language," *New York Times*, November 19, 1995).

The Code of Crack

In the 1980s, crack cocaine attacked the social fabric that was already under siege in the urban centers of America after the benign neglect of the 1970s. Cocaine, traditionally a drug of the high roller, moved into America's poor and black neighborhoods in the form of **crack** (so named because of the crackling noise made when it is smoked), cocaine with the hydrochloride removed, in small vials ready to smoke. The sale and use of crack (a.k.a. **cane, crills, nills, mi amigo,** or **shooby**) has been, sadly enough, largely the enterprise and problem of young people. With it has come an alarming culture of violence, jail, and hopelessness.

Yet, the crack cocaine business has produced a dynamic body of slang, some of which, such as **candy man** and **monkey,** go back to earlier drug argot. **Behind the scales** (working on the selling—**scrambling** or **slanging**—end of the business) are the **pitcher** (the dealer, known also as the **candy man** or **ice cream man**) and his bodyguard (**back**), the **cooker** (a person who prepares the freebase cocaine), the **crew** that **bags up** the cocaine, the **steerer** (a person who directs customers to the dealer), and the **spotter** (a person who warns dealers of police). The place where a dealer conducts business is known as the **spot** or **trap,** while a **sack** is a hiding place for the product.

The sale, or **hit,** is made of vials of crack (**criles, jumbs,** or **bottles**). Although measured in ounces (**zips**), most sales are based on cost—a **deuce** ($2 vial), **trey** ($3 sale), **nic** ($5 sale), or **dime** ($10 sale). One exception is the **8-ball,** which is 3.5 grams of crack.

Users—**cluckers, crackheads,** or **beamers** (from the *Star Trek* catch phrase of "Beam me up, Scotty")—are known by their characteristics. For example, a **chaser** is an overly obsessive user, and a **searcher** is a user who looks for **p.c.'s** (lost pieces of crack) or vials of cocaine. A craving for cocaine is a **monkey,** while a **feanin', fiendin',** or **thirsty** user is one who is yearning to use. An addict is a **chronic, on the pipe,** or just plain **whipped.**

To smoke is to **base, boof, bong on,** or **hit the pipe;** to achieve intoxication is to **beam up** (again the *Star Trek* allusion), or **get nice,** or **get stupid,** while the high is the **cloud.** Another weather word is **blizzard,** the thick white cloud of smoke in the pipe. A **master blaster** is a large piece of crack cocaine, while a **coolie** is a cigarette laced with cocaine. The pipe is known affectionately as the **devil's dick, bong bowl,** or **maserati** (an improvised pipe). Oils trapped in the pipe after smoking are known as **con-con, due** (resi-), or **res** (-idue).

To be high from drugs is to be **based out, blisted, blunted, bonged, booted, bopped out, buzzed, chopped, coked, cracked out, dancin' with the devil, dusted, geekin', looted, puffed out** or **up, red, ripped, rushed, skied up, splifted,** or **zooted.**

To **stay off the pipe** is to avoid use of crack cocaine, a good idea.

Much of this look at the language of crack cocaine is drawn from *Crack House: Notes From the End of the Line* by Terry Williams (Reading, Massachusetts: Addison-Wesley Publishing Company, 1992) and from *Clockers* by Richard Price (Boston: Houghton Mifflin, 1992).

Drunk in Rap

Beer and malt liquor (**40** or **forty** for 40-ounce bottles, **64** or **sixty-four** for 64-ounce bottles, **can** for beer in general, and **eight-ball** or **Olde E** for Olde English 800 malt liquor) are substantial parts of urban street life, and the slang of hip-hop has a modest group of words for drunk—**blasted, chopped, full, looted, puffed out** or **puffed up**, and **zooted**.

These early uses notwithstanding, *rap* was at best dormant until the 1960s. *Rap* was used in the civil rights movement of the early 1960s in a sense similar to that which would come to be described as "criticism/self-criticism" later in the 1960s. Basically, rap sessions involved the airing of internal differences within the movement, often drawn along racial lines and often resulting in the self-destruction of the movement. Perhaps prophetically, one of the leaders of the civil rights movement, H. Rap Brown, wrote in his autobiography that he was given the nickname "Rap" in his youth because he could rap so well.

In any event, *rap* meaning to discuss or debate soon entered the mainstream of both black and hippie slang. The earliest recorded use of the new sense was by Eldridge Cleaver in *Soul on Ice* (New York: McGraw Hill, 1968). In a letter from Folsom Prison dated September 19, 1965, Cleaver had written: "He thinks he is another Lenny Bruce...and I dig rapping with him." *Rap* permeated the two cultures, such that in relatively short order it had been tamed enough to appear in the *Peanuts* comic strip of July 21, 1969 ("I have more to do than sit around and rap with a bird.").

As the hippie movement faded, *rap* took on an arcane feel to it, branding a speaker who used it as locked in the past. This stigma, though, would not affect the word for long, for a new and potent meaning awaited. *Rap* in its latest incarnation—signifying rap music (music characterized by heavy use of rhythm and rhyming)—was first used in its new sense in 1979 in the titles of two songs, "Rapper's Delight" by the Sugar Hill Gang and "Rappin' and Rockin' in the House" by the Funky Four. Well into the 1990s, *rap* remains a vibrant and robust word, holding onto its hip-hop meaning, a fairly long run for one meaning. More importantly, rap as a cultural movement retains every bit of its vigor and drive.

* * *

[1]In dialect English of the early 19th century, *hip-hop* meant "with repeated hops." The *English Dialect Dictionary* contains the following quotation from 1827: "Fif. Arnold's nakit ghaist was seen...loupin hip-hop frae spire to spire." It is safe to assume that the *hip-hop* of

the modern day is not related to the *hip-hop* of 1827.

Sources and References

Excellent overviews of hip-hop culture are provided in *The Rap Attack: African Jive to New York Hip-Hop* by David Toop (Boston: South End Press, 1984); *Break it Down* by Michael Small (New York: Carol Publishing Group, 1992); and *Rap on Rap: Straight-Up Talk on Hip-Hop Culture*, edited by Adam Sexton (New York: Delta, 1995).

For the language of hip-hop, I worked primarily from the lyrics of rap music, and rap aficionado Jake Foster was an invaluable guide here. Also helpful was *Rap: The Lyrics*, edited by Lawrence A. Stanley (New York: Penguin, 1992).

Glossaries that were helpful in creating this chapter include *Rapper's Handbook* by Richard McAlister (Stone Mountain, Georgia: Mac and Mac, Inc., 1990); *The 376 Deee-Liteful Words* compiled by Lady Kier Kirby (New York: Elektra Entertainment, 1992); Fab 5 Freddy's *fresh fly flavor: Words & Phrases of the Hip-Hop Generation* (Stamford, Connecticut: Longmeadow Press, 1992); and *A 2 Z: The Book of Rap & Hip-Hop Slang* by Lois Stavsky, I.E. Mozeson, and Dani Reyes Mozeson (New York: Boulevard Books, 1995), as well as glossaries published in the *Yuba City* (California) *Appeal Democrat*, the *Oakland Tribune*, the *Los Angeles Times*, the *Washington Post*, and the *New York Times*.

CHAPTER 11
And Now...The 1990s

▼

"Cowabunga!"

As the 1990s edge towards the 21st century, youth culture in America remains without a unifying youth movement. To be sure, hip-hop culture and rap music continue to have a tremendous cultural influence; ironically, even as gangsta rap establishes an unquestionably black identity, it increasingly strikes a responsive chord in young affluent white boys.

At the same time, a range of ethnocentric choices of music exist for young white kids, including grunge, heavy metal, alternative music, and country and western. While the musicians, music, lyrics, and fans are not explicitly separatist, the sense of "us" is implicit in the music. While "us" is fine, it often implies a "them." One "us" whose implied "them" is not defined in racial terms is the resurgent Beat movement, which uses as its cultural model the counterculture of the 1950s and early 1960s and is reviving Beat jazz and Beat language (*cat*, *dig*, and *hipster* all being big words in these circles).

An additional expression of youth culture in the 1990s can be seen in the increased partici-

Illustrations by Matthew Martin

pation in outdoors activities—called extreme sports by some: mountain biking, snowboarding, and windsurfing, to name three. Entire subcultures have arisen around these activities, replete with dress codes, lifestyle, and language cues. In a similar vein, a growing number of young people, especially athletes, turn to ESPN's "Sports Center" each night, keyed and anticipating the use of a new catch phrase or slang expression such as *en fuego* ("on fire").

While the overall cultural setting in which American youth are coming of age may seem anemic when compared with the sound and fury that characterized the coming of age in earlier generations, manifestations of youth culture abound, from MTV to Quentin Tarantino's movies, from goatees to sagging jeans to graffiti-inspired graphic arts to Counting Crows and Pearl Jam and Snoop Doggy Dog.

birthplace. Simply put, it is far easier to recount what slang was in use twenty years ago than to describe what slang is in use today.

Despite the pallid and enervated state of youth culture as a whole, language production continues from the 1980s at a prolific, artistic, and enterprising rate. There are two basic trends within youth slang of the 1990s. Rap continues to exert a tremendous influence on the language of young people in America. Parental and governmental vilification of rap has had the inevitable effect of increasing its allure and popularity with the young, and this has hastened the spread of the rap idiom. Secondly, there is the clever and ironic use of standard English with a tendency toward bad-is-good meanings.

Slang of the 1990s

Reporting on the slang of the 1990s is more frightening than dealing with any other decade. Because of the transience of youth and the ephemeral nature of slang in general, youth slang changes extremely rapidly, and it is difficult to gauge what is likely to persist for more than a few moments or what is likely to spread beyond its

burning
Infected with a sexually
transmitted disease

Words of the '90s

banger
A STONER.
*Other synonyms for
this character type
include "burnout"
and "dirtbag."*

barred
Rejected

be sprung on
To like someone

beauteous maximus
A good deal

Believe that!
I agree!

biggums
Heavy

blaze
To leave

buckled
Ugly

bump
To idle or relax

bunk
Bad

burnout
A STONER.
*Other synonyms for
this character type
include "banger"
and "dirtbag."*

bus one
To leave

busted
Uncool, ugly

check it
To leave alone

chopped
Unattractive

circle of death
A bad pizza

clown
To tease or disparage

cool guy
An uncool guy

couch commander
A remote-control
device for a television

crib
One's home or apart-
ment. *"Crib" knew*

*this slang meaning
in the early 19th
century and entered
the lexicon of American
youth slang with the
infusion of Harlem jive
in the late 1930s.*

crushed
Ugly

crusty
Repulsive

dip
To leave

dirtbag
A STONER.
*Other synonyms for this
character type include
"banger and
"burnout."*

dirty
Abnormal

dog
A friend

duggy
Stylishly dressed

duke breath
Bad breath

easin'
Relaxing

epic
Great

fade
To crimp one's style

How Sweet it is

Although **cool** continues its long run as a slang term of approval, there are several other strong contenders for the current championship, most notably **sweet** and **tight**. **Sweet** is no slouch, having enjoyed a largely uninterrupted run of more than 20 years near the top of slang terms of admiration. Also in use over the last five years have been **all that, chillin', choice, cold-blooded, cool beans, crazy, def, dirty, dope, epic, fierce, filthy, fine, furious, hard, ill, kickin', killer, kooky, mad, on hit, shimmy, sick, slammin', straight,** and **thick**.

knuckle up
To fight

Fist it!
Shut up!

fly
Cool. *Making a strong comeback, "fly" is in its second or third generation.*

flex
To leave

frail
Precarious, iffy

freak
Attractive

fresh dip
Casual dress

front
To lie

full monk *or* **full nun**
Students who are sycophantic towards their teachers

fully
Completely

gaffle
1. To confuse or hurt

2. To steal

get up
To paint one's graffiti in a public place

grip
Money

grubbin'
Good food

heater
A cigarette

herb
A social outcast

high postage
A conceited woman

home slice
A good friend

hoochie
An attractive girl

hoopty
A car

hotty
An all-around attractive guy

houser
A group of friends

Howzit?
How are you?

in a grip
In a long time

jag
A social outcast

joints
Any pair of name-brand sneakers

kickin'
Smelly

L-12
Stupid times 12

laid-back
Well dressed

McJob
Any menial, tedious, mind-numbing, degrading job. *In the "Wayne's World" sketches and movies, Wayne Campbell at times refers to*

these types of jobs. The movie Clerks *glorifies one Generation X McJob, working in a convenience store.*

mobile
Attractive

mopped
Beaten up

non
A nerd

nosh
To kiss passionately

not hard
Bad

pimp
A cool guy

played out
Old

player
A boy who is always dating different girls

poser
A person who looks the part but cannot really play it

punk
A jerk

rack
To sleep

rag
To make fun of

rage
To engage in party activities with vigor

random
Completely off the wall

represent
To make a good showing

sauce
Beer. *"Sauce" was used as a slang synonym for alcohol by the Flapper of the 1920s.*

scam
To cruise in search of the opposite sex

scammer
Someone who dates many different people

Scandalous!
What a great put-down! *"You dance like that little blond kid on Barney!" "Scandalous!!!"*

shady
Deceptive

shine
To disparage

step off
To back away from a situation

sticky
Cute

stoked
Completely happy. *A surfer word that has migrated off the beach.*

stoner
A character type— dark moods, dark clothing, heavy metal music, and often drug and alcohol use. *Among widely used synonyms for the stoner are "banger," "burnout," and "dirtbag."*

stupid
Bad

suck
To be utterly inadequate, objectionable, or undesirable. *This is the same meaning the word had in the 1970s and 1980s, but now it is almost entirely devoid of sexual connotations. "Suck" has been the subject of considerable research*

by Teresa Labov and Ronald R. Butters of Duke University in conjunction with the court case of a junior high school student who refused to stop wearing a T-shirt that read DRUGS SUCK. Butters and Labov note that over the past 25 years, the older meaning of "suck" (with its clear allusion to oral-genital contact) has assumed a linguistically minor meaning. In fact, Labov showed that "suck" as a nonsexual pejorative is the most highly recognized slang term in use among high school students today. As Butters wrote, the former taboo sense of "suck" is a meaning that ony "dirty little minds" will find unless there is a clear sexual context for the phrase.

sweetness
Something great

syndicate
A group of friends

take the L train
To lose at something

test
To tease or disparage

Bart and Wayne

Television has supplied the young of the 1990s with an assortment of slang and slangy catch phrases. Two examples of the power of television to shape the language of the young are *The Simpsons* and the "Wayne's World" sketch on *Saturday Night Live*.

The Simpsons, a hip, iconoclastic, and antiheroic cartoon show has enjoyed considerable popularity since it first aired on a weekly basis in 1990, establishing itself as both a commercial success and an astounding phenomenon of popular culture.

From the lips of impish misfit antihero Bart Simpson have come a number of slangy catch phrases and words that have become emblems of the decade; while Bart (or his writers) coined none of them, he has certainly popularized them. **Been there, done that** is a classic Bart dismissal of an idea or opportunity that he has visited in the past. **Outta my way, man** and **No way, man** are definitive expressions of defiance. **Don't have a cow** is a plea to calm oneself, while **Cowabunga!** and **Aye, caramba** are well-established surfer interjections into which Bart breathed new life.

Wayne Campbell was the affectionately and carefully crafted creation of actor Mike Meyers, whose "Wayne's World" sketches on *Saturday Night Live* and two *Wayne's World* movies made community-access cable television host Wayne Campbell and his "best bud and most excellent cohost" Garth Algar household names in the late 1980s and early 1990s. Thanks to Meyers' excellent ear for teen slang, Wayne took from and then gave to the teen idiom in no small way. In part, Wayne spoke as any dude would speak—**excellent** as the superlative of choice, **hurl** as the verb of regurgitation, **take a pill** as an exhortation to calm down, and **babe** with its many Wayne variations (**Babe-elonia, babe-a-tude, babe-osity, babetious, McBabe,** etc.). Wayne's most popular contributions to the youth slang lexicon were **and monkeys might fly out my butt** (an expression of doubt), **Not!, Party time!** (Let's celebrate!), **Schwing!!!!** (the sound of an erection), **He Shoots! He Scores!!!** (He is triumphant!), and the ubiquitous **Party on!**

Think it ain't!
I totally agree with you!

to the curb
Rejected in a relationship

toss chow
To eat

twist a braid
To say good-bye

vid out
To investigate or explore something

virtual
Not quite real. *Derived from the term "virtual reality," the adjective is almost always used ironically, as in "He has a virtual job."*

Wat up?
What is new?
Obviously rap-inspired.

weak
Not up to standards or expectations

weesh
Weak

What's your damage?
What is your problem?

Whoomp, there it is! *or* **Whoot, there it is!**
An expression of joy.
The two versions of the exclamation mean the same thing. "Whoomp" was coined by rappers Tag Team, while 95 South originated "Whoot."

Yerp!
Boy this is fun!!!

zeke
A social outcast

The Language of Dude Sports

The 1980s and especially the 1990s have seen the proliferation of several dude sports, each of which has its own slang vocabulary.

Snowboarding, which was originally called **snurfing** (*snow* + *surf*), was the child of Sherman Poppen, who invented the first "snowboard" in 1965. After some years of dormancy, snowboarding has grown tremendously, and around it there has developed a unique subculture with its own slang and slangy jargon.

Given snowboarding's similarities to surfing, it is not surprising to find several direct borrowings from the vocabulary of the surfer, including **goofy** (riding a snowboard with the right foot forward), **shred** (to ride a snowboard very well) and **shredder** (a way cool snowboarder), and **tweak** (to twist or bend).

The words for winners and losers are also surf-derived, with **dude** and **shredder** on the accolade side and **cone, dork, dweeb,** and **nerd** used to describe the outcast.

One who snowboards fast and well is **raging** or **aggro**. When jumping, the space between the board and snow is simply **air** or an **ollie** (**hair sprayer air** is high enough to puncture the ozone), while a turn that is true to the radius of the snowboard's sidecut is a **carve**. A **half-pipe** is a trough dug out of a slope in order for snowboarders to perform aerial maneuvers off the sides. To **butter the muffin** is to spin on the board's nose.

When things go wrong snowboarding, there is a rich vocabulary for the occasion. Bad snow, often the cause of problems, is simply **crud**. If one abandons a jump or maneuver, one **bails**. To **bonk** is to hit something while riding on a snowboard, while to **jib** is to slide over a bump; a **butt plant** is falling backwards onto one's butt; a **head plant** or **face plant** is falling on one's head; a **sketch** is a near wipeout; to **biff** is to wipe out; to **lawn chair air** is to jump very high and then to collapse like a lawn chair upon impact; and a **yard sale** is a complete and total loss of control which leaves one's gear and clothing scattered over the snow.

A summertime spiritual equivalent of snowboarding is mountain biking, which also has its own slang idiom. As is the case with other dude sports, mountain biking has a variety of words to describe things going wrong, including **beartrapped** (what happens when a loose pedal comes back around and hits the lower leg), **boned** (to have caught the nose of your seat in your tail bone), **caterpillaring** (jerky pedal cadence after failing to preselect the correct gear for the end of a coast), **chain suck** (what happens when the chain flops between the chainstay and the tire), **clotheslined** (knocked off your bike by a suspended obstacle), **crash and burn** (any gruesome accident), **dabbing** (to touch the ground inadvertently with any part of the body), **face plant** (a face-first crash), **groin plant** (to catch your groin in the seat of the bike), **hellride** (a bad trail or bad ride), **porpoising** (reacting to the bike instead of controlling it), and **tweaked** (struck with a low glancing blow by a rock).

On the other side of the ledger, **clean** is to ride a difficult trail without **dabbing**.

The Dude & His Speak

In the beginning was the Surfer, who begot the Valley Girl, who begot the Dude. The dude as portrayed by Sean Penn in *Fast Times at Ridgemont High,* by Keanu Reaves in *Bill and Ted's Excellent Adventure,* and eloquently by Pauly Shore in movies and on MTV, is undoubtedly an accurate if caricatured portrayal of a young American male character type. That said, the depictions of the dude and his speech do not ring with the same vibrant authenticity as do the representations of the Valley Girl.

Much of dude slang relies on the unexpected use of intense standard English. To the dude, something good is **apocalyptic, beast, excellent, fierce, most atypical, most excellent, nasty, outstanding, rad, righteous, stellar, sterling, swell, triumphant, unprecedented, unrivaled, way gone,** or **way rad; clean** is very attractive. On the other hand, something that is **bogus, egregious, heinous,** or **weak** is uncool, and something that is **skanky** is ugly. **Crusty** is tired; **fully edged** is very angry, and **amped** is excited (to an earlier generation, **amped** clearly suggested the influence of stimulants; with rap came this more general application of the word).

In the realm of neologisms, **Latronic** is used as a parting remark ("Later on"); **fundage** is cash, and **grindage** is food. To **mack out** (derived from McDonald's) is to eat heartily, while a **brew-ha** is a beer.

Above all, the dude culture is one of **buds** (good friends) in pursuit of **babes** (girls). **Really!**

Word History: Cowabunga!

Cowabunga! carries with it a singular history.

It was first used by Bill LeCornec, who played a number of roles on the *Howdy Doody Show,* including Chief Thunderthud of the Ooragnak ("kangaroo" spelled backward). Speaking in racially stereotyped broken English as Chief Thunderthud, LeCornec prefaced his sentences with "Kawa," not unlike the Beat use of "like" as a prefatory filler in a sentence. He expanded on this, building words. When things went well, he pronounced "KawaGoopa"; when he was scared he said "KawaChicken," and whenever he came to grief, largely because of Clarabell's practical jokes, he exclaimed, "Kawabonga!"

It has been suggested that *Kawabonga* was some sort of subliminal or coded profanity, based on this quotation from scriptwriter Eddie Kean, which appeared in Stephen Davis's *Say Kids! What Time Is It?* (Boston: Little, Brown, 1987):

"Kowabonga (sic) was a nonsense word that originally meant an expression of anger, like "Dammit!" But the way Bill first said the line, it sounded more like an exclamation of surprise, and that's mostly the way we used it."

Buffalo Bob Smith strongly resented any insinuation of profanity and responded to the charge in *Howdy and Me* by Buffalo Bob Smith and Donna McCrohan (New York: Plume Books, 1990):

Some chowderhead started the rumor a few years ago that Kawabonga signified a profanity, and that when kids at home muttered Kawabonga, they were cursing. Believe me, I'd never teach a kid a secret way to curse, and I certainly have no wish to be remembered in that light.... The implications of Kawabonga were always squeaky-clean.

Kawabonga, in any event, was soon taken up by surfers, who changed the spelling to *Cowabunga!* It was an all-purpose cry of exultation, useful in any number of situations. *Cowabunga!* became known to mainstream youth as a surfer cry, as evidenced by its appearance in *Peanuts* comic strips and in the *Hy Lit Dictionary* (Philadelphia: Hyski Press, 1968), defined as "Surfer's yell of victory over a hard to ride wave"). If a hip AM radio deejay in Philadelphia picked up *Cowabunga!*, it had gotten around.

Cowabunga!'s next reported use was in Vietnam, as a latter-day version of "Banzai!" Although Davis and Smith both place *Cowabunga!* in Vietnam, none of the dictionaries or glossaries of slang used by soldiers in Vietnam that I have reviewed include it. It is not unlikely, but then again it does not appear to be documented.

Cowabunga!'s latest incarnation has been in the 1990s, from the lips of television cartoon characters to the ears of younger children, who use it effortlessly on the playground. Both Bart Simpson of *The Simpsons* and the heroes of *Teenage Ninja Mutant Turtles* often resort to *Cowabunga!* to express surprise or elation. Forty-five years old, *Cowabunga!* still holds its own with the young.

EPILOGUE

So yon teens, we're almost home. You've been hipped and you know what's happenin'. You've packed in your brown shoes and white socks and you're all woke up. It's time to split the scene and leave it clean, to get off our heels and onto some wheels. Toodles and peace—color me gone. It's been real, but I'm history. I'm out of here and—ciao for now. Enough with this spectacular vernacular, you've heard the word, and you're cool, no fool. Let's clear the joint of counterpoint and take a tacit for 24. We'll be back next black. Keep ya chin up and here's looking at ya. Solid Ted, nuff said. Later.

BIBLIOGRAPHY

At the end of each chapter, there is a list of sources and references for that chapter. The dictionaries referred to throughout the book include the following:

Barrère, Albert, and Charles G. Leland. *A Dictionary of Slang, Jargon, and Cant.* Edinburgh: Ballantyne Press, 1889-1890.

"B.E., Gent." *A New Dictionary of the Terms, Ancient and Modern of the Canting Crew.* Printed for W. Hawes at the Rose in Ludgate Street [London], 1696-1699.

Chapman, Robert. *New Dictionary of American Slang.* New York: Harper and Row, 1986.

Farmer, John Stephen, and William Ernest Henley. *Slang and Its Analogues Past and Present.* Printed for subscribers only. London, 1890-1904.

Gold, Robert S. *A Jazz Lexicon.* New York: Alfred A. Knopf, 1964.

Grose, Captain Francis. *A Classical Dictionary of the Vulgar Tongue.* London: S. Hooper, 1785.

Hotten, John Camden. *The Slang Dictionary.* London: John Camden Hotten, 1859.

Lighter, J.E. *Random House Historical Dictionary of American Slang: Volume 1 (A-G).* New York: Random House, 1994.

Mencken, H.L. *The American Language.* 4th ed. New York: Alfred A. Knopf, 1962.

Partridge, Eric. *A Dictionary of Slang and Unconventional English.* 8th ed. Edited by P. Beale. New York: Macmillan, 1984.

Wentworth, Harold and Stuart Berg Flexner. *Dictionary of American Slang.* New York: Thomas Y. Crowell, 1960, 1975.

Weseen, Maurice H. *Dictionary of American Slang.* New York: Thomas Y. Crowell, 1934.

INDEX